Visiting Africa

A Memoir

Jesse O'Reilly-Conlin

DEMETER

Visiting Africa
A Memoir

Jesse O'Reilly-Conlin

Demeter Press
2546 10th Line
Bradford, Ontario
Canada, L3Z 3L3
Tel: 289-383-0134
Email: info@demeterpress.org
Website: www.demeterpress.org

Demeter Press logo based on the sculpture "Demeter" by Maria-Luise Bodirsky www.keramik-atelier.bodirsky.de

Printed and Bound in Canada

Front cover image: Sandbar Island, Zanzibar © Jesse O'Reilly-Conlin
Typesetting: Michelle Pirovich

Library and Archives Canada Cataloguing in Publication
Title: Visiting Africa : a memoir / by Jesse O'Reilly-Conlin.
Names: O'Reilly-Conlin, Jesse, author.
Description: Includes bibliographical references.
Identifiers: Canadiana 20210294884 | ISBN 9781772583564 (softcover)
Subjects: LCSH: O'Reilly-Conlin, Jesse—Travel—Africa. | LCSH: Privilege (Social psychology) | LCSH: Race relations. | LCSH: Race awareness. | LCSH: Whites—Race identity. | LCSH: Empathy. | LCSH: Africa—Description and travel. | LCGFT: Travel writing.
Classification: LCC HT1523 .O74 2021 | DDC 305.8—dc23

For my parents

Acknowledgments

I would like to thank Di Brandt and Casey O'Reilly-Conlin for the work they did on my manuscript, which increased its quality leaps and bounds. And I would like to thank Demeter Press for publishing my work.

Contents

A Note on Method and Names

This is a work of literature, not journalism. My primary research tool is my memory. Thus, when I recreate a scene from twenty years ago or two weeks ago, I do not aim for brutal, overbearing realism. I do not strive to recite dialogue verbatim. I play with dialogue just as I play with time, but I do not misrepresent either—faithful and nuanced representation is at the heart of everything I do as a writer. The people I speak with in the African countries I visit are not my interviewees. I did not record their voices, nor did I take notes of their words because this would have violated the nature of conversation. We conversed. I listened, but I also talked. I processed and interpreted and filtered their words as well. I put their words to paper through memory alone. I do not pretend to be a human recording device, and my selections and omissions obviously represent a bias to some extent, yet their voices are always salient to the images I try to create on the page. I have endeavoured to present all the people in this book, including myself, as fully formed human beings, with all their contradictions and imperfections, to the best of my ability.

As a white man who wishes to trace his understanding of and engagement with Africa over the years, emphasizing my subjectivity is central. This book is not about Africa. This book is about my relationship with Africa; it's about my perceptions of Africa. I am not an expert on Africa. I have read many books about it, studied it at the undergraduate and graduate levels, written many papers, even a thesis, on it, but I still proudly flaunt my limitations, which is the only ethical position to have in such a project. I look forward to being wrong. I look forward to being challenged. The thoughts and feelings expressed herein are ever growing and evolving. This is what makes essaying so exciting: there is no definitive end point to reflection. Learning and debating should have no terminus. Doubt and uncertainty are my guiding principles.

I have changed all names of the people I encounter in this memoir to protect and safeguard their privacy and anonymity.

Introduction

Snapshots of Africa

It is a Saturday morning in March 1995, and I am ten years old. My town, Bradford, Ontario, has emerged from hibernation. Outside, it feels like spring. Clumps of grass have pushed through the melting snow. My toboggan hill has mostly turned to mud and muck; the sled's red glistening lip leans against the cedar rail fence near the bird feeders entertaining a group of grackles and sparrows. A frozen Coke can lies below the blue recycling bin. A chickadee blends into a birch tree's bark as it hops from twig to twig. Its call evokes memories of frozen lakes and hockey sticks.

At the moment, though, I have little interest in spring's first signs. I am not playing outside, nor am I in any rush to do so. I am sprawled on the downstairs couch devouring a bowl of Alphabets. In front of me sits the television, and on the screen, a huge orange sun rises over the dark savannah marked by a single acacia tree. I am watching one of my favourite movies—*The Lion King*. The action has begun.

The animals assemble to the call. A rhino raises its head; an antelope herd becomes alert. A meerkat mob stands at attention while a spotted leopard gazes across the plains. A vulture kettle glides past a teeming waterfall and gets covered in mist painted in pinkish hues from the early-morning sun. An elephant parade lumbers across the grasslands under a snow-capped mountain. Zebras gallop through puddles reflecting the rising sun in the sapphire sky, and giraffes saunter over rolling green hills. They all move towards Pride Rock.

With his walking staff, blue and red face, and flashy butt, wise Rafiki saunters through the parting animal herds towards Pride Rock, on which Mufasa stands overlooking his domain and subjects. He is majestic and noble. Little Simba rests in Sarabi's paws while Rafiki rattles his staff with grapefruit attached over the cub's big eyes. He splits one fruit open, smears its juices across Simba's forehead, and then sprinkles some sand on his face. Simba sneezes.

Rafiki takes Simba in his hands and climbs Pride Rock, its steep rock like a tongue sticking out over the plains. Below, all the animals wait. When Rafiki raises Simba to the sky, the elephants trumpet, the monkeys screech and flay their arms, and the zebras bray and stomp their hooves. And when a stream of light breaks through the clouds and covers Simba in a holy glow, the giraffes, elephants, zebras, and antelope all bow together.

The scenery is gorgeous. A half-dozen acacia trees stand underneath dark clouds and cascading mountains. The trees have so much personality; their trunks bend and sway like ballerinas. At their tops, their leaves clump together as if roofs or sombreros. They stand alone on the savannah, at a distance from each other, proudly individualistic and strong. Everything is so green, so fertile, so vibrant. The scene then cuts to raindrops, then a downpour, rivers splash and the ground softens, and then we see the baobab tree standing in lightning flashes and sheets of rain. The tree is beautiful. It's unlike any tree I have ever seen. Its trunk is tall, thick, and massive; it rises higher than the acacia, higher than the animals; the baobab is king of the savannah. Its leaves and branches emerge only at the top and entwine in dense, thick pockets. Underneath one canopy, Rafiki gazes at Simba's picture etched in the bark. He laughs in his maniacal way.

Mufasa and Simba sit on Pride Rock. The early light ignites the lowlands and rivers in a warm glow. Mufasa tells him that everything the light touches will one day be his, but not the shadows, not the elephant graveyard with its ribcages and tusks, where the savage hyenas bark and play. But because Mufasa does not tell him the truth about that dark place, Simba becomes intrigued and excited when Scar does tell him about the bones lying in dust and the fields of skeletons and carcases. And when Scar makes Simba promise not to go there, since only the bravest lions do, he knows Simba will.

Frustration nibbles at me. I know what happens because I've seen the movie dozens of times before. Simba should see the tragedy unfolding, should see the risk threatening him, the danger looming above. Instead, Mufasa and Simba only sit in the savannah underneath a starry night. Mufasa yells at his son for disobeying him and for endangering himself and Nala by taking her with him to the elephant graveyard. Simba has disappointed his father, and he weeps; his eyes grow as large and round as a baseball. He wanted to be brave like his dad, who isn't afraid of anything. But he is, Mufasa says, of losing his son. Kings are only brave when they need to be. Soon father has forgiven son, and Simba lies upon Mufasa's fluffy mane, and they both gaze into the stars. Mufasa says the kings of the past are the stars, the ancestors, and they look down on the living to remind them that no matter what, they are never alone.

I have a lump in my throat, not because of Mufasa's words, but because I know what happens. No matter how many times I watch the movie, I can't help but feel how unnecessary it all is. It is avoidable. It is not written in the stars. In my mind, I see Simba gently nudging his dead father, but he won't wake up. I cannot bear the idea of a loved one not waking up. I remember a few a years earlier watching *The Land Before Time* and bawling like a baby when Little Foot's mother would not wake up, even after her son pleads for her to. Please wake up, the little brontosaurus whimpers, alone amid cold rock and sky.

I pause the movie and head upstairs. I smell eggs. My dad is up. On the burner sits a covered skillet, and smoky little trails escape through its curved metal. It's Saturday morning, so underneath I know three eggs, twenty or so rectangular pieces of mozzarella, and a dozen sliced mushrooms cook and bubble and slowly form into an omelette.

At the kitchen table, my dad sits and reads the *Toronto Star*. He sips his instant coffee and glances through the sports section.

"Morning."

"Morning, Jess."

"Did the Blackhawks win?" I ask. My dad's favourite hockey team.

"Nope. They rarely win these days."

He has neatly separated the paper into piles, and I grab the front section, sit across from him, lay the paper out, and flip through its pages.

"Put it back where you found it after you're done."

I nod and pay little attention to the stories, only waiting for him to finish with the sports section. Then a headline catches my attention:

"Burundi's Hutus Fleeing Townships after Clashes"[1]

I know the word "Hutu." It means something to me. Last year, something bad happened with them in Rwanda, in Africa. Were they killed or were they the killers? I don't remember. I am ten. I don't know the word "Burundi." What is Burundi?

Above the headline, there is a picture and below the picture, a caption reads:

> "Hutu refugees fleeing their homes in the capital Bujumbura, carry their 9-year-old sister dying of AIDS through border to Zaire yesterday."

In the middle of the photo, a man stares at me. He has short black hair and a thin moustache. He's as thin as a sapling. His left hand extends to the picture's border, as if he were about to reach through the image and pull me in. His fingernails are trimmed and a bracelet clings to his wrist. His fingers are thin, bony, and barely covered by his black skin.

He has his mouth open and a front tooth is missing. Is he saying something? Maybe he's asking me for help, maybe he wants me to get out of the way, maybe he just wants my attention.

He pushes a dusty bike, and across the seat, someone has attached a cushion, and on it lies a young girl. Her bottom half rests on the cushion under a blanket while her top half is held in the hands of a second man, big and strong, walking behind the first. The little girl wears a hoodie, the colours of a zebra, and her body hangs limp and loose, her arms fragile like one of my sister's porcelain dolls. She's my age, and she looks at me.

My eyes move from the photo to the article's words:

> "Thousands of Hutus fled townships near Burundi's capital yesterday, swelling a weekend exodus sparked by ethnic clashes."

Burundi must be a country in Africa, and Hutus must live there like they do in Rwanda. But why are they fleeing? Who are they fighting with? I read the president of Burundi, a Hutu, says there have been 150 killings at least and fifty thousand refugees were leaving the capital.

> "The figure was much lower than the 500 deaths, predominantly of members of the Hutu tribe, based on witnesses' accounts after last Friday night's rampage by Tutsi militiamen."

Why are the Tutsis attacking the Hutus? Did they attack them too in Rwanda? I don't know. I don't remember.

> "The fighting between Burundi's two ethnic groups—Tutsi and Hutu—has provoked widespread fears the tiny central African country will go the way of its northern neighbour Rwanda."

The word "Rwanda" evokes a strange feeling—not words, only sensations. I cannot say anything certain about the country, but its letters stir something within. The name holds a special power. Nightmares. Rwanda reminds me of nightmares.

I had a nightmare once. I dreamt my mother had died, and I visited her grave. Her tombstone was grey and ugly with only her name carved on it and was identical to all the others rising from the grass. When I awoke in tears, I looked around at all my things—comic books, hockey cards, baseball glove—and they all meant nothing to me. All that mattered was the night outside and the maple branches shaking in the wind. In the morning, my mom said she would die, we all do, but it wouldn't be for a long time still, when I was old and grown. She said we still had so many years left together. "We only die after a full life", she said.

The next paragraph says:

"At least 500,000 people, mainly Tutsis, were slaughtered in Rwanda last year."

"Slaughtered" is a strange word, I think, and put the section back where I found it.

Downstairs, I fast-forward to my favourite part: the final battle scene. War has erupted between Simba and Scar. Light fights darkness. Good battles evil. On their hind legs, the two exchange blows and hard swats knocking and stunning the other. Their faces have transformed into masks of rage. They growl, snarl, and roar. Scar hits Simba hard sending the would-be king flying through the flames, and he lands just by the cliff's edge. Then Scar leaps through the fire, high in the air, a vision of menace, teeth sharp, claws out, eyes yellow and vicious, ready to rip his nephew apart. But when Scar lands, Simba reacts quickly, raising his leg, and flipping his uncle to the ground below. There, Scar stands again, only to be mauled and eaten by the hyenas. Amid the torn flesh and Scar's dying screams, Simba watches from above. He watches his uncle die.

The rains come and soon drown the fires. Simba embraces his mother and Nala, and Rafiki points to the tongue-shaped rock hanging over the once-great Pridelands. Simba climbs in the rain past skeletons and charred and burnt rock. At the edge, he looks unsure of what to do, how to act, until the clouds in the sky disperse and the stars become visible, thousands of twinkling balls of stardust. Upon seeing them, Simba's uncertainty vanishes. He remembers. And then he roars and roars and roars.

Before long, the green and animals have returned. Everything is as it was. Simba has restored order and tradition. Justice reigns. And when Rafiki holds Nala and Simba's cub over the Pridelands, the herds make their calls of thanks and gratitude. The circle of life resumes in Africa. Everything is beautiful.

The credits have finished, the tape begins to rewind, and the VCR flips back to the television. I sit in silence. Faces of Black children flash across the screen. Their eyes are downcast, faces sallow, bellies bloated, pants torn. Flies buzz around their closed mouths while a woman's voice speaks slowly from the sky. "Please help the children", the voice says. Please help the children.

This is how my interest in Africa, as a place, as an experience, as a haunting, began. I realized then, at age ten, that different Africas existed depending on where you looked or what you read. There was Simba, and there was Rwanda. And I could not understand how these two stories, so diametrically opposed, could unfold in the same place, but I did know that halfway across the world, in Africa, a different human story was happening, one which my privileged, white, and middle-class background had not helped me to understand. I wanted to know more.

On a day in 1998, I am fourteen years old and in a Chapters bookstore in downtown Toronto, in the travel section, and my eyes move from guidebooks with photos and maps to thicker ones filled with more pages and words. Without much thought or awareness, my fingertip stops on a spine with the word "Africa." I remove the book from its shelf and examine the cover. The background is white except for a thick black rectangle in the centre displaying the title in large lettering: *Into Africa: A Journey through the Ancient Empires* by Marq de Villiers and Sheila Hirtle. At the bottom of the cover stand three pyramids, which I recognize as belonging to Egypt. We learned in school that pyramids served as tombs for Egypt's great rulers, the pharaohs. We learned that ancient Egyptians would inject the dead pharaohs with liquids and chemicals and wrap them in cloth so they would appear lifelike forever. We learned about their gods and goddesses, their hieroglyphics, their calendars, their papyrus paper, their farming techniques. What an amazing civilization they had.

At the top of the cover, a black face stares at me, but not the entire face. No. The black rectangle has cut the mouth and chin. Only the eyes and head remain. On the head sits a beautiful headdress adorned with beads of every colour. Other looping jewelry hangs from it along with brown threads that may be leather. The headdress appears powerful, something a king or a warrior may wear. It is unlike anything I have ever seen. I flip through the pages, almost four hundred of them, and feel the breeze the rustling makes on my face. The new book smell enlivens me and fills me again with the promise of exotic and foreign places. It weighs heavy with stories.

On the inside page, an artist has sketched a map of Africa. It looks like a piece of old driftwood, warped by wind and water, a crooked stump similar to the ones my dad would go hunting for on the shores of Peter Lake, near Bancroft, and give to my mother, who would transport them to her garden and surround the bendy logs with red and blue tulips. The map contains dozens and dozens and dozens of countries whose names sound funny, so different from the familiar ones usually falling from my tongue, teeth, and lips. Some countries are as big as my thumb, and some are as thin as my shoelace. They come in all shapes and sizes. Zaire is large and showy and brash sitting proudly right in the continent's heart. Senegal wraps itself around the Gambia as if hugging or devouring the slim piece of land. Mali's borders bend and twist with no rules; its western border runs as straight as a pole while its southern lines resemble a seismometer during an earthquake. Rwanda and Burundi are tiny, jerky circles, hidden among the crevices and corners of bigger countries, almost completely invisible unless you know where to look. Sudan looks fat and plentiful while Togo appears sickly and thin. All the black lines separating one country from another wander and drift without balance, like a drunkard, like one of my parents' friends at one of their parties who couldn't walk in a straight line and whose stumbling and bumbling steps always made me laugh. I wonder if the drawer was sitting on a bumpy bus when he drew Africa, a bus that rattled and shook along a potholed concession road, and instead of erasing the zigzagging and crooked lines and trying again for those smoother, straight ones, like the long and perfect boundary running between Canada and the United States, he just shrugged his shoulders and went on with his work.

The map excites me. So many countries to know and memorize. I place my untrimmed fingernail underneath the names and practice saying those new words throbbing with strong vowels and consonants. Tanzania. Zimbabwe. Angola. I imagine shaking the map and watching each country fall to the ground, and I must gather each piece, each misshapen country, and put each back in place like a jigsaw puzzle, using only my memory, my instinct. I wonder if I could put them all back correctly. What harm could come to the continent if I accidently mistook Ghana for Guinea, Nigeria for Niger? Maps are important, and I understand them. They show the world as cut into blocks, perfectly ordered and tidy. They show where everything in the world belongs. They astonish yet soothe.

Book in hand, I rush to find my mom. She's in the fiction section looking through novels. I hand it to her, and she flips through it, her eyebrow rising in concern.

"Read it slowly and carefully," she says and passes the book back to me.

In my room, atop my bed, beneath my map of the world, and beside my globe, I follow her advice and read slowly. The main author, Marq de Villiers, is a white South African by birth but now calls Canada home. On the book's first pages, he sits on a plane flying over South Africa, a few years after apartheid's end. A nearby man watches *The Jungle Book* on the screen while they pass beautiful landscapes. Mowgli, whom I remember as carefree, feral child dressed in rags, wrestles with a British soldier in one comic scene. The author, a white South African by birth, finds this man's indifference to the outside world frustrating. He wants to tell the man that below, down on the earth, roam the animals and lie the jungles he admires so much in his film. The real thing is through the window. But he suddenly changes his mood and asks himself where on this continent could he discover the real Africa? Did the images he associates with Africa actually exist or were they products of his imagination? Who says what is real?

He recites a list of African horror I have come to know, names and images I have seen displayed and written in newspapers and heard broadcast over news programs: the genocides and massacres of Rwanda and Burundi; the slums of Dakar and Nairobi; the HIV-infested streets of Johannesburg and Lusaka; the corrupt anarchy of Lagos and Kinshasa; the child soldiers of Liberia and Sierra Leone.

The author says, though, Africa is more than the headlines, more than bloodshed, more than the Western world's fascination with exotic violence. He says despite crisis after crisis, Africa endures, Africa changes, Africa is always in a state of becoming. I like this word "becoming," something never begun, something never ended. He says borders, all those squiggly lines, are un-African, and before colonialism—I jot that word down—African groups moved around more, unpinned to any country. He talks about the awful effects of the slave trade, thirteen million Africans torn and sold from their homes, and I cannot believe that number. He talks about the variety and diversity of African cultural forms, the music and masks, about the sophistication of African religious beliefs, usually derided as simply spirit worship by outsiders. He says the negative images shared about Africa can never tell its complete story, can never explain its complexity, its fifty plus countries, hundreds of languages, thousands of cultures. He says Africa is so much more than blood and disease—something undefined, boundless, and becoming.

Before I go to sleep, I read about Great Zimbabwe, a series of granite stones, ruins in fact, belonging to one of Africa's greatest trading empires. The great stone city had sprung to life in the twelfth century, and by the fifteenth, it was the centre of a thriving trading network extending all the way to the Indian Ocean. It supported a population of twenty thousand and laid the foundation for later and greater Shona dynasties, including the Monomotapa. The author wanders through the ruins and touches and admires the cool rocks, amazed that this city was known throughout the continent, its riches and splendour eventually attracting traders from the Western and Eastern worlds. Yet he was even more amazed that despite growing up only a few hundred kilometres south of Great Zimbabwe in South Africa, he had never heard of the ruins and never learned about an Africa before the white world arrived. Nineteenth-century Europeans who visited the ruins similarly concluded that foreigners, from civilizations distant from the continent, must have built the grandiose city, for Africans themselves were outside the spirit of the world, powerless to match the creative genius and advanced cultures of the Egyptians, Greeks, or Phoenicians, incapable of joining the world's history.

A guide at the ruins asks the author to press his ear against one stone and listen. At first the author hears nothing, but then millions of tiny clicks and clacks sound from the boulder and swell in his ear, and soon those little noises fuse into one powerful sound echoing from within yet feeling far away like thunder exploding over the savannah. He asks the guide where the sound comes from, and the guide laughs and says many stories exist. Some say it's the sound of the ancient armies of Monomatapa sharpening their spears; The Christians say it's the sound of the dead clawing and scratching their way from the underground to confront God on Judgment Day. The archeologists believe the clicking comes from the shifting stones trembling under so much weight. Engineers arrive with tools, the guide says, and try to confirm the archeologists' theories, yet they often leave disappointed, unable to prove anything. Most of the time, they leave without even hearing the rocks because they listen in a scientific way, all head and no heart, only appreciating measurable things, things with a beginning and an end, things that can be felt in their fingers. Not everyone can hear the hidden sounds of Zimbabwe, the guide concludes. Some things should remain a mystery.

The questions Great Zimbabwe asks linger in my mind. Why couldn't European visitors to Zimbabwe accept that Africans had designed the complex? Why hadn't I heard about Great Zimbabwe? Why did Africa exist outside the world I lived in?

It's 2001, and I am in high school. We are studying, and I am sitting in the back row.

"The ships arrived on the West African coast from Europe and exchanged various goods for slaves," says our grade eleven history teacher, Mr. Smith, a bald and serious fellow who always wears khaki pants and buttoned shirts. He stands in front of a world map, pointing to Africa with a wooden metre stick.

He slowly runs the ruler across the blue Atlantic ocean before stopping in the Caribbean islands, Jamaica, Cuba, Barbados, Haiti—names through which I see only sandy beaches, rum bottles, and palm trees—and makes a large, sweeping circle swallowing South, Central, and North America.

"The slaves were brought to the New World where they worked on plantations, in mines, and within cities. They called the journey across the Atlantic the Middle Passage, and it lasted anywhere from six to eight weeks. Upon arrival in the Americas, the slaves produced crops and dug for minerals, which were then transported back to the European ports."

"Mr. Smith," I ask. "Why would Africans sell their own people to Europeans?"

Mr. Smith sighs, looks at the map, and then back at me. He scrunches his mouth and contorts his face. He opens his mouth only to close it again, each time peering at the map, as if it held the answer to my question. Eventually, he admits the increasingly obvious.

"That's a good question, and I don't have a good answer for you."

Pride swells within me as I have stumped the teacher. I glance around the room for recognition but am met with indifferent faces, faces blank with boredom, tedium. I return to the map and look at those regions in West Africa beyond the coast, the interior jungles and grasslands, and imagine what happens there. I hadn't really thought about people in maps. I had never really thought of Jamaica, for example, as housing people with history or culture, with a story predating the arrival of resorts and jet-skis. And I realize that if someone had asked me ten minutes ago why so many Caribbean people were Black, I wouldn't have known the answer. So with my conceit comes a tinge of secret embarrassment and a realization that if not by the grace of luck, of being in the right place at the right time with the right question, I might have been the source of ridicule, an example of ignorance. I might have earned my classmates' laughter and scorn, seen as a silly, stupid little boy, unworldly, so rural, so uncouth—as Rebecca did the following month.

Here she is now, rising from her desk. She collects her yellow Bristol board and stands in front of the blackboard. She has royal blue hair that falls across her forehead. She is short, five feet maybe, and walks the school's hallways in purple trainers and black sweaters. She likes Tori Amos. I've heard rumours floating through the cafeteria and library, little whispers that gain strength the more they are uttered, that she is a lesbian, preferring the company of girls to boys. I have often seen her standing at her locker, gazing at an attached mirror, and looking forlorn yet defiant. Today, she will give a brief presentation on a country, providing a quick overview of its history and industry, its geography and culture. She holds up the board, and I notice she has chosen the West African country Niger, a former French colony lying smack in the middle of the Sahara.

Rebecca has traced the country in red pencil crayon, and it resembles a fat thigh, a thin ankle, and small foot. She has written little notes on the board with arrows that run to various points on the map. The thigh portion, it seems, carries little in the way of information; it is a blanket blank space, indicating the desert, perhaps, the arid, sun-soaked land unsuitable for anything but survival. On the foot, in the country's extreme southwest, lies Niamey, the capital, and most of the information. A blue line bisects the foot, passing through the capital, and it must be the river, I think, for which the country is named.

Rebecca points to her country's name printed atop the board. She appears confident and strident, on the cusp of saying something vital, so unlike the mousey image I have of her.

"I just want to say before I begin that I find this country's name offensive. And I will not say it. While speaking, I will simply refer to it as 'the country I have chosen.' I will not say this word."

Those in the audience look at one another in confusion. Our white faces crinkle, our brows furrow. Faint snickering comes from the back rows and murmuring from the front ones. Heads turn and eyes meet. The students are aghast.

The teacher informs Rebecca that you don't pronounce the country like that. It is spoken with a soft "g" like the river's name or Nigeria. And since it's a French name, the pronunciation is different still. The "g" becomes an almost "sh" sound and the "i" is a French one, with the correct sound produced from the tongue tickling the rows of clenched teeth. *Knee-zhair.*

Rebecca turns red. She mumbles an apology and speaks in a shaky, rattling voice. She tries to concentrate on her written words, but she cannot seem to focus, cannot seem to move beyond her mistake. Every time she says the country's name, little giggles blossom from the seats. I cower, drop my head, and my body grows tense and apprehensive from her error, her colossal blunder. I want to laugh at her, too. I want to mock her as well. And when I catch the eyes of some of my classmates, my look, too, is less than sympathetic, empty of charity, filled with disappointment and displeasure. How can someone be so careless, I wonder. So oblivious to the rest of the world. How could someone mistake a country's name for one of the worst words in the English language? But when I gaze out the window to the surrounding, soggy farmlands, removing an errant dreadlock from my eye—dreadlocks I just got last month, which set me apart from the mundane looks and everyday opinions of my classmates—I suddenly picture her at home working on her Bristol board, writing that name out in big capital letters, anxiety rippling across her skin. How can I say this awful word, she asks herself? I, too, have been called horrific names, she says. I, too, have been bullied for being different. How can I be part of that hatred? If I say this name, even if part of a school project, even if it is asked of me, how am I any different from the boys who call me those terrible names in the stairwells and in the parking lot? She concludes that she won't say it. She will not say it, even if it means a lesser grade, even if it earns her the teacher's wrath. She has taken a stand. She will not say that awful word. But I keep these thoughts to myself, stay silent, and whenever acquaintances remember the episode, I snicker with them and mock her. How can people be so sheltered, so ignorant, so obtuse, I wonder, and when I shake my head in amazement, a dread loosens from my ponytail, but I secure it.

Stories of Africa change people around me. The name conjures up something inside of them and they become people I no longer recognize. A classmate of mine in grade twelve history, a girl named Sara with long brown hair and a face eager to smile and laugh, explains to me why so many people are dying from AIDS in Southern Africa.

She participates in everything. Sara sits on the student council and volunteers in a half-dozen student organizations. Sara plays basketball and volleyball. Sara studies hard and earns straight A's. Sara wants to improve and get better. Her clothes are modest and wholesome as she feels at home in jeans and sweaters. Sometimes I wonder if her humbleness and humility grow from her Christianity, her work ethic. Despite her meek and simple attitude, though, she exudes confidence and certainty.

"People are dying in South Africa because they have turned their back on God," she says.

Sara's face is soft and serious. She chews on her fingernail, as is her way when anxious, and becomes lost in thought and reflection. She believes it. This girl who shoots jump shots and spikes volleyballs, who gives speeches in front of the entire school, who studies each and every lunch hour, who volunteers in countless organizations, thinks that Africans are dying of AIDS as a result of God's punishment because he's annoyed that some people in the southern half of the continent have stopped saying their prayers or giving thanks.

I look at her, and my right leg vibrates. I am certain she is wrong just as she is certain she is right. Great Zimbabwe tells me she is wrong. Great

Zimbabwe tells me more reasons exist for why these terrible things happen. She has never read *Into Africa*; maybe she simply doesn't know, maybe she simply hasn't read any other books or talked to any other people. She is a good person, I still think, a good person who is horribly wrong about something important, a falseness that can have consequences. But I notice I am not saying anything, and she looks around the classroom waiting for the teacher to pull our attention back to the front. Why am I not saying anything? Why am I not challenging her? The moment has passed. We go on to other things.

In public school, a few years before, I challenged kids whenever they used "gay" in a negative way. I would tell them how hurtful it can be, how gay people are people just like us, how love is love, and it doesn't matter whom you love, just so long as you do love. After a recess of playing ball hockey one afternoon and another argument about how you shouldn't use "gay" to mean "stupid," my best friend approached me and suddenly asked if my uncle is gay. A few years earlier, my uncle brought his boyfriend to our home in Bradford, and we had a lovely afternoon chatting and laughing. Not long after that, his boyfriend died of AIDS, and my uncle was diagnosed with HIV. Yet without thinking, while flinging my binder on my desk, I simply said, "No. No he is not," and acted slightly surprised that my best friend could ask something so ridiculous.

In the classroom, the teacher asks a question, and Sara has shot her hand in the air. And when she answers the question correctly and her lips curve a little and a dimple forms on her cheek, I wonder how much responsibility comes with knowledge. Watching her move and speak and laugh, I feel fat with knowledge; it just sits inside of me useless and expanding, a bowl of empty calories. I want to use that energy to run faraway, further inside myself, and have no responsibilities, no feelings of guilt. My uncle shared something about himself with me, and I betrayed him.

I think of Great Zimbabwe's mysterious sounds. I think about the slave trade, the thirteen million taken and sold, the long, suffocating journey to the New World, to the plantations and mines and households. I think of Rebecca's blunder, her good intentions, and my promise to never be ignorant about anything. And I think of Sara and my uncle's cabinet of medication and his dead boyfriend and the million others dying in Southern Africa. I think about knowledge and responsibility. I think about betrayal. Can you just run away? When I place my ear on Great Zimbabwe's ruins and feel its coolness reverberate through my body, what do I hear? What will I do with such secret knowledge?

Growing up in Bradford, Ontario, as a white boy in the 1990s, I associated Africa with the big five animals—lion, elephant, buffalo, leopard, rhinoceros—beautiful landscapes, endless sky, and death. While I sang "Hakuna Matata" from Disney's *The Lion King*, I saw images, read stories, and heard reports of starvation, disease, and bloodshed on the continent. For every brave lion I admired, an untold number of African children perished. For every noble old monkey I listened to, a town vanished in flames. I remember African landscapes enchanting me—the wind-rippled Saharan sands, Victoria Falls' thunderous power, snow-capped Kilimanjaro, the savannah's poetic acacias—and I remember its stories horrifying me, its tales of famine, genocide, and poverty.

These were the images of Africa with which I grew up: beautiful landscapes, noble animals, and dying children. The characters in *The Lion King* had personalities and histories; they had motives and desires. Their actions could be rationalized and explained. They were intriguing and relatable; the viewer cares about what happens to them. Yet the remarkable thing about this quintessential African film is its lack of people. There are no human beings; there are no Africans. In my childhood, the only Africans I saw on screen or read about in newspapers were portrayed against the background of violence and suffering. They had no voice, no culture, no history. They were only bodies in need of food or medicine or saving. They were just biology. Africa was a place without a past or even a future; it was perpetual darkness. It was primordial, ancient. The Africa of my childhood was filled with powerful, complex animals, and silent, savage people. The animals deserved a story; the people did not.

I wanted to know why African history had been treated so cavalierly in most of the media and writings I watched and read about the continent. I wanted to know why Africans, the actual human beings living on the continent, had been relegated to the periphery in stories about their own homes and cultures. And this book's first half charts that journey, one marked by more failures than successes.

I studied African history at university as both an undergraduate and graduate student. I devoured book after book on African history and culture. I attended lectures, participated in seminars, and wrote essays. I spent hours at York University's Scott Library reading about how the transatlantic slave trade and colonialism—five hundred years of European interference—robbed the continent of its people and then its independence. I felt an equal amount of excitement and frustration poring over the chaos of history—the voluminous literature and often conflicting and diverging accounts—and stitching together a mosaic of meaning, something resembling a coherent argument. I wrote a one-hundred-page master's thesis on how religious practices among the Akan people, a cultural group in Ghana, influenced the development of religious practices among enslaved Africans in Jamaica during the period of the British slave trade. I visited neither Ghana nor Jamaica, but I still received an A+ on the project, and a year later, I was researching for my PhD applications.

I shifted my focus to East Africa—Kenya, Tanzania, and Mozambique—and excitedly jumped around from country to country. I disappeared into the literature. I read about the transition from slavery to capitalist economies, exploitative labour practices, and the emergence of independence movements. I read about the new national governments trying to create a country from the ashes of colonialism. I dove into books and rarely emerged. I read for eight to twelve hours a day, six or seven days a week. I tried for a book a day. I stopped seeing friends. I stopped going out. I stopped experiencing a world outside my books. Books became my life, academe my home. I measured myself through academic success alone. Nothing else mattered.

I was accepted at McGill University for its PhD in history program. My mother drove me to Montreal in September 2011, our van filled with all my belongings. She helped me move into my new apartment on Hutchinson Street. She helped me shelve my hundreds of books, hang my African maps, and unload all the kitchen appliances. I watched her drive away the Sunday before the new school was to start, her hand waving from the open window. Three weeks later, I had dropped out of McGill and was living back at home.

At home, fat with depression and shame over quitting, I switched my focus again to South Africa. I became interested in the history of labour migration in that country, of the Mozambican, Malawian, and Zimbabwean men and women who tramped to and then toiled in the gold mines outside of Johannesburg, who had come from thousands of miles away to earn a wage. Movement fascinated me—how it could be both a creative and destructive force. I loved how people on the move disrupted everything and revealed the cracks in many of modernity's most cherished notions: human rights, multiculturalism, the nation-state. I decided I would pursue a different master's degree at the African Centre for Migration and Society at the University of the Witwatersrand in Johannesburg, and to save money for the program, I decided to teach English in South Korea for a year, and in September 2012, I moved there. In Busan, my new home, I kept company mostly with migration literature. While my fellow English teachers were learning Korean and taking Korean cooking lessons and making Korean friends, I read alone in my apartment. I found old syllabi from the migration program and read everything on them. I downloaded hundreds of articles. I wrote thousands of pages of notes. I bought migration books from Amazon and had them shipped to Busan. I became fascinated with the movement of Zimbabweans into South Africa and the history of the relationship between the two countries. I consumed everything I could find on Zimbabwe. I crafted a research proposal aiming to explore the deportation of Zimbabweans from South Africa, submitted it along with my application, and in June 2013, I was accepted into the program. In February 2014, I moved to Johannesburg, and by May 2014, I had dropped out of the program and was living back home. I never saw Zimbabwe, and I did not much feel like living. In my mind, I had failed in my academic pursuits: I had failed at life.

Despite all I learned about the continent and despite my sharpened critical faculties, I never had a chance to visit Africa and experience it in any detail. Even at the University of Witwatersrand, in 2014, I never ventured far from its library or its gates. Africa, albeit in a more nuanced form, still existed for me as an image or as a page in a book. It wasn't until I landed in Mozambique in May 2018 at the age of thirty-three and felt the sun scorch my body and felt the people rush past me that I started to understand the difference between a book and a place, between history written in sentences and history lived and breathed, between history as something cerebral and history as something visceral.

In this book's second half, I recall my experience of finally exploring on foot the places I read so much about. At Cape Coast Castle in Ghana, the emporium of the British slave trade in West Africa, I descend into the darkness and heat of its slave dungeons. At Zanzibar, the principal site of the slave trade in East Africa, I stroll along the perfect beaches, the ocean lapping at my toes, and reflect on how many Africans said goodbye to the continent right there. Alongside my guide Ercilio, I walk Maputo's streets and hear him speak about the disastrous and lasting effects of Portuguese colonialism—the loss of languages and ways of life. In Johannesburg's Central Business District, on a bright Saturday morning, three men wrestle me to the ground, and as one man wraps his forearm around my neck and another pins my hands back, I wonder why no one comes to my rescue and then wonder why I expect such a response. At Victoria Falls, Zimbabwe, one of the natural wonders of the world, a dishevelled man walks alongside me for half a kilometre begging me for one American dollar to buy a loaf of bread. He calls me his brother. His brother. And no book had prepared me for how I would feel when I finally pay my brother to go away. In Kigali, Rwanda, at the Genocide Memorial, I reflect upon the country twenty-five years after the genocide and upon my twenty-five years learning about Africa.

Each chapter of the book's second half combines history and personal reflection. Although I consider myself an enlightened reader of African events and happenings, I remain irrevocably a product of the Western world, a person raised on cultural descriptions purporting to be objective and on images pretending to be reality. I take a critical, self-reflective approach in my reporting on the African countries I visit.

Ultimately, this memoir explores what it means to bridge the book and the place. It explores what learning and existing outside the book can look like. *Visiting Africa: A Memoir* is a personal journey as well as a physical one: It is about my ongoing and evolving attempt to approach difference with humility and modesty and about my struggles as a privileged white man to ethically encounter and live in a world marked by injustice and racialized inequality. It takes up the present challenge of resurrecting stories that challenge dominant narratives. It is an investigation of privilege and how the privileged must overcome their own defensiveness and feelings of guilt if they are to stand in solidarity with those people they meet and write about. Finally, this book is an investigation into the possibilities of empathy.

In 2012, I am twenty-eight years old, and I go searching for the remains of Toronto's one residential school—the Alexandra Industrial School for Girls. Opened in 1897, the school operated under the Industrial Schools Act of 1874 and intended to provide basic education and shelter for delinquent girls who had been sent there by the courts for truancy, incorrigible behaviour, or other morally suspect tendencies. In short, the school sought to redeem fallen girls and keep them from becoming fallen women. Yet it appears that alongside the truculent white girls were Indigenous ones who arrived to unlearn not only ill-manners but entire worldviews. Where these Indigenous girls came from is not known, nor is it known how many girls, Indigenous and non-Indigenous, died there, or when exactly the school closed. An October 2011 edition of a local Beaches paper, an upscale neighbourhood in eastern Toronto, published a story about the school. Although the article paints the school in a rather rosy, altruistic light and does not even mention its role as a residential school, it does provide the school's location—on Blantyre Avenue, just north of Kingston Road.

On a March afternoon, I am riding the Queen streetcar heading east over the Don Valley Parkway and towards Leslieville. I pass the Opera House where in my youth I heard so many bands play, and I pass Coxwell Avenue where, just to the northeast, I would drink and party with my friends before heading downtown to find mischief and deviance, and I pass Woodbine Park and its beach where I once watched the sunrise on a summer's morning while still slightly intoxicated. Today, I pass all those places and exit the streetcar at its terminus, Victoria Park, and walk a little farther east to Blantyre and turn north. Square houses sit in orderly rows under green trees. Each has a similarly shaped lawn; most have cars in their driveway. Yellow traffic signs warn drivers about children at play, of errant balls and little bodies, and most drivers seem to respect that this neighbourhood is residential and pass by with due diligence on the lookout for families with strollers or for little kids on bicycles.

As I approach Kingston Road, I take my digital camera from my backpack and ready it in my hands. I do not know what I expect to find, yet I prepare myself nonetheless. But standing at the traffic lights, looking around the intersection, I see no haunted-looking school looming in the horizon. I see no dilapidated building with broken windows or rotting walls or overgrown lawns. Instead, all I see is a Tim Horton's, a Beer Store, a Petro Canada gas station, and a Pizza Pizza. I cross Kingston Road and walk through Blantyre Park. I search for a marker, a plaque, anything memorializing Alexandra, anything recalling what was here, what happened here. But I see nothing, only children at play, only people enjoying an unseasonably warm March day. Maybe I have the wrong place, maybe the article was wrong about the school's location, maybe nothing at all happened here. Or maybe, on this very spot one hundred years earlier, Indigenous girls toiled in the gardens tilling the ground and planting vegetables, maybe right here on the very place where a family now sits, smiles, and laughs, an Indigenous girl sat upon the same grass and tried to remember that she, too, had a family.

Here, among homes and families at play, I feel something rising inside, and I want to direct it towards something tangible or productive, to aim it at some restorative project, but as it comes in greater and greater waves, the sensation does feel a lot like guilt, a lot like the shame you feel after stealing something, and I sense the collective eye-rolling of marginalized and dispossessed people the world over, scornful of my white, crocodile tears, amazed that I could take their stories and somehow make them all about me.

But I am learning to put those thoughts away and work towards some kind of affirmative project.

This book is the fruit of those efforts.

Endnotes

1. "Burundi's Hutus Fleeing Townships after Clashes." *Toronto Star*, 17 Mar. 1995, A15, https://www-proquest-com.ezproxy.library.yorku.ca/docview/1355572308/pageviewPDF/B8290917714431CPQ/2?accountid=15182. Although this story was published on a Monday, not a Saturday, I chose to include my reading of it in this scene because it well captures my simultaneous learning about two diametrically opposed, as well as equally false, Western visions of Africa: *The Lion King* and Rwanda.

Part 1

1.

Thinking of Africa

It is a Sunday morning in December 2007, and I am twenty-three years old. I am sitting at a desk in my girlfriend's apartment at Yonge and Eglington, mid-town Toronto. She is half-asleep in her bedroom, and I periodically hear a squawk emanating from there—her quiet rebellion against the encroaching morning aiming to rob her of her treasured sleep. I am wide awake and focused. My eyes dart between my laptop screen and the book before me resting open to the introduction. I am dressed in beige shorts and a black t-shirt; my long hair is tied back. I am dressed perfectly for a lazy Sunday morning.

I am taking notes from Judith Carney's book *Black Rice*, an important work I must read for my graduate course on the African diaspora. My master's in history program is only three months old, but I already feel burdened by the amount of material I'm expected to read. One must, it seems, read an entire library before adding anything new to it. Yet on this snowy Sunday morning, I feel at little more at ease because of what Carney writes and the ideas she plants within me. I see a path through the fog, an academic area in need of a little more scholarly attention.

Carney argues that enslaved Africans, not Europeans, transferred and adapted rice cultivation to New World agricultural conditions. She shows how traditional West African farming techniques facilitated the spread of rice in the Americas and provides an example of how some bonded Africans could retain some aspects of their cultural worldviews even under the hellish conditions of slavery. In my African diaspora class, we have entered a longstanding debate about the role Africa played in the emergence of new, creole cultural forms on American soil. How did enslaved Africans orient their lives in the New World? Could they resurrect Africa in any tangible sense when constructing communities under conditions of enslavement? How did African cultural forms blossom in New World soil? What does that history look like?

"Jesse, come back to bed. It's too early," my girlfriend shouts from her bedroom. She sleeps little during the week and relies on the weekend to revitalize her.

I smile.

"No," I shout back. "It's time to get up and experience the day."

I hear her sputter protest through her lips, and I try a different approach.

"I have made toast and coffee," I say, which is a lie.

"How come I don't smell the coffee?" she asks. "And how come you haven't served me in bed yet?"

I laugh. "If you want your toast, you will have to come get it."

"Fine," she says, and then she releases one of her playful shrieks, which, I always tell her, must have resembled the sounds of the extinct pterodactyl. I go to the kitchen, plug in the kettle, and throw two pieces of white bread in the oven, since she does not own a toaster, and set the knob to low, careful to adjust the correct amount of heat. I cannot recall how many pieces of toast I have blackened beyond recognition. The oven's interior glows orange, and I watch the toast brown and harden with a degree of happiness.

Back at the desk, I set aside Carney and see in my notes the word "shark" underlined. Sharks would follow ships filled with African life across the Atlantic because they had grown accustomed to a habit whereby crew members would toss dead African bodies, those who succumbed to the myriad of diseases plying their interior cages, into the churning waves. The waters would turn red from the sharks fighting over bodies and torn limbs. For some scholars, such an event serves as an apt metaphor for Africans' ability to retain any semblance of their old worlds in slavery. Once disembarking their ships in Charleston or Kingston or Rio de Janeiro, once setting to work in plantations or mines or cities, these Africans, who met and interacted with one another under the whip and shackle, had to be creative in forming communities and in making lives and had no choice but to forget certain memories, forgo some beliefs, and to work to assemble something coherent among a tangled mass of cultures, languages, and worldviews. What was birthed on New World soil, these scholars conclude, was undeniably new.

My professor, an eminent and white African historian, disagrees. He belongs to a new a crop of scholars, including Carney, who argue any study of African American cultural formation under slavery needs to begin in Africa. The continent oriented their understanding of New World realities; they remembered Africa. To understand what happened in the Americas, they argue, one needs to understand what happened in Africa. Slavery could not completely erase their memories of religion, family, and group. Slavery could not completely decimate their humanity, could not entirely reduce them to property to be sold and traded. Voices travelled across the Atlantic, from Africa to the Americas, and bypassed the sharks, survived the way of death, and revitalized and renewed African cultures and communities from Buenos Aires to Mexico City to Montreal. These traditions, of course, were not static, not mere rocks to be passed along; they mutated and changed, evolved and metamorphosed. But the creolization was explicitly African. In the maroons, amid the sugarcane, within secretive city alleyways, enslaved Africans—Akan, Ibo, Yorouba, Fon, Kongo—conversed in hybrid languages and recreated old ceremonies—Candomblé, Vodun, Santeria. They reached to Africa and plucked practices from Senegal all the way down to Angola.

In my girlfriend's apartment, while waiting for her toast to brown, I realize how much such a Pan-African approach to cultural formation fascinates me. I adore the idea that movement, no matter how coercive, is undeniably creative. Even in slavery, human beings can remember and can forge systems of meaning. During my undergraduate history courses, I always found it appalling that examples of African ingenuity, of creative output, had been lost or buried under European and American history. In my essays, I tried to resurrect that lost history, as I explored the African origins of Argentine tango, the forgotten African involvement in the South American wars of independence, and the hidden existences of African diaspora groups in Guatemala, Panama, and Colombia.

For me, history acts as a map to the present, and I like following the lines and legends to see how we arrived here from there. I like making connections. I like tying together previously disparate parts to fashion something new, vibrant, and brilliant. I like having an idea crystallize in my mind and feeling the excitement it produces within, feeling the potential and possibility lying within that little nugget of insight, which not long before had existed only in the deeper, untraceable recesses of my subconscious. And it is exhilaration I feel when I read about the religious practices of enslaved Africans in the Americas and the scholars who argue they represent not mere holdovers from a static African past but a reinterpretation and reengineering of African ontologies on American soil—of beliefs old and new.

These ideas come unexpectedly, but I find music waters and nurtures them, so when I work, I listen to music. And on that Sunday morning in my girlfriend's apartment, a song floods my headphones, only a falsetto voice and an acoustic guitar, yet its sound stops me dead. I stop typing and allow feeling to envelop me. Its power pulls emotion from me, like plucking clover leaves, and I feel remarkably sensory and vulnerable, so indescribably alive. Tears well in my eyes, and tingling sensations run down my legs. The song slowly draws me back to the present, to the book and the computer, and I start to jot down thoughts, mere scribbles, about my ideas about African religious practices in the Americas, about how, maybe, I could write about this for my major research project. The music fosters my creativity and holds it in place, not letting it slip back into blackness, and I work to unleash everything to the page, everything the music has excavated from within. Write, Jesse. Write. Write. Write.

I remove my headphones. I hear my girlfriend stirring from the next room. She walks, dressed head to toe in her pink pajamas, through her living room towards the window. Her appearance is adorable, so contrary to the aura of professionalism and proficiency she must exude Monday to Friday in her position as an ethics officer at York University. Her disheveled look, her unmanaged hair running past her shoulders, her eyes blinking with wakefulness, stands in gorgeous contrast to her usual polished appearance—the suits, the makeup, the perfume.

"Oh my God, look at the snow," she says by the window, and I go stand next to her.

Outside, along Holly Street, the snow has turned Toronto white. The road resembles tundra, a snow-beaten plain, which has long become fallow, long robbed of its nutrients and sustenance, long hardened and toughened. The wind rises and lifts torrents of snow down the street, erasing the footprints of any brave souls who had walked there earlier. The red and blue cars parked beside the Thai restaurant have almost vanished. No plows have yet come to rescue us. Snowflakes have spattered and smudged the windows of the apartment buildings across from us. Everything sleeps in snow.

Movement then catches my eye, and I look down towards the entrance to see a man in a red toque and black snowpants shovelling the building's walkway. He is agile and poetic. He pushes his shovel through mounds of freshly fallen show until he reaches the path's end, bends at his knees, lifts the shovel to his midsection, and then flicks the snow over his shoulder, which is taken by the wind, blown backwards into him, and blankets his toque, pants, and the walkway in white. He does not seem to mind, as he goes back to where he started and begins the process again. His work is purposeful, needed.

Snow reminds me to accept my vulnerability, and my vulnerability often makes me brave. All the brave things I have ever done were in response to my fragility. I listened and responded. Snow is threatening, deadly, but beautiful. It is the essential paradox. Standing in the warmth of my girlfriend's apartment staring at the snow, my work done for the morning, my aim, too, purposeful and worthwhile, I think how much I am willing to fight for something so maddeningly prosaic, so beautifully mundane: snow, warmth, and burnt toast.

In the kitchen, I open the oven just in time to salvage the pieces of crisp toast and smear them with cream cheese. I drop spoonsful of instant coffee into two mugs and add the hissing hot water. I put everything on a tray and take it to her enclosed balcony. "Breakfast is served," I say, and assemble everything on plastic chairs serving as a makeshift dining area. Then I see her again coming to me in her pink pajamas, her gloriously unkempt hair, and her pleasingly pouty face she makes whenever she feels robbed of sleep and demands vengeance for the slight.

We sit near the window. I hand her the coffee and watch her hands wrap around the red mug. She takes a sip, then another, and then another, and the sleepiness dissolves from her body, which becomes more alert, agile, attuned. "Would you like a cigarette," I ask, and she nods, so I hand her a Benson and Hedges special light, and she secures it between her lips. When I flick the lighter and produce a wavy flame, she touches my hand and draws it close to her, and I shield the fragile fire and smile as she tries to place the rolled tobacco within the bouncy flare until the end finally catches and ignites in red. She exhales and the smoke drifts to the ceiling. I light my own, and we sit together for a moment revelling in the stillness of a Sunday morning covered in snow, enjoying a fleeting moment of tranquility before the world awakes. "It's beautiful," she says. I nod twice. "Did you get much work done this morning," she asks, and I say "some," and feel her hand on my knee, which, without my knowledge, had begun its anxious twitch, and I watch as her touch orchestrates the return of the calm and serene, watch as her fingers massage softness back into my skin. "What would you like to do today," I ask. "Absolutely nothing," she says. I nod twice. "Then, would you like to hear a song?"

A few months later, in April, after she had listened to the song one too many times and I had ignored her needs one too many times, we separated, and I am sitting in a large seminar room at York University, Founders College, third floor. The room has couches and a piano; portraits of masters in robes hang from the white walls. The space screams erudite discussions and cerebral conversations. It feels hidden away from the world, beyond the burdens of noise and the incessant rumblings of people and their phones. Here, we are quiet. Here, we think.

Today is presentation day. Today, we four graduate MA students in this directed reading course on Caribbean history must present our thesis research proposals to our professor, a distinguished historian from Trinidad. Ashley Cook, from Winnipeg, goes first and speaks eloquently about her research goals, about how she has sensed a disconnection between antislavery scholarship in the French- and English-speaking Caribbean, how they do not talk to each other, and how she desires a holistic approach to abolitionist discourses in the Atlantic world to better understand how voices outside Europe pushed the continent to condemn the practice. Benjamin Smith, from Toronto, speaks about his desire to compare historical accounts of the Haitian Revolution and what he calls the "romantic" portrayal of the Haitian Revolution—in which the complexities of the event are reduced to heroic accounts of the oppressed overthrowing their oppressors—and what this narrative inevitably silences. I say I wish to trace the Akan contribution to the three main religious practices of enslaved Africans in Jamaica during the period of the British slave trade—burial practices, Obeah, and Myal—and how Akan religious beliefs, along with other West African practices, underwent an intra-African syncretism that facilitated the emergence of a Pan-African religiosity in Jamaica.

The professor has reacted blasé to the first three proposals, providing one or two cutting criticisms that though brief have served to undermine not only the validity of our projects but our confidence and our sense of self—the fragile and tenuous mess of intellect and insecurity lining the soul of every graduate student. He is not so reticent after John Curto speaks, however. John, a native of São Tomé, has written an anemic and shapeless proposal about women, slavery, and resistance in the Caribbean. Even I can see that the proposal lacks direction and specificity; it is too vague and cursory. He has not carved out his position; he has not situated himself in the literature. There is no direction, no research question, no methodology. And when John finishes discussing his topic, acknowledging that his research is only at a preliminary stage, pleading with his eyes and tone that he too realizes he should have offered more, begging with his gestures not to judge him completely on this one effort, the professor lets John know without equivocation and without grace what he thinks.

"I don't know what this," the professor says, holding the two-page proposal in his hand. "What is this?" he asks again, his voice layered with contempt. His question is rhetorical. He does not wish John to answer. He does not wish John to explain how he was only able to produce this meagre proposal. Instead, he wants John to know deep within himself that his proposal is an embarrassment and that he should feel ashamed to have wasted everyone's time with his paltry effort. The professor says that his proposal is unacceptable at the graduate level. He says this hard and steely, indifferent to how his words have begun to affect John. He says again and again that his proposal lacks the focus and analytical clout necessary for an MA in history, the insight and intelligence necessary to evolve from merely regurgitating history to critiquing it. He does not seem to notice how John has solidified and has grown almost statuesque, how his body and skin seem to have transformed into stone, into a wall, a fortress.

When he finally finishes his long and cruel diatribe and then segues to a different topic, John sits silently for a minute or two and then stands and excuses himself. Yet his legs do not seem to obey his command; his whole frame shakes and wobbles, and he must grab his chair and then the table for support. He is visibly upset; his carapace has cracked. "Excuse me," he says again, "but I think I am having a panic attack." He stumbles behind me and towards the nearby couch. "Excuse me," he says again, "but I must sit down." I am sure he wants nothing more than to leave the room, the college, and the university and to retreat to the outside world where his family and friends are, but instead he labours on the couch, taking deep, powerful breaths in the hope he may calm himself, in the hope he may restore his internal equilibrium that had been so violently ripped from him. The professor takes a seat next to John and instructs him to breathe and to breathe some more. And around them the portraits of learned men in robes stay silent as do we, his peers and colleagues, as we watch John disintegrate and die little by little. I think how awful it is. But more to the point, I think how grateful I am that John is not me.

On a May morning, I drive the fifty or so kilometres from my home in Bradford to York University in northern Toronto to study in Scott Library. Classes have finished, yet my last task remains the most daunting: researching and then writing my thesis. Yet despite that cloud of doom hanging over me, I have a feeling of pride sitting in the early-morning traffic with my fellow commuters. I look across the median to drivers smoking cigarettes, talking on cell phones, and listening to music and sense a camaraderie with them, an affinity with the daily slog, the quotidian struggle, for I have never experienced something similar. I have never held a real job forcing me to schedule my life around the hours of the day and to drill existence into the holes of routine. Even though my pursuits are not monetarily driven, and I have no family to support or boss to endure, and my work entails twelve hours of reading oriented around the transatlantic slave trade, I still feel wonderfully average and beautifully circumscribed. I feel I am working, and this sensation momentarily blunts my feelings of guilt that have for years followed me like a ghost haunting my every step and ambition—the ghost of unearned prosperity. Both of my parents teach at the university, so I did not have to pay tuition during my undergraduate degree. They also footed the bill for my residency, my food allowance, and supported me when I studied abroad in Copenhagen during my third year. So when I park my parents' car in my father's parking spot, swing my bag filled with books on the history of West Africa over my shoulder, and race over to the library, I hold something wonderful in my heart—something earned.

I stack my books on top my library desk, and they rise over my laptop like miniature mountains. I hold a feverish, almost maniacal, reverence for libraries as places of quiet contemplation and deep, fundamental learning. And if nature—mountains, lakes, and air—represent to me the ideal setting for physical exertion, the pinnacle place wherein the body can blend seamlessly with its environment, then the library represents a temple of erudition, a holy place for the mind to wander, play, and make connections between various faces and disparate forces. The stories and facts and figures all speak to me while the information fills me, lifts me, and sends me floating towards the sky like a balloon. I am part of a conversation, part of a community of people and places I have never met but still know, somehow, whose cases and arguments I understand, even if I cannot claim their words as my own. Knowledge paves a path towards not only personal growth but power—the power of critique and the power to remember.

Fuelled by my few first sips of caffeine and the lingering effects of nicotine, I set upon my task of devouring each and every book before me. But this voracious appetite for knowledge often proves my undoing. Each book I meticulously prune over, making hundreds of notes with my pen or pencil—marks I am ashamed to admit can still be found in dozens of African history books lining the Scott Library shelves—leads to another and then to another. I dread the reference section because those detailed, single-spaced pages inevitably reveal another dozen books I must read, and before long, my reading list has multiplied tenfold. I cannot just stop. I cannot just read for the book's general idea, its overall thesis. I cannot just summarize the book's main findings, methodology, sources, and evidence in a page or two. One page of notes turns into two and then five and then ten, and soon I am simply rewriting the book verbatim, sentence by sentence, word by word, and punctuation mark by punctuation mark. I cannot distinguish between parts; I cannot craft a hierarchy of importance. Everything is essential. Everything matters.

As a child, my family and I would spend a few weeks every summer at our cottage. I hated packing. I hated choosing between which toys I would take and which I would leave behind. I remember one action figure—a Teenage Mutant Ninja Turtle, Leonardo, I believe—sitting on my bed. I knew I probably would not play with him at the cottage and would probably forget about him once I arrived, but I still could not bear the idea of leaving him behind on my bed alone. So I stuffed him deep within my bag, and I suddenly felt so much better. He was with me. He was part of me.

In a similar way, sitting under Scott's bright lights, I sense each word, sentence, paragraph, and page becoming part of me. And even though I will never use each and every one, even though the specific, intricate details of Akan culture and its historical contours will remain peripheral, maybe even ephemeral, to my project, I digest all of them in the hope they will become fastened to me and glued within my mind and body and soul. I wish the history would invite me into its home and welcome me with a handshake and, maybe, a mug of coffee. I believe knowledge itself is enough to grant me access to a stranger's home, and, over time, I will transform into a brother and then into a member of the house, the family, and the community.

I savour those wonderful moments, in the throes of words and music, when I see connections between places and dates and people, when I sense among the chaos of history, the infinite bodies moving through the unorganized and unhinged melee of the everyday, patterns emerge and then coalesce into an argument, and when I hack back the weeds of the past to make what remains mine.

At the bottom of my screen, MSN flashes yellow, notifying me of a message she has sent.

"Absinthe Pub, 5:p.m.?" it reads.

"Sounds good," I type.

On my Word document, I move people around here and there. I draw lines where I want: there and here. I make connections between then and now. Now and then.

In the Absinthe Pub, in the basement of Winters College, she sits at a table nursing a pint of Moosehead. She is dressed in her finest business attire—grey and black colours wrap around her body. She is immaculate, professionalism personified. Nothing appears out of place. She is neat and tidy.

I sit across from her and drop my bag of books on the table. She smiles and goes through its contents, repeating the titles with feigned interest:

Robert Rattray. *Religion and Art in Ashanti.*
Kamau Brathwaite. *The Development of Creole Society in Jamaica, 1770-1820.*
Vincent Brown. *The Reaper's Garden: Death and Power in the World of Atlantic Slavery.*
Richard Burton. *Afro-Creole: Power, Opposition and Play in the Caribbean.*
Walton Claridge. *History of the Gold Coast and Ashanti—Volume 1.*

She takes her eyes from my books, satisfied it seems, and lays them on me, as mischievous and playful as ever yet now hidden behind formality and the new rules of the game.

"A little light reading?" she asks.

"Yes," I reply. "My entire summer is in that bag."

"You had better get a beer then."

"Indeed."

The Absinthe Pub is a stereotypical student place where youngsters high on alcohol get to rant about whichever theory they recently read about. They get to apply what they learned to the real, somatic world. They get to taste how those long words feel in their mouths, taking shape over their teeth, tongue, and lips. They get to learn how to argue with a pint in hand.

The décor is perfunctory yet workmanlike. Humble. There are dartboards and space for a band to play or poets to read or comedians to joke. There are tables and booths. There is a patio with picnic tables and ashtrays and lights. There is a restaurant serving nachos and quesadillas and club sandwiches. There is a bar pouring a wide variety of draught beer and handing out shot glasses filled with tequila, Jägermeister, or whiskey.

I spent many Thursday nights—Pub Night—here during my undergraduate years. I spent many Pub Nights here drunk and arrogant and uncouth. With her. We would drink rum and smoke and listen to music in my dormitory room and then go to the bars. I would argue, and she would check me. She would collar me as if I were a misbehaving dog. She would put me on a leash and tie me to her. And I would get drunker, and she would stay calm and collected. She was cool. She was the adult, and I the child. She would go to work the next morning, and I would sleep until the afternoon. She was my first, and it happened one night after the Ab.

"Do you remember when they cut you off here," she asks when I return to the table with my pint.

"Of course. They had a policy against serving six rye and cokes within a forty-five-minute time period."

"I've never been cut off anywhere," she says with a grin.

One night, she told me something personal outside on the patio, and I did not know how to react. I felt heavy and useless. A stone or a rock or a tomb. She stared at the ground and smoked her cigarette. The night was cold, too cold for snow, a deep February tundra, and she sat huddled next to me on a bench. The sky was black and frozen. She stared at her hands in silence.

Inside, she asks "How many Pub Nights did we come here?"

"A few. I was always so well behaved, wasn't I?"

"Oh. You were a treat—a cute little drunken ball of arguments."

"How did you manage to go to work all those Friday mornings?"

"I get my sleep on the weekends."

Outside, I did not know how to comfort her or even whether comfort was what she needed. I felt myself slowly form into ice. I felt myself slowly solidify into a wordless statue, a soundless mannequin who possesses all the appearances of humanity but none of its essences. She looked fiercely at the ground, purely entangled in her own thoughts and streams of consciousness, and when I did say a word, she glared at me more out of reaction than genuineness and said, "No. Do not say that. I am not that." She said again, "I am not that." And she possessed for me the feeling of strangeness, so incompatible with how I understood the world, so difficult for me to pin down to paper with sentences and punctuation. I could not reconcile her body with my image of it. I could not align her experience with my expectation. I was humbled in her presence by her life and by her spirit because she had earned her sentiment, however roughly or unfairly. She had lived so much more than I had, and I feared this because she had arrived to herself, and she spoke her truth based on her experience, whereas I sounded so bookish, my thoughts so disingenuous, my life so memorized. I feared her because she was so much truer—in all her dizzying contradictions—than I was. She was so much better. She made memories; I read books.

Inside, I ask about her trip to Spain and Morocco with our mutual friends, and when I hear about her adventures, her maybe romances, I struggle to swallow those feelings of jealously I find so juvenile and unbecoming. I struggle to smile when she does or laugh when she laughs. I struggle to eat my emotions. I fight to shut myself down.

I want her to become a book I can just put on my shelf and ignore. I need her to become a page I can just turn at a whim. I need her to become an argument I can dissect, dismiss, and disavow. I see my books resting on the table. How comforting and attractive they seem. How I long to lose myself into their carefully crafted arguments, their meticulously detailed endnotes, their fifty pages of references. How I long to seek sanctuary in a library and never emerge again.

"We are still friends, right?" she asks.

"Of course we are."

"And we will always be friends?"

"Yes. We will."

She sips and savours her beer, and I feel lost in her presence. How do I respond to her friendship? Do I respond as a man who embraces both vulnerability and insecurity, who allows himself to melt and thaw and drip under the spotlight of doubt, under the sun of grace? Or do I respond as a boy who believes it when he hears the world belongs to him and him alone?

In the library, I have settled on the title for my thesis's introduction: "The Life and Times of Philip Quaque." I throw together the following sentences:

> *Quaque, né Kweku, was born in the Cape Coast community on the Gold Coast (modern Ghana) in 1741. This settlement was on the outskirts of the Cape Coast Castle, one of the largest British slave castles on the West African coast. In 1754, at the tender and impressionable age of thirteen, young Kweku was sent to England for education as part of a treaty made between the Fante and the British. Sponsored by the Society for the Propagation of the Gospel (SPG), Kweku spent eleven years in England and returned Philip Quaque, the new and first African chaplain of Cape Coast Castle. He returned a changed man; he lived in European fashion, with books and mahogany furniture, and his first wife was an Englishwoman. Like many others at the fort, he engaged in trade, including that lucrative one in human beings. But it soon became apparent that a large rift was growing between him and*

> *his traditional origins: He ceased to be fluent in Fante or any African language, relied on an interpreter, and mercilessly attacked traditional Akan religious practices. Towards the end of Quaque's life, a profound, it seems, spiritual and moral crisis enveloped him. After being a victim of European cultural imperialism and then an agent of that very same system, Philip Quaque reverted back to his ancestral culture and religion. By the 1790s he left the castle walls and built a family house in Cape Coast town.*

I have this man's story in front of me and have cut it into manageable chunks. I have pulled themes from this man's life like pulling quills from a porcupine: they are abundant and sharp. He represents a transnational existence. He was cut in half. He held duelling ontologies in his mind and heart—on his skin. He was African and European. He was creole. He beautifully yet tragically revealed how culture never disappears and never becomes subjected to complete erasure. *He survived the sharks*, I write.

> *He survived the sharks.*
> *He survived the sharks.*

In that moment, all else fades from me, except Quaque and how I dress him with my words. My ex-girlfriend fades from me, and I mark his body with my words.

I mark his body with my words.

2.

In My Mother's Office

It's a Tuesday evening in February 2011, and I am twenty-six years old. I am sitting at a desk in my mother's office on the second floor of Founders College in York University. McGill University in Montreal has just accepted me into its history PhD program. I start in seven months, and before then, I must learn everything about the history of East Africa.

It's been over two years since I finished my master's thesis on the religious practices of enslaved Africans in Jamaica, for which I was awarded an A+, and it's been over six months since I returned from a year-long trip volunteering and travelling around South America, a trip which my parents financially supported in no small part. Since returning, I have watched people move on. From the basement of my parents' house in Bradford, I have watched colleagues from my master's program enter PhD programs. I have watched friends and acquaintances start careers and families. I have watched an ex-girlfriend of mine find a new boyfriend and begin an exciting life with him in one Toronto's trendiest neighbourhoods. I have watched this all with a deep feeling of consternation, a burgeoning sense of shame. I have been left behind.

But this PhD program has given me a chance to finally stand on my own two feet and to cast off the support my parents have always so generously provided. I will become a man apart. There will be no more excuses. I will globetrot no longer, meander no further. I will no longer fatten myself on the food of others. Procrastination ends tonight. It's time to grow up. I will seize the opportunity laid before me. No distractions. No outings. No social calls. I will learn everything about East Africa. It's my ticket to self-reliance. I will prepare myself for this program, dedicate myself to it body and soul, for in it lies my future. My independence.

I tell myself this sitting in my mother's office reading Frederick Cooper's *From Slaves to Squatters: Plantation Labor and Agriculture in Zanzibar and Coastal Kenya, 1890–1925.* When I take a break from working, I turn in my chair and stare through the slender window behind me, which provides a generous view of York University's workmanlike campus located in northern Toronto. Its aesthetic is severe, serious, Soviet inspired. The buildings are mechanical, devoid any of personality except purpose. They are dreary and colourless, like skin devoid of blood flow or a body devoid of health. Yet somehow these structures inspire diligence like few others, and I am not sure why. Perhaps they inspire pupils with dreams of elsewhere, as if their hard work will somehow take them far away to places of light and fecundity. They inspire me for the exact opposite reason: They offer a lesson in the dictum "function over fashion." They are ugly yet of the mind. Their exteriors are bland and grey designs; the facades are chipping and peeling in age and neglect, and their windows are cracked and smudged and regimented. Yes and yes and yes. Yet I feel wonderfully refreshed staring at these structures, especially now in February, blanketed as they are in snow and ice, because they remind me what matters is the intellect, the interior. The walls whisper erudition is the only currency worth having.

I return to reading Cooper. To speak more succinctly, however, a trademark of any good academic in training, I am not reading Cooper but typing Cooper out. I have already read Cooper, and now I must note the most salient parts, the parts that may condense his magisterial work into a few bite-sized chunks. His book lies at the bottom of my laptop, and I am dutifully typing the parts I have underlined or made an asterisk or written "NB" beside. I believe this will make the information part of me. I believe if I keep typing those words and keep rewriting those sentences, the knowledge will become second nature, intuitive and instinctual, as if I had known these things all along and can recall them at will, as if memorized, as if fathomed from birth. It will become a second language.

My mother's office is a shrine to her accomplishments. A tenured professor of women's studies as well as editor-in-chief of her own academic press, she is the living embodiment of hard work and perseverance. She has almost single-handedly created a new discipline, motherhood studies, and has resolutely fought to have the study of mothers—their work, experiences, and struggles—recognized as a study worthy of academic exploration. She has articulated how motherhood freed from the imprisoning clutches of patriarchal control can become a practice of empowerment for women, a source of persistent frustration, pain, and exhaustion, sure, but also of pride, purpose, and power. And she always underscores how mothering is a practice, something learned through doing and doing again and again, an art form full of errors and mistakes, yes, but eventually one filled with voice, style, and grit. No one is born a mother; it is not of blood. She herself learned through doing; she, along with my father, had to juggle PhD requirements, teaching loads, and caring for us, her children, me along with my two sisters, in an environment—the academy—that often perceives children to be anathema to the cerebral, largely masculine, pursuits of higher learning. She accomplished all her goals while wrestling with three unruly children and placating all our unrelenting demands. She was younger than I am now. By twenty-six, she had responsibilities beyond the book and beyond the mind. She had little ones depending on her for their survival. She did not have her own office space, or the money to spend liberally on buying books, or the time to read for hours on end, book after book after book. She did not have my head start.

Gazing at her books lining the shelves, I think about these parallels, as well as the divergences, between my story and hers. I admire how she took her own experiences—a young woman with three young children navigating the halls of academe—and crafted a research project. I admire how she unapologetically made the personal political. I think, sitting here among her accomplishments, that I too, could become a professor and a researcher and dedicate my life to actively pursuing topics both of interest and of worth. I imagine how delightfully rewarding it would be to have the time and freedom to excavate the world and to shine a flashlight into unexplored crevices and untrodden passageways. I imagine how I could upend the taken for granted, the so-called natural and traditional, and how I could link the personal to the academic and eventually to the political, just like my mother did and just like my father did, too.

My father, a professor in the social sciences, often told me about the early giants of sociology, particularly Adam Smith and Karl Marx, and how they were both fascinated and alarmed by the effects of the Industrial Revolution and how seemingly overnight entire societies irrevocably changed, their means of production transforming from agrarian, rustic to mechanical, modern. He loved recounting the story of the pin worker in Smith's *Wealth of Nations*. The pin worker was once involved in each stage of the pin's birth—from raw material to artifact—and he worked the wire himself. He drew it out and measured it and cut it and straightened it and grinded it and shaped it. "This was his skill," my father said, "and his craft." He might make a dozen a day, for the process was intricate and involved particular diligence and care; it was work of the hands and eyes. It was art. But like all art, or any work that was as much about the idiosyncrasies of the worker as the product itself, it was incredibly inefficient and unproductive. "So what do you do?" my father said. "You divide the labour." Where once a pin belonged to the hands of one man, it now passed through twenty. One man drew it out and another measured it and another cut it and another straightened it and another grinded it and another shaped it. Pins were now assembled in a factory, and each worker became an expert in one specific part of the process. The men worked together as a machine and produced thousands of products over the course of a day. Yet for the individual man, over the course of the same day, he did only one task over and over and over again. For hours a day, he would only straighten or hammer or grind. He became skilled at one specific task and was a master of nothing. He was divorced from the fruits of his labour. He became indistinguishable from the other men, indivisible from the machine. And what made him unique and what provided him purpose—his work and art—were swallowed by the logic of productivity.

"Marx called this alienation," my father said. The factory pin worker never saw the final pin; he could not even say for sure whether it was a pin he was making. He cut metal for twelve hours a day. He cut again and then again. The same repetitive motions again and again. He was a gear, nothing more. A cog. The efforts of his labour were not his. They were meaningless; the value and worth were stripped from him, and he stood naked in front of his tool, only a body to be instructed, whose work enriched others, whose efforts were not his to enjoy. He was alienated from his work; he was alienated from himself.

And this new capitalist means of production robbed the worker not only his relationship with himself through his work but his relationship with his fellow workers. He was a stranger among his fellow workers, standing and working alone on the assembly line, as if he were his own island state surviving alone in the Pacific or the only planet orbiting a star. Yet it was Marx's hope that the workers could see themselves in one another, a reflection speaking to a common affliction, a singular goal, and that they could recognize themselves in opposition to the managers, the owners of capital and production, the overseers, and masters of profit, who saw their underlings as nothing more than tools to be used and exploited, but tools, all the same, that were completely necessary to extract profit from raw material.

My father witnessed this division of human beings and their labour during his time working at Firestone, with his father, and how each worker had his task in transforming a piece of rubber into a tire the size of a man. He witnessed how the factory worked as a laboratory of sorts to see how workers could be manoeuvred and assembled to maximize efficiency and productivity. Seemingly invisible hands moved them from one station to another and from one job to another to experiment with which arrangements worked best, and sometimes there were accidents, sometimes men died, hands were cut, bones broken. The work was dangerous, demanding, and, at times, dehumanizing. Yet my father also witnessed how the workers understood their own labour power as theirs to withhold or extend as they saw fit, a weapon to be used to improve their lot and position vis-à-vis the managers and overseers. My father witnessed the small acts of daily resistance, the little wars over smoke breaks, and he eventually witnessed how these little acts evolved to work stoppages and then months-long strikes that tested the workers' resolve, decimating, as they often did, their families and livelihoods. But this collective action nonetheless illustrated without doubt that workers were awake to the systematic logics of capital and to how they could wield such power to wreak havoc on management's mode of production, its way of accumulations, and its ability to extract profit on a whim. Organized labour was capitalism's check; it forced a morality on a system birthed only to take and then take again.

In my mother's office, not far from my father's in McLaughlin College, I adjust my eyes to Cooper's words and one particular chapter of his. Cooper concerns himself with the transition from slavery to freedom—or, more accurately, to wage labour and capitalism—along the East African coast, particularly Zanzibar, at the turn of the twentieth century under the beseech of the British colonial overlords. British abolitionists were as concerned about the immorality of slavery as they were with the inefficiencies of idle and free bodies, about what to do with the repercussions of liberty—the recalcitrant slave owners, the untethered slaves. Cooper dissects British thinking around work, wage labour, and productivity, teasing out these discourses from the grandiose archnarrative of abolition and freedom, to reveal how these abstract concepts produced concrete results: a capitalist system of production. Work as well as relationships had to be redefined. A new way of thinking had to be implanted in the minds and hearts of the former slave owners and former slaves. Yesterday, Zanzibar was the epicentre of the East African slave trade, a vast trading network that sent both spices and human beings to far reaches of the Indian Ocean. Today, Zanzibar has stopped sending the slaves, and the slaves who had picked the cloves and other spices linger around the island, squatting in old plantations, without tools, without orders. Labour was no longer owned by another; it was now owned by individuals, tethered to them as if their soul or conscience, and they were free to rent their labour out on an open, competitive market, for which they would be compensated freely and, allegedly, fairly.

What fascinates me most about Cooper's analysis is how the new capitalist conception of work imposed itself on the newly freed. The impetus to work no longer came from a whip; it came from within. The desire to hold a tool and then use it was internalized, until it became instinctual and unthinkable, as if that yearning were oxygen passing through the lungs or blood flowing through the veins. The British colonial state in Zanzibar instructed its subjects to embrace this idea of work, wished for them to willingly and lovingly tie themselves to a particular estate or plantation, to fight the scourge of idleness, to commit to the same daily work routine day after day, and to understand that time was not something that just passes but a measurement to evaluate the success or failure of a particular endeavour. And in return, the ex-slave received the gift of a wage—the epitome of both freedom and civilization. Dignity was less of a concern. Of course, the British failed in completely transforming the slave into a rational economic being. Officials routinely criticized ex-slaves for their laziness and idleness, yet for ex-slaves, what mattered just as much as the wage was the manner through which they obtained it. They understood the options this currency provided and reacted to the allure of choice as any agent would, yet they desired control of their work just as much as their British overlords. They desired land and mobility. They desired a life outside of work. Freedom was of little use if they had no land upon which to enjoy it or no time through which to experience it, time understood here as only the space between birth and death.

Outside my mother's office, night has come, and students scurry and dart under the streetlights. Cooper still lies below me, and his words still shine from my laptop's screen. I have spent the last eight hours copying his words verbatim and have accumulated ten pages of single-spaced prose detailing the complex and messy transition from slavery to freedom in Zanzibar. I take a sip of coffee, my third this afternoon, and it tastes particularly bitter, awful, in fact—the normal rejuvenating effects of caffeine have vanished, leaving only a heavy, cumbersome feeling, as if my head were too big for my body and wishes so very much just to rest itself on the desk. The words seem to glare at me and mock me in their weight, heft, and number. I suddenly feel overwhelmed and vulnerable in the face of such an information deluge. Naked. I am naked and exposed standing in a winter forest. I have nothing to offer and nothing to do. I do not know what to do with these words. I do not know how to read them, use them, place them, analyse them. I do not know how to connect them to my life. What have I missed?

Seven years earlier, in a university lecture hall, a grey-haired woman stood in front of a podium, arranged her notes, and adjusted the overhead. The projection over the blackboard read "Joseph Conrad's *Heart of Darkness.*" The overhead listed several topics in bullet form but with no further information. Professor Smith always told us that we must make our own notes and must separate the important from the mere dressing. "Filtering," she said, "is a great skill." The ability to take buckets of complex and dense information, condense and edit and parse it down, and then write a succinct and pithy sentence remained the Marcel Proust of academic skills. "And such economy of language," she said on the first day of class, "is of great importance to us, since we will spend the year studying English literature and modernisms."

The students made little noise; only a few pages rustled. All eyes were focused on her, and all pens were readied to fill workbooks and blank pages. The professor was short and frail, yet she intimidated with her intellect. Only a few classes in, and I feared her. I feared disappointing her. I feared answering a question not to her liking. Most of all, I feared her showing just how ignorant I was. She scanned the hall while tapping a pen against the podium. We all came to attention, and she began.

"Why have we begun this semester reading Conrad's novella?"[1] she asked. All hands remained down. All we heard were her notes rustling in her fingers. "For the rest of the year, we will read authors whose works better exemplify the tenets of modernism—Fitzgerald, Woolf, Faulkner, Stein, Madox Ford, Eliot, Pound, Hemingway—so why have we bothered with Conrad? Why have we spent hours combing through this dense book, whose prose, I think you would all agree, resembles the sentiments of a romantic and not that of a modern writer." Silence cooked the room to an unbearable tension; all heads stayed downcast, all hands pretended to scribble notes, and all egos prayed not to be called upon.

"What is the significance of Conrad's *Heart of Darkness*?"

Silence.

"Modernists mistrusted authority," Professor Smith intoned. "For them, a stable, straightforward narrative was anathema. Since such security did not exist in nature, why should it exist in fiction? Modernists brought uncertainty and doubt to narrative. Could any story be actually trusted? For Conrad, specifically, he saw firsthand the cracks and splinters embedded in ideologies masquerading as truths. He saw with his own eyes how civilizing missions—how the entire European colonial project—turned urbane men into savage beasts. He watched Europe's elite—the upper class, the university educated, the posh and privileged—transform into marauding hyenas in search of ivory and rubber." She paused to catch her breath. "Don't forget, *Heart of Darkness* takes place during the first systematic slaughter of the twentieth century."

She spoke about the Belgian Congo, about how King Leopold dressed his colonial desires, his need of land and resources, in talk of advancement, progress, and development. He had teamed with explorer Henry Morgan Stanley and formed the International Association of the Congo to further explore the Congo River and its interior. He told potential investors he wanted to bring European enlightenment to Africa's darkest jungles. He spoke enthusiastically about the "free negro republics" emerging under his tutelage. He would build roads, towns, and cities—civilization's infrastructure.

"Behind such rhetoric," Professor Smith told us, "unfolded a very different story." Africans would never gain political power. Leopold wanted their land. He demanded their labour. He craved their ivory. Stanley persuaded Congolese chieftains—through trickery and presents and gin—to surrender claims to their land. For pieces of cloth, Stanley bought large swaths of rich rainforest. And in 1884, at the Council of Berlin, the other European powers recognized Leopold's claims to the Congo. He named it the Congo Free State, and he alone ruled over it. It was his personal fiefdom, his pet colony, and it was seventy-six times bigger than Belgium itself.

For twenty-three years, Leopold singlehandedly ruled the Congo Free State, and the population declined from twenty to eight million. Professor Smith said Leopold's rule was barbarity personified. Forced labour was the rule; beatings were the norm. Leopold employed his Force Publique—a ragtag band of African mercenaries—to scare the population into submission. They kidnapped family members of Congolese men and held them until weekly ivory quotas were met. Whippings and mutilations met insubordination. Insurrection was punished with village burnings and arbitrary executions. Amputations were commonplace. Millions died.

"This is the violent setting into which Kurtz wandered," she said. "And remember his principal occupation—he is an ivory trader. And although we never learn in any great detail the barbarous practices he has participated in, we can, on account of the historic context, be reasonably sure they were many." As she spoke, I understood more clearly the function of Kurtz. He represented nobility polluted, brilliance tarnished. He went into the jungle as representative of benevolence, a light in the dark. He brought progress, justice as well as commerce, and democracy. He brought development, righteousness. But deep in the interior, away from laws and learned society, Kurtz bowed to the dark and embraced the latent horror within us all. Indeed, in the dark, as servants of war or colonialism, not much separates us, the civilized, from our ancestors, the apes, who reacted only to needs, who killed and massacred and ravaged for a slab of meat. When there are no rules, when chaos resides around every turn in the river, how does the moral man react? Kurtz is a cautionary tale for us all.

As I finished scribbling my notes, I looked to the overhead to see where we were in the lecture. After the bullet "*Heart of Darkness* in History," the next one read "Is *Heart of Darkness* Racist?" I stopped writing and checked the subtitle again. Indeed, I correctly read it. The air emptied from me. Racist, I asked myself. How is the novella racist? I felt my breath quicken, my legs twitch, my muscles flex and tighten. I overheated. I flushed. I sweated. I prepared my defense in my head. I laid out my arguments. Conrad is neither Marlow nor Kurtz. He does not profess the opinions of either man. He critiques their exploits. He critiques their ideals. He critiques the enterprises they represent. Conrad is a critic of empire. He dissects its germ. He is not his characters. But below the cursory arguments, the ranting and raving, I knew what really troubled me was the possibility I could be an admirer of a racist text. Impossible, I reassured myself. Not I. Not I.

"The Nigerian writer and critic Chinua Achebe," Professor Smith said, "has argued the novella is racist because it uses Africa mainly as a literary device, as a foil to Europe, day juxtaposed to night. It fails to draw the continent with any discernible human traits. In Conrad's Africa, darkness reigns. Conrad's Africa is outside culture and history. It is land civilization has sidestepped. It is void. It is lack." She stopped, and I was transfixed. "Who are the Africans in the novella?" she asked. "They are the cannibals. They are the deranged subjects of Kurtz who follow him around as if a god. They are the Europeans before civilization. They are only the first steps on the ladder to human. They speak in grumbles and slurs. Their language is basic, childish. They are merely limbs and eyes. They are one mass filling the forest. Indistinguishable." My hand shook, trembled. "Africa is the place where a European enters at his peril, a land where a man can all too easily revert back, devolve into an animal existing only on appetite." She lifted her eyes from her notes and settled them on us: "I want to ask you then, how can such a work be considered a masterpiece of English literature?"

I felt ashamed not because she was right but because I failed to see it. Why didn't I see it?

"In many ways, in both form and context," Professor Smith concluded, "*Heart of Darkness* birthed the twentieth century. In its structure, in its questioning of the perceived order of things, and its racist portrayal—or, indeed, treatment—of Others, Conrad's little book set the stage for a century of questioning both in literature and the larger world, for a century of unimaginable violence both in literature and the larger world."

Professor Smith looked us over.

"Are there any questions?"

Silence.

"See you next week."

I escaped towards the exit sign and out of the lecture hall. I could not bear reflecting another second upon what I might have missed—I, the child born from critical minds and piercing intellects.

Growing up, I hated sharing the music and films I liked with my sisters because they would always pinpoint with great precision some misogynistic line or sexist undertone I had failed to see. Their analysis would ruin my enjoyment. And I would argue and argue and argue with them, almost to the point of tears, and the more I argued, the more I knew I was wrong, and the more I knew I was wrong, the harder I screamed because I couldn't bear not seeing it. I couldn't stand being outside it. What gave them such insight that bypassed mine? Later, among my friends, when we would watch the same film or listen to the same song, I had to decide whether I would act. Would I share my sisters' insights, or would I enjoy an evening with my friends?

A few days before Smith's lecture, I was driving my sister to school when I played a burned Xiu Xiu album, one of my favourite bands, fronted by Jamie Stewart, a gay white American man. Stewart is an enigmatic, vulnerable frontman with a whispering falsetto that devastates with its intimate portrayal of pain and torture, of abuse and homophobia. His voice and lyrics draw me not because I can relate to their specificity of being a young gay man but because the music and wider themes of alienation and regret do resonate. On this particular drive, Stewart was delivering his bare and harrowing interpretation of Tracey Chapman's "Fast Car." Accompanied only by the barest of guitar strings, Xiu Xiu's interpretation haunts and hounds the listener. Stewart has inserted details of his own life into the narrative, fitting his personal troubles into the larger rubric of desire frustrated. Like Chapman, he yearns to get free, to get away beyond his imprisoning life, his duties and dependencies, to finally seek his dreams just across the bridge, over the border, a place where he belongs, where he can be someone.

I drove our car over concession roads coated with the season's first fallen leafs, past the big maples that had turned crimson red from the cooler air. I drove over knolls and flat farmlands, whose grey barns were slowly dilapidating under the bluest of skies and among the most orange of pumpkins. I drove without noticing my speed increasing, without noticing the loose papers next to me fluttering from the wind flowing through the opened window. I felt the urgency of the song, no matter the specifics of Chapman or Stewart—the universal urgency to choose, to act, and to live while I still can. There is still time, I assured myself. There is still time.

I looked at my rear-view window and saw my sister, Casey, gazing at the passing forests and bungalows. "What do you think of the song?" I asked. She shrugged: "Another example of a white man ripping off a Black musician." And from the moment she muttered her sentence fragment, I knew that she had forever tarred Stewart's version for me. She had forever opened a door I would have rather stayed locked. In an instant, I knew she was correct. I knew you cannot take a piece of art made in a particular cultural milieu and sung by a voice socialized and raised in a specifically oppressive environment and then insert your own details, your own tidbits, and expect the meaning to stay true to the original. But I didn't say this. Instead, I reacted and defended a piece of music that had meant the world to me. I said, "Stewart, too, as a gay man, knows something about oppression and violence; he knows intimately the desire to be free from the world's hatreds." Casey swatted away each of my arguments as if only annoying black flies and calmly refuted each's assertion. She had practiced this. She said words like intersectionality and institutional racism and white supremacy and white privilege. She said: "Experience is not a buffet where you get to pick and choose which you would like to sample. Experience is lived. And particular experiences are only lived by particular people, and people who have not lived those experiences should simply listen to people who have, instead of taking a life story, a narrative, and moulding it to make it more palatable to them. That is a privilege. You become a mere tourist in the life stories of others. You sample their foods and drinks. You take photos of their homes. You sleep on their beds. You claim a universality of experience only because yours is the only one that really matters."

Beneath my defense mechanisms, below my intellectual shield deflecting each blow, I knew she was right. Of course, she was right. But that was not the point. What bothered me was that I was wrong. I could not see it. Why couldn't I see it? Why had I become dependent upon others for wisdom? I turned Stewart off and let the wind fill the silence.

Outside the lecture hall, in fall's coolness, I calmed down, slightly, and concluded it best never to love anything. Attachment brings with it a certain jaundice clouding judgment and analysis. Closeness disables criticism. Passion induces parochialism. I promised myself then to never allow my positionality to soften and dull my critical knives. I would cut and dissect each and every argument thrown my way, until all that remained was the fat of that raw and uncooked thesis. And I would drop each morsel into my mouth above the vanquished man kneeling in front of me in wonderful submission and total surrender. My god, I would know everything. I promised and promised. I would master it all. Never again would they think me a mere charlatan with clever parents. I would insert my voice into the melee until it rose above the rest.

It's past midnight, and the lights of my mother's office have begun to hurt my eyes. I am tired and will return to Cooper and his cloves tomorrow. I shut down my laptop, flick off the lights, and curl myself into a ball on my mother's floor surrounded by boxes of books for her press, which she has just had printed. I am encircled by books.

I try to coax myself to sleep with gentle reminders that I still have time to make myself worthy of a doctoral program. You will take these books and eat them and digest them until you are fat with knowledge, so fat, in fact, that no one would dare question your position or approach or argument because theories, facts, and dates burst forth from your belly whenever you speak. You are knowledge embodied. You are walking intelligence.

But just as I am on the edge of sleep, I see myself leading a tutorial group of eighteen- and nineteen-year-olds, and I am speaking eloquently about a particular epoch of African history or the contributions of a particular African thinker or the lasting effects of the transatlantic slave trade, until a young woman of colour raises her hand and says, "You don't know any of this, do you? You may have it memorized, but you don't really know it, because you can never see it or feel it. You are a usurper of experience, a pillager of distant, foreign lands." And I cannot respond because there is nothing to say, no clever retort or comeback, only the realization that I will forever be a stranger in these fields, no matter the books I have read, the things I have thought, the wonderfully subversive episodes I have imagined. I have nothing except my books and my imagination, and while they may be good enough for me, they will never be good enough for her and many others.

Endnotes

1. I have recreated the professor's lecture from memory. Information regarding King Leopold was taken from Hochschild Adam, *King Leopold's Ghost: A Story of Greed, Terror, and Heroism in Colonial Africa.* Random House, 2010.

3.

Three Weeks in Montreal

August 31, 2011, 2:00 p.m.

Beneath a map of Mozambique, a country blessed with over 700 kilometres of coast and beach, I sink into my bed, grab fistfuls of mattress, and cry. I am twenty-seven years old, and I am alone in my apartment in Montreal. In between my gasps, a sound my neighbour might describe as primal, I smell lingering traces of the coffee I had prepared this morning. Coffee grind odour has always forced me to think about productivity or, perhaps more accurately, about all the things I have not yet produced. I hear water dripping into the sink, full of unwashed pots and plates from last night's bland spaghetti dinner. Each drip functions as an act of torture. The kitchen, a rather grandiose term for a stove and refrigerator, is a mere metre from where I lie now, from where I presently bite into an old bed sheet and scream, only producing muffled, inaudible sounds, a rather apt metaphor, it would seem, for my entire existence.

The verb "cry," I conclude, feels inappropriate to describe what I experience—a bludgeoning. Someone has taken a sledgehammer to my abdomen, and oxygen now refuses to flow as effortlessly as it once had, similar to when I was child and I fell from a playground apparatus and had the air beaten out of me. I remember stumbling through the grounds amid the swings and slides, like a staggering zombie clutching and clawing not for flesh but for breath.

From the corner of my reddened eyes, I see the books scattered across my apartment carpet; their hard library covers and colours—oranges and reds and yellows—remind me, for a moment, of a Southern Ontario fall, of dead, crimson leaves falling and floating on the placid surfaces of some freshwater lake hidden in a forgotten forest. And I, sitting upright in my green canoe, paddle over and through them, and the sounds of my paddle cutting through the water sing a lullaby planting me forever in the present, in the glorious solitude of water, trees, and sky. My corneas strengthen and focus the afternoon light streaming through my glass sliding door, which leads to a balcony overlooking Rue Hutchinson, and I begin to see the book's blurry letters form into words and phrases and sentences. Alan Jeeves's *Migrant Labour in South Africa's Mining Economy*, Charles Van Onselen's *New Nineveh: Studies in the Social and Economic History of the Witwatersrand, 1886-1914*, and Patrick Harries's *Work, Culture and Identity: Migrant Laborers in Mozambique and South Africa, 1860-1910*. Their presence only wounds me more.

Not four hours ago, I sat on that blue lounge chair across from me, a lovely gift from McGill Graduate Housing, and flipped through the monographs and wrote notes for SSHRC applications concerning my nascent PHD project: The Evolution of Modes of Migration in Southern Africa—From the Slave Trade to Human Trafficking. I looked at my map of Mozambique, which I had thumb-tacked onto my wall a week earlier, when I arrived to Montreal, as a reminder to what I was working towards, as motivation, as a subtle kick or push when things get real dark real quick.

But now, pounding on my bed and screaming self-hating words, I feel Mozambique has floated from my grasp, the country feels a distant dream, a different planet, extraterrestrial, a destination for more worthy pupils who have the intelligence, the poise, to take those books on the floor—also the hundreds upon hundreds of books lining my shelves, stacked in my closet, thrown across my desk—and to fight through the fog of previously published work and bring something fresh to the world. This is not me. I believe this now, as if I have always believed it, as if I am now only excavating a truth buried beneath false confidence, under fake intelligence, a soft sheen of self-worth softly watered over the years by encouraging loved ones and well-meaning professors. I believe it as strongly as I believe the earth is round, the sky is blue, and the sun rises and sets each and every day.

I do not belong here. I whisper the words delicately, enunciating each deliberately, as if prayer, as if confessing my sin of self-distortion to men dressed in dark robes hidden behind panels made from the strongest oak. I do not belong here. I smile. I do not belong here.

I imagine what a friend may say, or a counsellor, if I had either. I imagine the feeling of their touch on my shoulder and listening as they say to me "Breathe, Jesse. Breathe." I hear my mother's soothing words of encouragement while she reminds me of all my accomplishments, feats I typically slander as meaningless. Yet for all their soft, gentle words, I refuse to believe them, and their saccharine praise and empty platitudes further infuriate me. I despise their disingenuous pep talks, the type of motivational speech often reserved for a shy or stubborn toddler who refuses to use the toilet to defecate. And a remarkable thing happens to me there sobbing alone on my bed—those feelings of inadequacy harden into an apathetic resolve. I feel my body toughen to steel. I feel my muscles flex and become marble. My breath calms. All those eyes I have associated with scorn and judgment I have thumbed backwards into their skulls. I ignore their screams until only empty sockets stare at me, until I have killed all their power. I feel wonderfully numb and invincible. Indifference is my reprieve from the world. "Fuck you," I whisper. "Fuck you."

I look at my Mozambique map, and facts and themes float through my suddenly tranquil mind. The capital is Maputo. The country was a Portuguese colony until 1975. During colonialism, thousands of Mozambicans migrated to South African mines for employment and to escape Portuguese forced labour campaigns. After independence, the revolutionary party FRELIMO fought with the South African-backed RENAMO to destabilize Black rule in Southern Africa. After a brutal seventeen-year war, both parties signed a peace treaty and became political parties in a democratic, multiparty Mozambican state. Now in power, FRELIMO has shed its socialistic sensibilities, embraced neoliberal reform, and has received kudos from international organizations who laud the country's growth and ignore its continuing poverty.

This chronology means less than nothing to me—only words and dates I have memorized to have something relevant to say in this milieu. I stare hard into the map, noting the principal ports and remembering the names of the regions, and realize that I will never see Mozambique in any somatic sense. The country will forever remain only a map to me, an assemblage of lines drawn by white men in suits and bowler hats, smoking pipes in some parlour room in Berlin. And that is fine. Perhaps saving the world from the opinions of another white Africanist could be my little gift to the literature.

I rise from my knees and move towards my computer. Outside, the sun shines, and I know young men and women ride their bicycles through the network of leafy one-way streets, full of stop signs and townhouses, on their way to McGill, with their backpacks strapped tight and containing textbooks and laptops full of ambition and dreams. McGill is often called the Harvard of the North. Lots of history. Lots of graduates who have done great things. Lots of leaders of men. Leaders of institutions. Leaders of countries.

I log onto my McGill email account and see a note from the secretary of the Indian Ocean World Centre informing me of an employment opportunity. My stomach knots. I hear a dog bark, and a car slam on its breaks. The wind rises. I read another note from a professor I will be working with starting next week. He wants to meet with all first-year teaching assistants to discuss expectations and workshop problem-solving strategies. I imagine myself sitting at a table surrounded by undergraduates who look at me with expecting eyes that demand explanation and expedience, who crave knowledge worthy of their tuition fees, who do not feel it inappropriate to pin me down and draw speech bubbles around my sewn lips when I can only mumble words, when my silence proves inadequate for a centre of critical thinking and of devastating reflection. What wonderful words will they write, I wonder.

The final email I read has been sent to the entire McGill community. The support staff at the university—librarians, lab and information technology assistants, and other clerical workers—have rejected the employer's latest offer, and MUNACA, the union representing them, has declared a work stoppage commencing the following week to align with the official start of classes. A representative of the union informs students to expect picket lines at every entrance and to anticipate inconveniences to their education. Relief pours through me. *A student shall not be penalized for exercising their conscience and respecting the picket line* I remember reading somewhere in the McGill literature. I will not compromise my ethics for the sake of my education. I say it again. It sounds so haughty, so holy, so self-sacrificing.

I turn once more to my Mozambican map and run my eyes from Maputo, to Johannesburg, and to the mines of Witwatersrand and Kimberly. I fashion the rhetoric, the line of argument carefully and skillfully. How can I in good conscience and in good faith cross a picket line to study the social lives of Mozambican mine workers in apartheid South Africa? I will not insulate myself in the warm ivory tower when the realities of what I study are transpiring below the tower's windows. I like the way it sounds. I feel empowered and emboldened. I have fortified my defenses and sharpened my palisades. Before shutting down my laptop, I forward the email to my colleagues, my classmates, my competition, whom I only just met a few hours ago under the hard glare of our supervisor and with whom I had just shared a beer and listened with ineffable anxiety about their research interests and academic histories. I doubt they will share my enthusiasm for the work stoppage.

At the kitchen sink, I wash my dishes. I feel calmer, better. I have a plan of attack. I have chosen my mode of self-defence. As I reflect on this, I accidentally knock a glass from the counter, and it hits the floor with a predictable thud. I notice a piece, the size of a tooth, has chipped from the edge. And I think nothing of the cut glass when I instinctively place it in the rack to dry, even though it is not wet.

September 9, 9:00 a.m.

My father likes to tell me that I participated in my first picket line when I was barely four months old. York University's teaching assistants had gone on strike in 1984, and he proudly marched along Jane Street with me slung to his chest. Fellow strikers would stop and applaud my dedication and comment that I was the most socialist-leaning infant they had ever met. I stood up for workers' rights, the joke went, before I could even stand myself. My father always talks about the joyous spirit of the line and the unbreakable will of a people bound together in a common struggle warmed by solidarity. He talks about the chatting and chanting, the singing and the music making, the visiting with colleagues with whom you haven't conversed in years, sharing stories, and learning about one another's passions and research and interests. He recalls the camaraderie birthed there on the line, in the simple act of walking together towards a common goal. You cannot help but be moved by the resolve of a picket line in motion, he says.

So a warm, prideful sensation wraps around me when I write to my supervisor and to the professor whom I am assisting that I stand in solidarity with MUNACA, and I refuse to cross a picket line and legitimize the day-to-day workings of a university that has failed to negotiate in good faith with its employees and that has continued to hold classes when half its workers remain without a contract. My union has informed me, I write, that MUNACA supported graduate students when they last went on strike, and I plan to stand with them this time around. Soon my supervisor responds in curt and flavourless sentences that the decision is indeed mine to make, but he has set aside time this semester for these comprehensive-exam-preparing tutorials, and I should not expect any missed sessions to be made up.

An image of this man, whom I have met just once before, forms in my mind. I watch from my seat as a pair of white legs and arms, a head and a torso, come together and lock. His body attaches itself, piece by piece, before my eyes, and comes into being below his shelves of books and framed maps. On his face, just above his greying beard, there is a mouth, and when it opens and closes, I suspect that he senses each syllable a gift to whoever stands within his reach. Years of study have bestowed upon this man the title of expert, and he will use it to demand things not his to have.

At Ruddick Gates, right on McGill's mouth, we march in a narrow circle, more oblong in shape, as our feet edge close to Rue Sherbrooke packed with cars and buses and trucks on this early weekday morning. The vehicles almost touch us as they crawl by. Many picketers raise white signs saying "McGill Works Because We Do" or "We Want What Other Universities Already Have." A young man in white shorts races up and down Sherbrooke waving a blue sign encouraging drivers to honk if they support MUNACA, but as the road dissolves into a cacophony of shrill, blaring horns, I cannot say for sure whether they result from support or frustration. The man in white shorts spots a transport trunk plodding down the pavement and sprints towards it. He punches the sign skywards and shouts and motions for the man in the cabin to blast his horn, as he believes, I suspect, that all truck drivers embody union ideals and would support a work stoppage whatever the cause. And in this case, his stereotyping proves sage. The driver waves, reaches for his pulley, and yanks, which releases a long, discordant honk into the air. We cheer and our voices become louder and bolder. Other commuters are not so supportive and feel the need to share with us in not so diplomatic phrasing their thoughts on proper management-labour relations. In response, one man in a green turtleneck strums his ukulele with more vigour, sings his song with more enthusiasm, and welcomes the naysayers in their parked, motionless cars to sing along.

A traffic light hovers over us, and whenever the orange hand transforms into a white man in mid-step, a stream of students cross Sherbrooke to enter McGill through the gates. As I watch them move with sanguine steps, the gait of those who still believe in bright futures, I guess which ones will wait for a gap in the line before they enter and which ones will plow right through. Picket lines, my father says, bring out the very best and worst in people. One adolescent male, donning the attire of affluence, his appearance sharp and well moneyed, struts across Sherbrooke and pushes his way through a pair of picketers who glare at him but do not lose their temper, for, as they must think, such an expenditure of energy would be as useless as screaming at a puppy pissing on a rug. I track his movements as he marches under the solemn gate, this future leader of business and men, as he passes along an asphalt path underneath swaying, green-leafed branches, and the university opens like a meadow around him and welcomes him with sublime greenery and historic buildings, whose grey, stately exteriors give the illusion of intellect. I imagine him forgetting about the melee behind him and focusing on the increasingly silent atmosphere, such a sedate and serene ambiance, perfect, he must think, for serious study, away from the bustling outside world filled with noise and protest. He glances towards his left, at McLennan Library, a place I frequented regularly before the strike, checking out a dozen books on South African history, the librarian looking at me while she scanned each, saying she was from South Africa and asking had I ever been there. I simply shook my head.

I soon lose sight of the man behind the trees and instead picture him walking towards the Arts Building, dating from 1839, McGill's oldest existing edifice, and looking up at the wooden cupola, the university's well-known icon. Standing underneath the imposing structure, the young man must reflect on his school's past, how, for example, only two hundred years earlier no buildings stood here, only private property, a rather novel term for the time, and a hill, some mistakenly called a mountain, nothing much. A plucky Scotsman and fur trader named James McGill thought it scandalous that the settlement of Montreal had so few institutions to teach young boys how to think, being as he was a product of the Scottish Enlightenment, and decided to rectify such outrage and wrote a will in 1811 bequeathing ten thousand pounds and his forty-acre Mount Royal estate to the Royal Institution for the Advancement of Learning demanding a college be built there within ten years of his passing and bearing his name.

I envision the man moving left, past the Leacock and Morrice buildings, through a tight passageway, and emerging at Rue McTavish, turning left again, until he arrives at placid Peterson building, climbs its steps, opens its door, and upon entering, to his immediate left, appears another door. But this one is locked, impenetrable, and he must press a button and wait until a voice sounds from the intercom asking him his purpose for being there, and he must explain he is there for the seminar, that he is there to learn, and he convinces the woman he belongs at the Indian Ocean World Centre, and he enters and sits on a chair surrounded by encased knowledge and beside three other students, equally eager to impress their new master, who sits across from them, steely and unmoving.

And the man, who suddenly seems much older, who suddenly looks a lot more like me, more beaten and jaded, shakes and stumbles over his words and sentences, the first of thousands, since he has forty-five minutes to talk about one area he studies, and today he discusses slavery in Africa and in the Indian Ocean World, in Madagascar and Mauritius, along the Swahili coast and among the clover plantations of Zanzibar, and about how slavery in those places was often quite distinct from its Western, more infamous, counterparts, how it was often a method of incorporation, of tutelage, of apprenticeship, violent yes, but also a mechanism of advancement, upward mobility, social cohesion. But the man soon sweats and stews over each word, until long silences appear between sentences and then between words, until he knows everyone silently mocks him, until his supervisor, God himself, moves on to the next, more gifted graduate student.

My eyes and thoughts return to the picket line. The increasing number of walkers has pushed the line down Sherbrooke so that we now walk in the shape of an axe: down the Sherbrooke handle and around the Ruddick blade. The traffic has once again stopped. Noise fills the air, yet I walk my round in silence.

Monday, September 17

Near my apartment is a Second Cup, and every morning, I stop to buy a coffee, check my email, and sit among the legions of young students typing away at their Macs and working diligently and conscientiously towards a future full of more cinnamon lattes and delicious pastries. I have an email from my supervisor, and the anxiety comes as it always does. I had sent the man my reading list for the year attached in an email—the hundred or so books to help me prepare for my comprehensive exams, broken down into such thematic sections as comparative slavery and emancipation in the Indian Ocean World, postslavery labour regimes, colonialism and labour migration in Eastern and Southern Africa, contemporary migration patterns within Africa, and the rise of the human trafficking discourse.

I open the email and the first line reads "Jesse, this is a face-to-face course not a correspondence one, so it is difficult for me to respond by email." My body temperature rises, and the first beads of sweat emerge on my forehead. He critiques two of my section titles, mentions two authors I need to include, and finishes his message with this: "What I have asked from everyone else is a revised outline with, underneath the titles, a one-paragraph list of issues to be raised in that particular session—it will help clarify the debates." He offers me his best wishes.

I hold two contradictory emotions together, and each vies for my attention. Relief tells me that I have fulfilled my prophecy. Relief tells me I have successfully created an atmosphere in which I can flee, nay depart, with a degree of self-respect and dignity. Relief tells me I have successfully saved face. Anger, though, rebukes my assent to defeat. Anger tells me that this man, this supervisor, this scholar with whom I am expected to work for the next five-plus years, has robbed me of my right to protest. Anger tells me this man deserves more of my attention.

Outside, I am walking towards Concordia University and its library, my refuge for the past week or so, a space in which I can read and work in relative peace and calm for twelve-hour bursts of intellectual expenditure. And as it always happens, my mood improves once I am away from McGill, once I am walking away from its orbit, its pull, its influence—and away from him—I become more defiant, more reckless with my thoughts, more bellicose in my lines of argument. Anxiety is wondrous in its ability to prepare you for the worst. Anxiety has groomed me for the apocalypse, to verbally attack any self-proclaimed advisor who dares speak to me as if I were less simply because I lack the requisite initials following my name, those little titles guaranteeing respect and worship. As a result, I have sublime defense mechanisms, so sharp, so threatening. On the walk, my body tightens, solidifies. I personify nervous, unpredictable energy. I let my thoughts flow undisturbed, let them go in an incendiary stream of vitriol. I focus on him. I look at him. You, I tell him, expect me to acquiesce to your demands? You expect me to laud the time you have taken out of your busy research schedule to help supervise a bunch of lowly graduate students? You, a scholar of slavery, of African labour regimes, expect me to cross a picket line, to ignore the plights of workers here and to enter your million-dollar research centre so to discuss the social lives of African migrants a century ago? Do you simply treat history as a puzzle to solve, a complex mosaic forever divorced from the present? Is history simply your income? Is history simply a way for you to pass the time? Is history your hobby? You disgust me. You, professor, disgust me. You sitting there behind your immaculate desk, surrounded by old scrolls protected by glass, you sitting there dictating to us your expectations, your fucking goals and agendas, you, sir, are an embarrassment to history, a historian of the worst kind, a profiteer of the past, a carpetbagger of the archives, a colonial academic who rips and ravages the annals of Africa to serve his personal whims. Fuck you.

In the library, I calm. I take out my books, start my laptop, and open my notebook. Libraries have always provided me a space of solace and reflection. They are repositories of knowledge, containers of the world's collective wisdom. Whenever I can, I try to bury myself in a library's remotest corners, on the floors and in the workspaces furthest from the exits and other students, deep in the stacks and among the forgotten dusty aisles, and here in Concordia University Library, it is no different. During breaks, I walk down the rows of shelves and run my finger along books' spines, catching their titles and realizing it would take innumerable lifetimes to read and learn all this place has to offer. When I was younger, this knowledge depressed me, but now I find it surprisingly soothing to see that a single lifespan, eighty odd years of reading and writing and learning, only makes one slightly less ignorant than the day of their birth.

On the desk in front of me lies Harries's *Work, Culture, and Identity*, a history of Mozambican workers who lived and worked in sugar plantations, diamond fields, and gold mines of South Africa from 1860 to 1910. He explores in minute and vivid detail the social histories of these migrants, and how they negotiated, with varying degrees of success, their relationships with their employers and the nascent apartheid South African state. Specifically, he resurrects the ways in which Mozambican migrants understood themselves in South Africa and how they could resuscitate rituals, traditions, and beliefs even deep in Witwatersrand gold mines. Through oral testimony and the reading of symbolic forms (folklore, metaphor, dress, drink, and habit), Harries tries to recreate the cultural lives of ordinary migrant workers, a history from below, a history from their point of view, in their language, through their customs and belief systems. He has grown tired of a historiography that treats these human beings as mere objects of exploitation, as only tools for the Randlords, the capitalist and racist classes, as only comprehensible through Western epistemology, through its crude binaries and essentialist categorizations. He has grown weary of historians who ignore the agency of migrants themselves, who drown their humanity in economics and structural forces, who treat the cultures of mines and plantations as something to be glossed over, something reduced to exploitation.

I have always admired how scholars can come to view gaps in the literature and to see how an entire generation of work has missed a salient point or to reinterpret the same evidence in novel and fascinating ways. "You are creating new knowledge," my mother said when I asked her years ago what one does in a PhD program, when she herself was finishing her dissertation on African American mothering in the novels of Toni Morrison. How daunting such an idea sounded to me then. "Most of women's history has remained buried," she told me later when I expressed my interest in the discipline. "Male scholars never saw its value. They never looked beyond what they already knew."

When I was a child, I would play along the shores of my grandmother's cottage near Bancroft, Ontario. With my net held high above my head, I would hunt the muddy shoreline looking for frogs to add to my pail. On the other side of the dock, though, the bottom was rockier, and my dad, when he saw me traversing that section, would yell from the deck, "Lift a rock and see what you find." And I would smile because I had come to know what to expect and when I bent to lift one glistening rock from its spot, I would brace myself because every now and then a crayfish, pinchers extended and ready, would come shooting out from the darkness, swim past my bare feet, and find refuge under a distant rock. No matter how prepared I was for it, its presence and movement always startled me. What unseen and unexpected wonders do live right beneath our sight, our touch.

In Concordia's library, I think about Mozambique and crayfish as I open a Word document titled "SSHRCApplication." The page is a series of ideas and sentence fragments, half-formed thoughts, barely articulable notions and whimsies. I must cohere and shape these tangents into something comprehensible, I tell myself, again and again, as if I cannot believe such a feat is feasible. I open folder after folder scanning the copious documents I have created containing page after page of notes from the hundreds of sources I have read preparing for this PhD program, remembering the months and months I spent isolated in my basement or sequestered in a library poring over each page, every single paragraph, sentence, word, remembering the mornings, afternoons, and evenings I spent hunched over a desk, digesting each thesis and structure, noting the supporting evidence, recording if and how the source has taken the literature further, expanded the conversation, produced new knowledge, remembering all the social events I forsook, all friends I condemned to the trash, all the nights I wished I had been doing something else, all for this, this moment sitting alone and bewildered in a Montreal library.

I look over the documents I have about contemporary migration within and from Southern Africa, and I notice how most discuss the increasingly feminized form it has taken: In the face of globalization and changing gender dynamics, more African women appear to be migrating than ever before. Another literature suggests that the women who migrate clandestinely, without papers, undocumented, are at an increased risk for sex trafficking, a practice labelled contemporary slavery by many observers. Even another, more critical, literature argues that this obsession with sex trafficking among policymakers masks their real intension: border control.

By focusing on women's alleged victimhood and silencing their agency, their desire to move and work elsewhere, this protection discourse keeps women at home, locked and sequestered in their perceived homelands, condemned to a sedentary life.

I sense something missing from these discussions. I begin to piece together echoes of half-started conversations, whispery dialogues I have heard throughout my readings. Why does so much literature treat globalization as a recent phenomenon, I ask myself. The advent of the internet and other technological advances has, indeed, made the world seem smaller, more connected, more accessible and knowable. Yet mercantilism and capitalism, the brutal economics of plundering and pillaging, have for hundreds of years reluctantly brought the world closer together. Capital was the first cosmopolitan citizen who cared little for differences separating human beings, cared even less about borders, and who saw the vast economic potential in each and every one of us, regardless of race or creed.

I further scan my notes. Even before European intrusion and their eventual conquest of the region, the peoples of Southern Africa never lived in splendid isolation from one another. People moved. And when diamonds and gold were discovered in the Kimberley and Witwatersrand regions towards the end of the nineteenth century, and Africans from the north, south, east, and west migrated there to fill the labour shortages, they only continued a practice, albeit in an accelerated and radicalized form, they had long known: movement, adaptation, creation, survival. I look in awe at the amount of literature about the thousands upon thousands of male migrants toiling in the emerging South African extractive industries. I revisit my notes from the early works centring the exploitative nature of the migrant system and the dehumanizing conditions of the mine work itself. Divorced from their families and communities, this literature asserts, these men transformed into expendable chattel, disciplined into becoming more efficient and productive workers to benefit the mining capitalists.

I look back to Harries's monograph lying open next to my laptop. Yes, mining the Witwatersrand was brutal, I hear him telling me, but it was never so brutal to completely sever migrants' attachments to their homelands, never so harsh to make them forget from where they came. Within the horrific mines or inside the cramped hostels, men could, at times, resist the intrusion of capitalist work regimes into their lives, reinvent important rites of passage, reconstruct a masculine-centred universe, and recreate an understanding of work invested with cultural significance. I type the word "transnational." I type the words "strengthen home," as many male migrants moved to sustain or save for a home and family in the countryside.

What about women? Did most African women tend to their domestic duties while their partners were gone earning wages in the mines? Were African women merely the physical manifestation of an anchor, reminding men of their origins and their patriarchal duties and keeping them to only a temporary absenteeism? Did women not move too?

The lights in the library brighten. It is late, and I am the only person within sight. In the silence, I feel my internal buzz. I am buzzing with connections and creativity. I sense I am close to something, an avenue of inquiry worthy of a PhD project, a topic worthy of excavation. I feel it, the reason why, the reason I am here, the reason why I have sacrificed so much to be alone here in the library. I feel it so acutely that I suffer no shame when tears well in my eyes. Purpose. Yes, it is the feeling of purpose.

I turn back to my notes and look for an explanation. Scholars, I discover, have rationalized this scant attention to female migrancy based on the premise that African women simply did not migrate. Only in the 1970s, the argument goes, did women begin to migrate to South African cities en masse because of increased rural impoverishment and in search of their husbands, who, after becoming increasingly attached to wage labour often did not return home. Once in the cities, the argument concludes, female migrants found themselves in exploitative relationships with men in cities, often exchanging sex for a measure of security.

This line of reasoning ignores the whispers I have uncovered in the literature, little hints of African women living and surviving in the mining communities, little mentions of women acting unruly, wantonly, unwomanly, brewing beer and selling sex, little bits of evidence suggesting women moved outside the sphere of male proletariatization, moved to solidify the rural base not in response to its collapse, moved for many of the same reasons as their male peers.

I pause. I am on the cusp of something. I am on the edge of a cliff. From the bricolage, from the mess of sources and theses, and from the months and months I have spent tapping my pen in frustration thrusts a nugget of novelty, a string of sentences that perhaps separates me and my work from everything that has preceded them. I place my fingers on the keys and let the words flow:

> Building upon these efforts, I hope to research the phenomenon of female migrancy by centring African women's experiences. I wish

> to explore how labour migrancy offered them both opportunities and constraints. Although Sesotho, Zulu, and women from other cultural backgrounds will inform my analysis, my focus will be on Mozambican women and the effect their presence had on the Witwatersrand mining communities. Specifically, I wish to elucidate—what until now has only been haphazardly studied—the place of sex and sexuality in the female migrant experience in a way which centres power, negotiation, and agency.

I write that scholars have only afforded such delicate and holistic treatments to male sexualities developing within the South African mines. I write that Marc Epprecht has studied the practice of "mine marriages" and has argued this relationship between older men and more passive, "womanly" boys were not only initiation rites from their home culture aiming to perpetuate patriarchal roles but also an example of changing patters of African same-sex desire. I write that Dunbar Moodie has highlighted the benefits the boy received in these relationships, despite the unequal power dynamics at play: protection, financial remuneration, and a quicker graduation into manhood.

But the migrant women who sold sex in the towns and communities above the mines have not received similarly nuanced treatment in the literature. Some scholars, I note, have paid cursory attention to the "town women" who performed types of sex work but have focused on the ways African miners attempted to avoid these so-called loose women because of the various threats they posed: financial ruin, dissolution of rural connection, and infections. But I do remember reading about relationships between African women and men forming in the mining compounds and in the towns. I remember at times men called these women "prostitutes" and at other times "girlfriends." I think such categories and constructs are never absolute, their borders never so rigid to avoid leakage. They are fluid, porous. My attention falls on these ambiguities, these aspects of human existence defying easy categorization. It is these complexities and subtle negotiations and contestations of sex and power that I am interested in exploring.

More questions come in sharp bursts. Did South African officials panic about women selling sex or about their existing where they should not? Were these officials concerned about the women's wellbeing or concerned about the partial opportunities selling sex or brewing beer or hawking wares afforded them? Was it because women were exploited or was it because they upended certain perceived absolutes about where African women were thought to belong? Can I draw parallels between the hysteria surrounding urban women of the young Witwatersrand and the contemporary panic over sex trafficking? Why are certain forms of mobility deemed so threatening? What did mobility give women? What did it take away?

I stop and look around. The library is silent, beautifully so. The artificial lights give the place a vibrancy it does not deserve. In reality, everything here is tired, including me. And it's in these moments of exhaustion, when my defenses weaken, that I feel vulnerable and soft, approachable and welcoming. I gaze lovingly at the words glowing on my computer screen and feel proud I have filled the empty whiteness that was once there. There is still much to be done. I must kill about two hundred or so words. I must provide better linkages between paragraphs. I must delete some nominalizations. I have overused the passive voice. But for now, I am satisfied with the work done. I am calm with accomplishment. Productive. I have been productive.

I gather my things, float down the escalator, and breeze through the doors out into the night. When I was younger, on a New Year's Eve, my friends and I stumbled along this street, drunk and silly and stupid, along with thousands of other Ontarians who only understand Montreal as a hedonistic playground, a stereotyped city where inhibitions and anxieties are unknown. And how exhilarating everything seemed to me then. Life was an unopened Christmas present. Of course, in the back of my mind, in the unaffected and sober parts, I knew such a feeling could not last. The realities of yesterday and tomorrow ruin today's pleasures. All excitement eventually dulls. And now, many years later, I sense the same inevitability walking back to McGill. Beneath the joys I have just experienced, I know I will never see my work to completion. Those words will die on the page. My excitement will vanish. But, my god, how nice it was to feel it again.

August 31, 12:00 p.m.

He speaks:

"These sessions will essentially act as practice for your comprehensive exams, which you will take in a year's time. This program has no coursework. As a result, what we do together in this room—discussing and debating ideas, fine tuning your own approaches, improving your speaking skills—becomes that much more important."

Four of us sit in front of him. We met a dozen minutes ago waiting outside the Indian Ocean World Centre. The three of them—two men and a woman—lounge on comfy chairs in the hallway when I enter from outside. I busy myself looking at the notice board and reading about upcoming talks and conferences. I listen to their conversations and soon conclude they are here for the same reason I am. I approach them, feebly, and ask if they are waiting for the orientation session for incoming history PhD students. They nod, and the woman tells me they buzzed the intercom and a voice told them to wait patiently for another five or so minutes. I turn to the door, which is black, heavy, and shut.

He speaks:

"I am dedicating the entire fall semester to these sessions. We will meet a few times a month for about four hours. Each of you will talk for forty-five minutes followed by fifteen minutes of group discussion and critique. You need to become comfortable speaking about your topics. You may bring notes, of course, but I urge to become better at conversing than regurgitating. You must know your material inside out. You must convince us you know the theories, the arguments, the lines of disagreement. And most importantly, you must situate yourself in the literature. Where do your nascent topics sit? What does the literature already say about them? What doesn't it say?"

I look to my right and see my colleagues scribbling down notes. The pen in my hand has momentarily stopped writing. My eyes swing over the room. It is spacious and decadent and learned. It is the type of place one would expect to get work done unencumbered. It is inoculated against the outside world. It smells of the cerebral. It smells of expectation. It smells of inevitable failure. Something damning and destructive lurks within me. I feel it coming, rising. It demands my attention.

He speaks:

"By next week, please send me a list of the topics you wish to cover in these sessions. Each topic should be based on ten to fifteen sources. Each topic should be large enough to warrant such research but concise enough to allow a thorough investigation in forty-five minutes. Once I have your list, I will offer suggestions about whether I think a topic is too big for one session and, of course, whether you are missing any key sources."

I raise my hand.

I have been practising this question in my head for the last few minutes. I have dissected it into pieces, rearranged them in my mind, and reformed them for better syntax, clarity, and conciseness. For each word, I have debated whether the usage is correct, wondered whether a better word exists, deliberated over whether each preposition is really needed. What is filler? What is necessary? Is the question pithy? Is it succinct? Is it worthy of a PhD candidate?

"In terms of sources," I ask, "what ratio between monograph and articles should we aim for? What would be appropriate?"

As I ask the question, as the words release from my mouth, I step back and above myself and watch my peers gently turn their heads in unison towards me, watch the professor stay steely and detached as he absorbs my question, watch myself wave my hands as if a conductor, as if by the magic of movement I can place each word in its proper syntactical slot, as if such a display may dispel them, however briefly, of the belief that I do not belong here. He answers me, and my colleagues jot down a few notes. He offers a few final words of encouragement and acknowledges how daunting the task seems at the moment, how intimidating, but he assures us that we are building a base, a knowledge foundation, which will serve us well in the long run. I suddenly become aware of the door. I suddenly notice my leg twitching and bouncing. I suddenly hear my curly-haired colleague ask a question and am convinced it is more intelligent than mine. I am convinced that the professor knows it too. I suddenly fixate my attention on the outside—the sky, earth, and air—and think how lovely it would be to disappear completely into it.

In the late-morning sun, we, the baby PhD students, congregate on McTavish lane. They talk and laugh, and I force a smile upon my lips. I want to run to my apartment and bury myself in the literature, prove to myself again that I am worthy, I do belong, and I do deserve to be here. The older man from Israel, a graduate from the University of Tel Aviv, suggests we get a drink at the graduate pub just up the street. The curly-haired man, from McMaster University, enthusiastically agrees, as does the woman, an alumna from Carleton University. For the sake of convention, to adhere to social etiquette, I, an alumnus of York University, follow them. The woman from Carleton University walks next to me and asks whether I consider myself an Africanist in my orientation, as she has a background in South African history and plans to do her PhD on the Mau Mau revolt in colonial Kenya and its effects on the children there.

"Not yet," I say, "but maybe after this program."

"Of course, of course," she says. "I only mean whether an academic, a historian, can limit herself to the confines of a single category. I mean, look at Frederick Cooper."

She stops and looks at me.

"You have read Frederick Cooper," she asks, and I nod.

"Well, Cooper started out as an Africanist through and through with his brilliant analyses of slavery on the East African coast as well as his detailed studies of labour regimes in English and French colonies and the nascent African labour movements there and their roles in decolonization. His later work, though, has primarily focused on comparative approaches to the study of colonialism both within Africa and outside of it. He seems to have found the Africanist label too constricting to study what he wants to study. It makes you wonder how useful these labels really are, wouldn't you agree?"

I nod.

"That's why I find the Indian Ocean Centre so enthralling, so intriguing, because it looks at places not existing in splendid isolation but as part of a system, a network, that has existed for centuries."

"Connection," she says. "It's all about finding connection. I mean look at us. "He," she says pointing to the man from Israel, "studies the Philippines, and he," pointing to the man from McMaster, "studies India. You study Mozambique, and I study Kenya. It's incredible, wouldn't you agree?"

I nod.

In the bar, McMaster has ordered a pitcher of beer and has filled four pint glasses. He hands them out, careful not to spill any on the table. Tel Aviv raises his glass and motions for us to follow. Our four glasses gently touch in mid-air, and Tel Aviv says, "Here's to beginnings, here's to hard work, here's to great accomplishment, here's to the future." McMaster says, "Amen," and Carleton says, "Cheers." Our glasses touch, and we all say cheers together, our voices blending into a chorus of well wishes and hope.

The alcohol quickly depresses me. The expected buzz has turned to mud. I feel so heavy, cumbersome, a rock dropped in water, sinking down and down and down, further from the sun, further into the dark. Tel Aviv and McMaster have begun to argue about some point in some time period in some literature. They are sizing each other up, I conclude, measuring each other's intellect. They bark and jab at each other, circling each other, scouting for weaknesses, as if mammalian alpha males in some forest somewhere. It's all in good fun, of course. McMaster laughs, and Tel Aviv smiles.

I stay silent and detached. I speak only when spoken to. Carleton asks me questions, and I reply with one word answers.

"Are you TAing this semester?"

"Yes."

"Do you plan on doing research in Mozambique?"

"Yes."

"Do you speak Portuguese? "

"No."

"Do you plan on learning it?"

"Yes."

"Do you intend to learn any African languages?"

"Yes."

"Do you play any sports?"

"Yes."

"What sports do you play?" McMaster asks as he wiggles his way into this interrogation.

"I lift weights," I say.

"Really? I lift too," he says. "I used to work out with the Tiger Cats back at McMaster. We should work out together this semester. Make a routine of it. Get out of the library every now and then. Work the body as well as the mind. It's all about balance and moderation. You need to balance if you want to survive. Right? You need a life outside the work. Or you'll drown. You will drown. You will drown in words and sources and arguments."

I have stopped listening.

"Do you like the Maple Leafs," he asks. "Do you think any bar in Montreal would show Leafs games? We should find out."

He says he is so happy and excited to be here in Montreal.

By the men's washroom, an employee mops the water flowing over the floor towards the tables. I watch him sweep the tails over the liquid in a serene way. He sweeps until the tails become heavy, and then he drops the mop head into the wringer and squeezes until the water empties into the bucket and the mop becomes light again. He sees me waiting and watching.

"You'll have to use the women's washroom," he says. "As you can see, we have a little plumbing situation here."

Eight years earlier, I worked at a similar kind of pub at York, and I mopped the floors in a similar kind of fashion. I served drinks and cooked typical pub fare. The employees there became close, and we became friends. We would drink and socialize together. Do things together outside work time, outside the university. We learned what one another studied, but it was peripheral to our core. Only one dimension. Only a single piece. We talked about everything. Everything was fresh. Everything felt vital. Life intoxicated me.

The pub was located on the seventh floor of the Ross Building, and it had a balcony overlooking the university and the grey, industrialized landscape of northern Toronto. Before it was a pub, I heard, it was an office. And one night, long ago, a student broke in, stepped onto the balcony, climbed to the edge, and jumped. They said he was overwhelmed from studying. Too much pressure, they said. Too much. Or they said he had suffered too much shame from a failing grade. Too much shame, they said. Too much. And I often wondered, as I emptied the mop bucket onto the balcony, and smoked a cigarette overlooking the glittering lights of York University, what the young man thought in his few seconds of falling, in the last moments he had. As the pavement approached, did he regret his decision, did he suddenly remember all the good times he had forgotten in his turmoil, the smiles, the laughter, the unacknowledged joys? Or did he crave the impact more than ever?

Friday, September 21

Outside my apartment building on Rue Hutchinson, next to the rent-a-bike stand, is a telephone booth and on this particularly sunny morning, I am standing inside it. I have my hand firmly wrapped around the receiver and have it pressed against my ear. I have just told my mother in clear and resolute words that I can no longer stay in Montreal, can no longer carry on this routine, this charade. The situation has devolved into something untenable. I have not spoken to another person in days. I am full of anger and hatred. I despise it here.

"Then you should come home," my mother says. "Tell your supervisor you are struggling and need a few days or weeks to rest and recover. They will understand given the circumstances. They will understand what the last few weeks have done to you. They will make certain allowances. They will accommodate you. There are a million different ways to do something," she says.

As she speaks, I examine the Band-Aid covering the wound on the lower reaches of my thumb. The bandage has reddened from the blood, and the adhesive has loosened. I note, with mild indifference, the stubborn trail of blood emerging from the dressing and gently sliding down my palm and towards my wrist. I have already gone through a dozen Band-Aids, and each one has proven ineffective in slowing the blood or in closing the jagged, snarled wound.

It happened last night. The kitchen sink was full of water and plates and forks and glasses. I stood at the counter's edge washing them. I would drop my left hand into the murky suds, retrieve a dish, and with my right, would wash it with a rag before placing it in the rack to dry. During the practice, I fell into a calming routine. The rhythm of the simplistic pattern momentarily soothed me. I felt adrift and light. Washing was relaxing, so relaxing that I did not remember about the chipped glass and did not think to take greater care when it came to my left hand. And when I stuffed the rag and my right hand into the glass, I did not notice that the fat skin of my thumb had lodged itself into the sharp opening and did not think to stop and reflect before I turned my hand with great vigour.

My mom tells me to come home.

"Just come home Jesse. Take the train tomorrow. Leave all your stuff there. Just take what you need for a week or so. Be among your family, and we can talk about this. You know your father and I will support you either way. But please don't be impetuous. Make this decision with a clearer and calmer head. This doesn't need to be the end. Will you come home tomorrow?"

I breathe deeply and tell her I will. I tell her I will leave Montreal tomorrow and come home. I tell her I will think about my decision, but I know this is a lie. I have made my decision. I am done here. This decision provides me a measure of satisfaction, a dash of power, but something within me has broken.

In my apartment, on the balcony, I light a cigarette and sit on the ground. The nicotine blocks my mounting tears from releasing. I feel so thick and uninspired, yet I have such desire to move and run. I want to believe in a future. I want to believe this failure is only a blip, a bump in the road, a learning experience. "Maybe academe isn't your passion," my mom had said. "Isn't it better to know that now as opposed to ten years from now?" she reasoned. Yes, I think, maybe I could write. Maybe I could teach English abroad again. Maybe I could travel the world again. Maybe history no longer aligns with my passions.

I stuff my cigarette out on the railing. I watch young men and women carrying books and backpacks walk beneath me. An attractive woman passes by on a bike. Just around the corner, strikers are fighting for their rights on McGill's periphery. Inside, students are working towards their futures.

I turn back to my apartment and see my books lying across the floor, see the maps tacked to the wall. My thumb still bleeds, and a few drops escape from underneath the band aid. The scar is jagged. My skin heals in zigzags. I will have this scar for the rest of my life, I think, until, maybe, the skin rots and decomposes, until, maybe, I am only bone. This is fine because I have nothing else from Montreal. No other souvenirs. No other mementos. Only a scar. And if I study the cut long enough, if I squint my eyes and pretend, the scar's shape resembles Mozambique a little. Just a little. And as the blood runs towards my palm and down to my wrist, I imagine the migrants of Mozambique spilling out over borders, over the dead and artificial, their bodies full of not only blood and muscle but dreams and memories. Yes, I see it. I see Mozambique and its coastline. I see the passage between Maputo and Johannesburg and think of the thousands who marched there.

And then my body tightens and then crumples.

I surrender.

4.

Teaching English in South Korea

South Korea is the bottom rung on my ladder to redemption. I do not mean redemption in a religious sense; I do not believe in a god capable of washing me of my sins or past transgressions. Redemption, for me, signifies surmounting past failures and challenges to emerge stronger, wiser, and more confident. Redemption is rebirth.

After McGill, I stunk of failure. I reeked of opportunities wasted. I had to purify myself. I had to find my sense of self-worth, which I had lost in the streets of Montreal. I wanted a path back to academia to prove myself able to withstand its rigours and demands. I needed a chance.

I discovered an MA program in forced migration offered at the University of Witwatersrand in Johannesburg; after Montreal, history as a discipline no longer interested me as much. I still believed in its power to shape and influence the present, but I wanted my work to be more fully anchored in the here and now. I wanted to explore more contemporary forms of movement, forced or otherwise, in Southern Africa, and this program seemed to offer all the requisite tools I would need. More to the point, the university was in South Africa, not in some Western country. I would be learning about Africa in Africa; I would move from the book to the place, from words on a page to sentences spoken directly to me.

I decided to teach English in South Korea for a year to save the money for this master's program. Toronto recruiters told me about Busan's natural endowments when they pitched the city as an ideal place to teach English as a second language. Despite Busan's growth, they told me, those apartment buildings persistently rising in between mountain ranges, the city, as well as the country, respects and reveres the nature it has. There are limitless avenues for exploration, they said. They told me about the hidden

Buddhist temples and shrines I could find deep in the pine forests. They told me about the beaches and Busan's famous film festival; they told me about its history and culture. They told me these are the things I should mention in my Skype interview with a representative from the Korean Ministry of Education. Stress your cultural interests in the country, they said. Do not mention money. Do not mention benefits. Do not mention vacation days. I agreed and followed their advice. But I was interested in the money, just as I was interested in redemption, and redemption costs money.

Today, I am twenty-nine years old and walking from my apartment towards Dongnae metro station in Busan, South Korea. It's a Wednesday morning, December 19, 2012, yet Busan's typically busy streets are uncharacteristically vacant. Fewer people clog the sidewalks and fewer cars crawl along the asphalt. Today is election day in South Korea, a national holiday, and citizens have the entire day to perform their hard-won democratic duties and to cast their vote for their preferred president. This year's contest pits Park Geun-hye—the daughter of Park Chung-hee, the general who took power in a 1961 military coup, brutally ruled the country for eighteen years, quashing human rights and appeals for democratic reform, and who laid the foundation for South Korea's transformation from economic backwater to powerhouse—and Moon Jae-in, a former human rights lawyer and self-described "common man." Since the candidates share many similar policies, including further social spending and engagement with North Korea, differing mainly in size and scope, political scientists have dubbed this election a referendum on Korea's past. Older generations remember Park's father as the initiator of the "Miracle on the Han," the man who pulled the peninsula from the ruins of the Korean War to prosperity and international respect. Younger Koreans, meanwhile, have renamed Park Geun-hye "the General's daughter" to remind everyone that from 1974 to 1979—the years in which both her mother and father were assassinated—she served as the de facto first lady and was complicit in the torturing, disappearing, and killing. If she is elected, Park has promised to heal the past's wounds. Today, Koreans vote on whether they believe her. Today, Koreans vote on their country's future as well as on their past. And today, perhaps more importantly for me, the country's English teachers have the day off.

I am used to running this stretch of cement, weaving through pedestrians and dodging cars, but today, I saunter by and savour the sights of quieted commerce: the closed auto shops and real estate offices, the plastic surgeon clinics and barbeque joints, the taekwondo gyms and golfing simulators, the love motels with their sultry lights and veiled glass doors, and the endless convenience stores, which never close, and their fridges full of kimbap and iced caffeinated drinks and bottles of soju. This morning everything has a drowsy air; Busan is wondrously listless.

Up ahead stands Dognae station; its hulking metalled frame resembles the skeleton of some kind of prehistoric leviathan found rotting in the sun. The elevated tracks stretch north towards Busan National University. A group of hikers stands outside the entrance deep in conversation, their bodies dressed in a collage of the latest hiking clothing and accessories—the poles, the hats, the pullovers, the boots—with colours as bright as chameleons. To my left, just beyond my sight, stands Guemjeongsan Mountain, the highest point in Busan, and below it the fortress of the same name. They must go there. A myriad of trails climbs up and around the mountain. In Korea, mountains moonlight as catwalks.

In Dongnae station, I wait for a southbound train. Amy told me over Facebook she would meet me in the fifth car of the 10:30 a.m. train from Myeongyum-dong station. I told her the likelihood of our finding each other was slim to none, and she simply reminded me it was the best we could hope for, since I refused to buy a smartphone or use the antiquated one my Korean co-teacher forced me to buy. To that, I could not argue. So when I watch the train enter the platform and rumble to a stop, I am amazed to see Amy's head poke out from the doors and scan the station for any strange-looking foreigners. Her pitch-dark hair flows to her shoulders. An equally black overcoat covers her body, while Uggs protect her feet.

She waves to me, and I rush to her side just as the doors rattle shut.

"I cannot believe that worked," she says.

"A Christmas miracle," I reply.

"Speaking of Christmas, I need to buy a present for Sara. I got her for Secret Santa. After Gamcheon, can we go shopping for a bit? Do you have any ideas what she might like? I still cannot believe you are not participating in Secret Santa. You can still come to our Christmas party, you know. Why don't you come?"

"Which question would you like me to answer first?"

"Is it because Claire might be there? Or Brenda? Look at all these women you are terrified of Jesse. I am surprised you are spending any time me."

"I didn't tell you I saw Brenda the other day on the train. I was sitting and listening to music when she came running in and sat down only three seats away from me. She was so engrossed in her smartphone she didn't see me. I sat there terrified she would. All it took was one glance from her phone, one sideways look. I was so petrified that I got off at the next station, which wasn't even my stop."

"Were you afraid you might have to revisit the fact that she tried to undress you at the bar?"

"Perhaps."

"Well, you should stop making yourself irresistible to women. What do you expect?"

"Cats."

"What?"

"Sara likes cats. Buy her something catty."

Today, Amy and I visit the artistic hamlet of Gamcheon, a colourful burrow hidden deep within Busan, whose history dates to the war that split the peninsula in two. In September 1950, the Korean War was already almost over. The Korean People's Army had pushed the UN troops—a motley crew of South Korean, American, and British fighters—back to the "Busan Perimeter," a 230-kilometre horseshoe around Busan and the greater southeastern portion of the peninsula. The UN troops eventually, and somewhat miraculously, held the line and checked the northerners further and further back. During the violent engagements, however, thousands of South Koreans fled the wreckage and many sought refuge in Gamcheon, then already home to members of the Taegeukdo religious order. Members had built the village in tiers, long slashes in the side of the mountain, to prevent one house from blocking the view of another, conforming to a basic tenet of Taegeukdo: One may not impede the prosperity of another. Members had also begun to paint their homes in gentle pastels, transforming the area into a veritable painting amid the ruins of war.

In 1955, in gratitude for their generous hospitality, the city expelled the Taegeukdo practitioners to the neighbouring mountains. In the subsequent decades, as the descendants of these internal refugees rebuilt their lives and their small, compact country underwent rapid industrialization, the citizens of Gamcheon continued to live trapped in poverty, yet in recent years, encouraged by city officials, artists have arrived to further decorate the community in colour.

From Toseong station, close to the Jalgachi fish market, we emerge from exit six, find the bus stand in front of Busan National University Hospital, board a minibus, and ride up a mountain and through steep side streets with precariously placed shops and holiday-enjoying kids out and about. With every sharp turn and near miss of a pedestrian, Amy turns to me and asks if we are heading in the right direction, and I offer a half-hearted smile and say we must be, but my mind floats back down the mountain to the university and then to a forwarded email I received that morning informing me that Ashley Cook finished her first edited book on Olaudah Equiano, the eighteenth-century Igbo man turned American slave turned emancipated writer turned famed abolitionist. The email also says she has completed her dissertation, teaches the history of slavery and human rights at both the University of Manitoba and York University, and is the director of the Alliance against Modern Slavery. Ashley and I completed our master's degrees together at York, and then I volunteered at the Alliance for the six months preceding my departure to Montreal. She was tireless and intelligent and decent. She had the remarkable ability to juggle a dozen different things without dropping a single one. I admired her for how she connected the past with the present in her study of slavery. I admired her desire to take what she learned in the academy and apply it to the world. I admired her passion for telling anyone who would listen that slavery is not simply a part of our collective past and that there are an estimated twenty-seven million slaves today. For her organization, I researched and wrote reports about the realities of contemporary slavery, about its various manifestations, about its trajectory from past to more present forms, and about relevant international laws and protocols. I helped Ashley promote and run conferences. We talked about expansion and finding partners with whom we could work. We were interested in locating forced labour in corporate supply lines. We even talked about writing a book together on the history of chocolate and slavery. And as the date of my departure to McGill approached, she gave me survival tips and warm words of encouragement, as she neared her doctorate's completion. But once I returned from Montreal and closed all my books and severed so many ties, I stopped responding to her emails, for I couldn't bear the idea of explaining Montreal to her, couldn't bear the disappointment in her eyes, couldn't stomach the idea of asking her to forgive my shame, but soon, a few weeks after my return, it no longer mattered, since her emails stopped coming.

"Jesse, we're here." Outside, the sky is a sharp blue, the air crisp and enlivening. The sun shines from its mid-day position, and in the distance, the sea twinkles and glitters. Below us, Gamcheon unfolds in colour. Amy leads me to the visitor's centre, where she purchases a map with recommended routes and spaces where you can collect stamps from each endorsed highlight.

"Aren't you getting one?" she asks.

"I think I'll live vicariously through yours."

"Come on Grandpa Jesse, live a little."

"It's far too much work."

"You are no fun."

We descend the nonsensible, direction-defying contours of Gamcheon's labyrinthine layers and levels. The pinks and blues and reds overwhelm and disorient the eyes. We walk through a painting. The paths are thin, emaciated, and starved of space. We climb past homes with families going about their daily routines, men hauling plastic piping and other wooden goods, women sorting through produce to determine the day's menu. Laundry hangs along a tied rope at eye level; the cute children's socks flutter in the breeze. Below we see the green, brown, and orange corrugated roofs congregate in a mosaic of human creativity. Long electrical wires race up connecting poles standing at opposite ends of the hill. They look like ski lifts. Gardens grace many rooftops; others are under perpetual construction. The red and yellow metalled and cemented shacks sneak up the gentle incline, turn, and then snake up a little further before turning once again. I imagine candy bars on a shelf or Christmas presents stacked under a conifer. We stop at a viewpoint next to a statue of a little prince dressed in green and his dog enjoying the same view.

"I think I am enjoying my Christmas lessons more than my students," I suddenly say.

"I would never have pegged you as a Christmassy person," she says.

"When I was a child, I lived and breathed Christmas. I believed in Santa Claus for far longer than I should have."

"I love teaching my little ones about Christmas. This week, we are writing letters to Santa."

"My high school students are a little old for it. When I asked why Rudolph had a red nose, one replied because he was drunk."

She laughs.

"I remember, as a child, when I moved from Hong Kong to Canada, how struck I was by how big a deal Christmas was. The snow. The presents. The trees. And whenever I talk about Christmas now, I am always reminded of my first ones. Why does Christmas give such nostalgia?"

"A reminder of childhood innocence, perhaps."

Two weeks ago, it is snowing in Busan. That morning, I emerge from Deokcheon station and see the streets paved with white. A few cars slide across the snow. I step carefully inside my bus shelter, my coat drawn to my chin, my head hooded. The snow falls in long, persistent arrows. Inside the shelter, the screen detailing the bus schedule is blank, just a vacant blue displaying nothing. Outside, the sky slowly lightens from black to a glowing grey. The streets are silent. The hawkers and employees have not yet come; their stores and stalls stay forlorn and abandoned. I watch the snow pile the streets, the tracks of those few automobiles disappearing. I wonder where the plows have gone before checking my stupidity. What plows? Busan has no contingency plan for such events; snowstorms are once in a blue moon. I imagine the plows trying to navigate the steep roads and alleys leading to my school beneath the pine-heavy mountain full of hidden and nondescript shrines, where people come to worship their ancestors and offer gifts. I understand my foolishness.

Then I see them: broken, uneven lines of people tramping through the snow with the gracefulness of a drunken brown bear. A misstep here, a near collapse there. I break from my shelter and follow them crisscrossing their way over the tundra, slipping regularly yet determined, as if walking for the first time. We step down the middle of the street. Families with excited children play in the snow, toss handfuls in the air, close their eyes, and feel the cool powder hit their outstretched tongues. Uniformed teenagers with big, dark-rimmed glasses shriek into their glowing cell phones, while others lurk behind buildings meticulously moulding the perfect sphere of snow, a soft centre coated with a layer of ice. Outside the restaurants, hair salons, craft stores—those that have survived the merciless slaughter of Home Plus's and E-Mart's low prices—their owners manically clear the sidewalks with brooms, the frantic sweeping clears but an inch, for thin bristles are helpless against thick snow.

At a steep intersection, we ignore the flashing lights and giggle to other approaching snow walkers that technology no longer has any authority. Green, yellow, red, the colours have lost their significance. The quiet, broken only by sounds of human merriment, paints a tableau of such transcendence—one of those rare moments when we abandon our conditioned selves, break from our beaten and whipped appearances and hug the extraordinary, hold the creativity. In the falling snow, amid the decaying greyish light, beside the silent stores, we are all artists, and we are all amazed. In the rare breaks from the modern, the choked and the clocked, when we may glimpse into another reality, past or imagined, we, again, let the human in and we, again, are astonished.

I reach my high school, Sung-Do, enter the premises and expect to see the old security guard greet me with his bemused indifference. But not today. I am the only one here. And as I walk through the snow-covered football field, my tracks unequivocally marking my presence, under the sprawling, derelict, and metallic buildings of my school, looking more like a factory than a site of education, and below the snow-dusted evergreens standing sentinel in silence and wrapping themselves around the frosted mountain, I feel in awe of a first snow. How it transforms, makes beautiful again what had become perfunctory and practiced to the eye. A first snow is like the start of a relationship: the excitement of new beginnings, the desire to start afresh, the potential.

Inside the school, the classrooms are vacant, no sight of even the most-determined pupils ready to start their sixteen hours of study. My steps leave little wet trails in their wake. A chill runs through the corridor. My breath lingers in grey vapour streams. The lights above flicker and flash. I unlock the door to the English classroom, switch on the lights, deposit my things at my desk, and turn on my laptop. English posters and lettering decorate the walls; English-language books fill the shelves; English textbooks rise in stacks on my desk. The room is a little refuge of English.

As my students have a mock test today, another in a never-ending series of practice examinations for university entrance, I had planned to work on my graduate application to the University of Witwatersrand in Johannesburg and complete my response paper to the question "What distinguishes displacement and migration in Africa from similar processes elsewhere in the world?" I find the relevant Word document and read the following:

> Much of the literature on African migration and displacement casts it as quintessentially different from other similar processes occurring elsewhere. Whether the migratory issue is the enduring legacy of colonialism, the prevalence of circular migration, the feminization of migration, the impact of globalization, or the alarming levels of forced migration, Africa is consistently presented as essentially unique. Beyond the problematic nature of essentialism, methodologies that underscore Africa's differences can isolate the continent from a broader discussion about contemporaneous global migration processes (Bakewell and de Hass, 2007; Berriane and de Hass, 2008).
>
> The astute researcher uncovers Africa's distinguishing migratory processes by placing them within the context of the continent's own historical, political, and economic development, without succumbing to the temptation of presenting these phenomena as inherently African. Although certain African regions, for example, might have higher levels of forced or informal migration, these same attributes

> characterize migration processes throughout the world. In what follows, I will provide a broad sketch of what distinguishes migration in Africa, without essentializing the continent as the "strange other" (Mbembe, 2001).

I am about to write about the lingering effect of colonialism on African migration, about the artificiality of borders and the burden of the nation-state model, about the imposition of a cash economy and hut and pull taxation, about colonials' attempts to control and direct mobility into mines and plantations, when I hear commotion in the hallway. The vice-principal and a fellow English teacher have arrived, and they are chatting outside the office. The vice-principal, a stern and serious man, sees me and shouts something in Korean. The English teacher then swiftly screams the translation: "He says it's a miracle you have made it through the snow." I give a slight bow in thanks before I watch them both disappear into the office. Soon the halls fill with rambunctious students covered in snow. Their laughter and jubilance are contagious, and I follow some back outside and watch as dozens of students play on the football field. Some write messages in the snow; others wrestle and throw snowballs. One student taps me on the shoulder, and he shoves a smartphone in my face. On the screen stands a solemn snowman with a torso, two arms, and a face. Then, within seconds, a flurry of kicks and punches and wacks decimate and massacre the man to mere a pile of snow and slush. The teenager smirks, as do I.

Amy and I watch the sun. "I want to teach in England someday, maybe," Amy says. "Somewhere in Europe. I've never been to Europe."

"And what about Brendan in China? Have you thought about him?"

"Of course. We'll see."

Overlooking Gamcheon, I think this place should not exist. On few tourist maps and itineraries, it would seem that this community sprung from the ground like some hallucinogenic mushroom. It is a dreamland.

"And you, Grandpa Jesse. What are your plans after Korea?"

"South Africa for a degree in forced migration studies."

"Forced migration?"

"I want to study refugees."

"Back to school, then, for Grandpa Jesse."

"Yes. Back to school."

Below, other tourists muscle their way through slim openings, past people working and living, past a woman sweeping her walkway, past a girl scurrying up a hill, past an elderly man shuffling through a lane, hands behind his back, cigarette hanging from his mouth, lost in thought.

"Why the interest in refugees?" Amy asks.

"I believe in the freedom of movement."

"Is that why you run?"

In early November, I am completing my first marathon. I run through southern Busan, through its industrial heart, past dreary factories and smokestacks and electrical wires, overhead the threat of rain again looms in the encroaching clouds. I approach kilometre sixteen, and since the runners have already dispersed, with an equal amount both ahead and behind, I find myself wonderfully alone. My stride is consistent, my pace efficient. And at the moment, passing the kilometre marker, the streets bare and sullen, the music building in my ears, nothing seems as easy or as natural as running. I think about neither the inevitable pain of kilometre thirty-eight nor the hours I still must run. For that moment, kilometre sixteen, everything locks into place. Mind and body become one. My thoughts anchor to the now, to the present, to the effortless beauty of putting one leg in front of the other, to the simplicity and essentialness of movement. I am explicitly attuned to my surroundings. My anxiety disappears in the sweat oozing from my skin. I have neither a past nor a future. I am only now. I am only this moment of indescribable energy and fluidity. So when the music explodes into a symphony of power and hope and determination, and takes my body and propels its legs, arms, and feet forwards, forwards to the next kilometre and the next and next, and pushes me to a swelling crescendo of love and purpose and creativity, I punch my fist skywards and draw the attention of other runners, who return their fists in kind, and then, in that moment, however illusionary, however temporary, a solidarity emerges based on movement, based on the felicity of bodies in motion.

"Is that why you're here?" Amy asks. "As a step to something else?"

"I am here to work and save money like everyone else."

"Don't forget to stop and smell the roses. People can always tell if there is some other place you'd rather be."

"I do have a tendency to only appreciate moments years after they have passed."

"Let me help you remember this one," she says, pointing to the camera slung over my shoulder. "Take a picture of me."

Amy steps back to the railing's edge while I bring the camera to my eye. I turn the lens until Amy and her black coat and black hair and infectious smile come into focus. Behind her, rows of colourful, ramshackle homes rise and fall over the rippling hills. While the wind rises, ruffling and unsettling her hair, and the sky blossoms into a dark blue, I take her photo and almost forget that most of those homes are now empty, almost forget that art installations have replaced families inside those buildings that blind with their beauty.

"How cute am I," Amy says when I show her the photo.

"Absolutely adorable."

"Let me take yours."

"No thanks. I am of the opinion that people ruin pictures."

"Jerk," Amy says. "Tell you what. You let me take your picture, and I'll tell you a story.

I hand Amy my camera.

"Remember to smile," she says.

On the night of Claire's birthday, a pack of wild English teachers descends on Gwangali beach and become intoxicated in its party bars. I am one of them. Weekend nights, the long, curving beach transforms into a debauched port, rivalling any from Europe in its mercantilist heyday. Foreigners throw slushies at parked cars while others urinate in parking garages. In the smoky rooms of Thursday Bar or Sharky's, boys and girls talk in English to each other over loud, obnoxious music, spilling their plans and dreams, their feelings and fears to any listener close enough to hear. Some then fuck in the bathroom; others run naked through the bar. The tequila flows. Eyes grow hungrier and more covetous, more demanding, audacious, and expecting. And in the environs of such expectation and hegemony, the hard unspoken, everything unwinds in long seconds, and the desire to judge burns brighter than any sun fuelling life in some otherworldly galaxy. I imagine them wandering back to their apartment, the young teachers, drunk and in love. They feel the crisp sun on their tired bodies and hope, as the faithful may, the long depression does not follow, as it always does. Gwangalli seduces them into believing that night will race into perpetuity, the sun will never rise, and consequence has no currency, but just as a fog lifts, so too does the sun shine and romance die.

"What the fuck is your problem, man?" The burly, forty-year-old Australian snarls at me from the bar. He holds a beer against his protruding belly. "If I weren't dating Rebecca, and Claire came on to me like that, I'd bury my tongue inside of her so quick." I turn and watch Claire flee through the crowd and exit onto the street. "Is it that she's not your type? What is your type?" A Canadian man asks me this with shining and probing eyes. "Are you saving yourself for a Korean woman?" "I don't think of women as a buffet to be sampled," I say and immediately despise those words. "Oh, good answer. Smart. Very smart." The Canadian man finishes his beer and then draws the bartender's attention to ask for another.

I skirt and sidestep the patrons, dodging lit cigarettes and shakily held pint glasses, and soon I am outside and see Claire, tall and athletic, crossing the street, maneuvering through the stationary, waiting cars, and walking onto the sand and drifting towards the sea. I ask myself why I am following her, why I feel the need to explain myself when I do not even understand my actions. Have I led her on over the last weeks, talking and conversing over Facebook, agreeing to attend her birthday party, consenting to celebrate an event important to her? Was I only being friendly, or did I secretly like the attention?

Claire sits in the sand with her arms wrapped around her knees and stares out towards Gwangalli Bridge glowing in the distance. I sit down next to her in silence. To my left, a hawker has sold a firecracker to two teenagers, and the young men secure the rocket to the sand, light it with trepidation, and flee to a secure space. It crackles and shoots, fires and screams, into the black night, leaving a trail of soft smoke before exploding over the flashing neon lights.

"I'm sorry Claire. It wasn't my intention ..." but my words falter. "What I mean Claire is that I don't want, I mean, I cannot ... I cannot get in ..." She looks at me hard. "It is difficult to articulate what I want to say," and I no longer try with any sincerity. Vague and ambiguous words fall from my mouth, as I stumble and bumble over clunks of sentence fragment, but then an interesting thing happens: My mind floats to safer pastures.

I think about Wimmer and Schiller's article about the shortcomings of methodological nationalism, about how the social sciences have had an unfortunate tendency to take the nation-state as an unproblematic unit of analysis, effectively silencing the way social processes (e.g., migration) operate transnationally, rendering invisible the alternative ways people may claim membership or project identity. Claire's eyes sparkle and fill with malice, and my words still sputter and fall from my mouth in loud, meaningless clunks. My mind, though, concentrates on what Wimmer and Schiller's insights can reveal about the Southern African context, what a transnational approach can uncover about the recent Zimbabwean exodus to South Africa, and what this multi-sited methodology may say about notions of belonging in an area where the permanency and saliency of the nation-state may be withering.

"What is it that you want Claire?" I finally manage to ask. She turns to me then, her face rigid yet so expressive, and says, "Never mind, Jesse. Never mind." She rises and walks back towards the bar. I stay seated in the sand and listen to the water crashing upon the shore. I feel rather drunk sitting alone on the beach and contemplate the inevitable hangover I will experience in a few hours, which is unfortunate because I have much work to do. I will write Claire an email explaining and apologizing for the entire misunderstanding, and then I will learn the entire history of Zimbabwe.

"*Have You Filled a Bucket Today* is a story I often share with my students," Amy says. "Do you know it?"

I shake my head.

"Every person in the world on any given day walks around carrying an invisible bucket. And in this bucket, you carry all the good things you think and feel about yourself. You are at your happiest when the bucket is full and at your saddest when the bucket is empty."

While Amy speaks I listen, just as I listen to Mr. Lee, a Korean English teacher at my school, when he tells me about Korean history and Korean cuisine or when he gives me his opinion on Said or Foucault or T.S. Eliot. He is older, nearing retirement, and he dresses in modest, unassuming clothing, a far cry from the suits and ties of the younger, more socially mobile generation. He speaks English with a thick accent and always ends his sentences with "anyways"—a curious idiosyncrasy of his, which, I'm sure, helps him orient his thinking and speaking in the strange world of English. He never studied English in Vancouver or Los Angeles or Toronto, unlike his younger peers who did and who can now speak the language far better than he. He must, I feel, resent the fact he never experienced the language as lived and breathed, rather only grasped it through lessons from dusty old textbooks that did describe the subjunctive in wonderful detail but could not put it into practice. I sense this disdain and derision not only from the way he interacts with his underlings, quite dismissively, but from the great enthusiasm he exudes when talking about his daughter, who has just finished her degree in England and now travels through Southeastern Europe. I tell her, he says, not to hurry back here. I tell her to experience life as much as she can before finding a career or starting a family.

"People, however, cannot simply fill their own buckets all the time," Amy says. "You must fill other people's buckets, and people must fill your bucket. Through saying something nice, a small act of kindness, or even just a smile, you can fill other people's buckets and they can fill yours. And the wonderful thing is when you feel good helping others, you are also filling your own bucket. This is called being a bucket filler."

Despite his vast knowledge and penetrating intelligence, Mr. Lee has never left the peninsula and has only seen and learned about the outside world through Google searches and online articles, books, and videos. So Mr. Lee always asks me about my former travels, about the things I learned, the moments I experienced, the countries I've seen. And when I tell him I am saving money to pursue another graduate degree in South Africa, he extols my prudence and ambition while noting how too many waygooks, or foreigners, waste their money on less reputable pursuits.

"There are also bucket dippers," Amy says. "These are people who steal from other people's buckets. These are people who take other people's good feelings when they say or do something mean. They drink from the happiness of others."

After school, on some days, Mr. Lee drives me back to my apartment, and on one particular Friday afternoon, we sit in traffic amid the honking horns and exhaust smell. He asks me fewer and fewer questions, as it seems he has acquired all the information he cares to know about Canadian culture, or, and perhaps more likely, he has become uninterested in my terse and uninspired answers. But then, while my mind drifts towards my weekend of studying and running, he suddenly declares he knows little about Africa in general but has a particular fondness for South African history. He says he is fascinated by the diversity of the country, by the ways in which, post-apartheid South Africa has tried to fashion a rainbow nation, has begun to write new national narratives, has attempted to create something total and complete out of its disparate parts. And as he admits his admiration for South African determination, I, too, think about the power of national myths, about how all stories are inevitably distortions, history as only a power struggle, but I wonder if they can ever serve a greater purpose—does a legend redeem itself if it tells a nobler story, a more inclusive one? But the curious thing is I do not share these thoughts with Mr. Lee; I simply nod and listen and stare out the window. And even more curious is the reality that I will see South Africa and he will not.

"Are you a bucket filler, Jesse?" Amy asks. Her lips gently expand into a smile. "Why do I get the feeling you'd enjoy drinking from other's peoples buckets?"

"I was never given a bucket," I say. "I have to dip from others' in order to survive."

"Come on, Jesse. Have you filled a bucket today?"

"Look how you smile, Amy. You tell me."

She playfully pushes me.

"What a bucket dipper you are," I say.

We both pause for a moment to savour Gamcheon. The mid-day sun has ignited its colour, and the houses blaze in vibrancy.

I want to ask her if she ever feels guilty about being here, and I want her to say "No, no I do not because I make an effort. I try." But I don't ask this. Such a question would ruin the moment.

I play along.

"Any plans for the winter break in January?" I ask.

"Maybe Thailand with Brenda. I don't know."

"And Christian?"

"I don't know."

I watch the grandchildren of refugees go about their day.

"Let's head back down," Amy says. "I need to buy something for Sara."

"Christmas shopping in Korea," I say. "It does roll off the tongue."

We walk towards the bus stop.

"Won't you come this weekend for our Christmas party," Amy asks.

"I can't. I have work to do."

We pass more Koreans on the street. And as they march past the quiet and pretty and art-filled houses, I wonder for whom each will vote.

In classical Greek mythology, the Phoenix represents immortality. And its story goes like this: One day, as the bird suns itself under a clear blue sky—his plumage, brilliant streaks of gold and scarlet—he catches the eye of the Sun, who says the Phoenix will live forever. Overjoyed, the bird takes to the sky and travels the world. After five hundred years, though, the beautiful bird grows tired and weak and sad. He returns to the mountainside, climbs to the top of the tallest tree, and pleads for the Sun to make him young again. In an instant, the Phoenix bursts into a glorious ball of flickering orange light before dissolving into a mound of silver ash. From the heap spring the claws, bones, and beak of a young chick, who like the early morning sun rises from the nothingness. He grows strong. He grows fast. He is rejuvenated. And every five hundred years, he returns to the same spot and the sun casts him alight and watches him reborn confident and courageous from his older remains.

The night before New Year's Eve, I exit gate one of Hongik University metro station, ascend the staircase, and meet the neon lights of downtown Seoul. I walk along Yanghwa-ro, with a printed map in my hand, and look for the road leading to the Orange Guesthouse. The air is sharp, biting, and each gust of wind cuts into my skin. Pedestrians are bundled up, their faces hidden behind hoodies and scarfs, and at each intersection, we all, in our respective languages, curse the orange hand telling us to wait.

Seoul is showy, ostentatious, and demands attention. I pass all the familiar landmarks of Korean capitalism—7-Eleven, KFC, Papa John's, Tous les Jours, Hyundai Motors, Samsung adverts—and under the skyscrapers, I pause my cynicism and just admire the creativity and power of it all. Sixty years ago, Seoul was a wasteland, a pile of rubble, just ruined pieces of old building, wrecked cement, and metal. Now, it stands confident and powerful, twinkling in a black, winter sky. In its entire history, the city has undergone many episodes of death and rebirth, destruction and restoration. Seoul has suffered a plethora of burnings, pillages, sackings, and bombings only to emerge strong, only to be reborn triumphantly. The city is defiant. Immortal.

The guesthouse is busy. People socialize over drinks. The atmosphere is cordial and cozy. Everyone seems merry. I stand at reception, and a young Korean woman appears and motions me to follow her. She is beautiful, and I quickly chastise myself for the thought. She leads me to a dorm room with three bunkbeds and motions me to a free lower one. As I drop my backpack, I notice that she sits on the bunk across from me and ruffles through some clothing lying on the blanket. She catches my curiosity.

"I don't actually work here," she says. "The owner was busy checking people in, so I asked if I could help."

"That was kind of you," I say.

She smiles.

"What brings you to Seoul?" she asks.

"I am an English teacher in Busan, and I have a few days off around New Year's, so I decided to see the capital."

"An English teacher," she repeats.

"Yes, an English teacher. One of those people."

"One of those people," she says with a smile. "There are many English teachers in Korea."

"Yes, there are," I say.

Two large suitcases sit open below her bed, and she takes each piece of clothing from the bed, folds it, and places it in one of the suitcases.

"And you?" I ask. "Are you visiting Seoul?"

"I'm leaving it actually. I'm moving to Geneva. I was actually supposed to leave this morning, but my flight was cancelled. I depart tomorrow instead."

"What's in Geneva?"

"I'm starting a job at the United Nations High Commission for Refugees. Do you know it?"

I nod.

"Yes, well, it has been a lifelong dream of mine to work there."

"Congratulations," I say.

She looks at me and smiles, and I decide against my better judgment to tell her.

"I am actually interested in forced migration myself. I hope to do a master's program in Johannesburg studying it in the African context."

"Small world," she says. "I research protracted refugee situations in Asia, particularly with Afghan refugees in Pakistan, and look for durable solutions."

She closes her suitcases and puts on her coat.

"Listen," she says, "I have to meet a friend now, and I probably won't be back until late, but I will have some time to chat tomorrow morning if you're around. Or if you're an early riser, just wake me up and we can exchange contact information."

"Sounds like a plan," I say.

In the morning, I shower and get dressed. I put on my shoes and see her torso rise and fall under the blanket. I picture myself tiptoeing toward her, touching her shoulder, and whispering "Hey." I grin at the absurdity of it, and when I leave, I gently pull the door closed, careful not to make too much noise.

I spend the morning touring Seoul and studying its contrasts. The old and the new. The ancient and the modern. Buddhists rub shoulders with bankers. Confucian collectivism challenges the ethos of twenty-first-century capitalism and its reverence of the individual. Centuries-old palaces and temples sit underneath metal towers. People venerate their ancestors before sipping a latte in a coffee house. Seoul is a cocktail of thousands of years.

In the afternoon, I climb the south side of Mt. Inwang, or White Tiger Mountain, to visit one of Korea's most sacred shaman sites, Guksa-dang, buried within the urban entrails of northern Seoul. I pass the gateway, enter the secluded shaman village, and climb further until I hear the chanting. Only softly perceptible at first, barely audible, the chanting increases in intensity and pitch. Inside the Guksa shrine, a shaman bows in prayers, and his cries sound alien. Paintings of different spirits hang from the wall; flickering candles adorn the room. On tables rise trays of fruit—apples, oranges, pineapples, berries—beside them are plates full of rice cakes. It is a room of offering and devotion.

I scramble farther up the mountain until I reach Seon-bawi. These are wonderfully weird, weather-eroded boulders formed from outcroppings of volcanic stone. Sizeable holes scar the gigantic boulders as if they had been shot by cannons. Confucians, Buddhists, and Shamans all hold this site in deep reverence. For Buddhists, the rocks appear as two monks sitting in deep reflection; for Confucians, the rocks' energy connects with the heavens to ease enlightenment; and for Shamans, the rocks resemble Sanshin, a mountain-king spirit, siting next to his tiger.

The path disintegrates as the pine trees grow thicker and the snow becomes deeper. In between branches, dressed in snow, Seoul spreads out before me. In the distance stands Seoul Tower on top of Namsan Mountain. Guksa shrine used to reside on Namsan Mountain until the Japanese burned it to the ground during the occupation. Shamans rebuilt it here in secret, and they worshipped it in defiance.

Apartment buildings rise from the frosty grounds, and smoke billows from their tops as if from a dragon's nostrils. I hear car horns below and watch vehicles drift through the city's many arteries. Seoul is awake and is evolving. It is shedding yet another layer and is metamorphosing before my very eyes. How much has it already survived? How many times has it already rebuilt itself? During the Korean War, the city had been crushed, flattened, hollowed out. It changed hands between the Soviet-backed North and the American-backed South four times. Scores were dead; hope appeared lost. Yet the city, like the Phoenix of ancient myths, rose again from the ashes and refused to submit. Like the old bird, the city forever transforms and reinvents itself. It redeems itself. It pushes forwards. Seoul inspires me.

A week earlier, with the snow around Busan melting, I am standing in my school's cafeteria drinking a glass of water and gazing into the pine forests. Mr. Lee, who has been upset about the General Daughter's election victory, stands next to me, and he, too, stares out into the fading white.

"What would you say is the most famous line in English literature?" he asks.

"I wouldn't have the faintest idea," I say.

"April is the cruellest month," he says, quoting the opening line to T.S. Eliot's *The Wasteland*.

"Not a bad choice," I say.

"Yes, but what does it mean?" Mr. Lee asks.

I remember reading the poem in university and trying to wrap my head around its language. I remember reading the library of interpretations of the poem, its meaning and its significance. And I remember never completely understanding any of them.

"What do you think it means?" I ask.

"April is the cruellest month because the narrator wishes to die," Mr. Lee says. "Yet all around him he sees rebirth. He sees the buds on the trees. He sees the cherry blossoms. He sees the flowers. He sees the snow melt. He sees spring. He sees the world shedding the cold and embracing the warmth yet again. He experiences the beginning of another cycle."

Mr. Lee sips his water.

"And he must ask himself whether he wishes to try again. Is it worth it to struggle on when failure is almost a certainty? Is the experience of living worth more than a goal itself? Can you accept that life is more disappointment than happiness?"

At five minutes to midnight, I stand in Seoul's main plaza with thousands of others to countdown the end of 2012 and welcome 2013. Strobe lights emanate from the ground and pierce the black sky. Local celebrities parade across a nearby stage and shout messages to the crowd, which cheers and claps. Large screens project images of smiling faces, and soon they laugh and wave when they realize they are on camera. A band plays music next to a clock that counts the minutes to the New Year. The fervour is spectacular.

Two minutes to go.

Office towers rise around us, and I see shadowy figures in the windows looking down on the festivities. People nearby have their smartphone cameras held high, aimed at the stage, ready to capture whatever happens at midnight forever. Images they will share with friends and families. Images they will share with hashtags telling of the resolutions they have for 2013, the things they wish to accomplish, the things they wish to do, all the bad habits they will discard. New Year's is the time of redemption. New Year's is the time of hope.

One minute to go.

In front of me, a daughter sits on her father's shoulders. She is wrapped in layers. I watch the grey breath exhale from her and float to the night before disappearing. Her brother below jumps in excitement. Their mother raises her camera and takes a selfie of the young family. I cannot help but smile. I, too, have big plans for 2013. I, too, have resolutions. I, too, like the Phoenix before me, like Seoul itself, dream of redemption and resurrection. I will come back from the night.

The crowd sways and buzzes. The energy is everywhere and astounding.

I clap my hands.

Five

I will succeed.

Four.

I will be good again.

Three.

I will become better.

Two.

I will earn all of this.

One.

5.

In the University of Witwatersrand

I have finally arrived in Africa. I am twenty-nine years old, and it's February 2014. I am studying forced migration at the University of Witwatersrand in Johannesburg, South Africa, and heading to class. I pass through the Senate House's thick Romanesque pillars, which serve as helpful landmark to orient visitors in the university's East Campus. They are difficult to miss. I climb the stairs, and along the House's upper floor, part of the Department of Engineering, I stop to survey a series of photographs gracing the spartan walls. When I have time before class, I like to examine these photographs because they reveal much about the city and country.

The university's history, as well as Johannesburg's, owes its existence to a particular kind of engineering, the mining variety, for it was the discovery of gold in the surrounding countryside that prompted capitalists, industrialists, and entrepreneurs to flock here in the second half of the nineteenth century to open the earth and remove its contents. And as to be expected from savvy and conscientious and adventurous businessmen, they established a school to learn better and more efficient techniques for ripping the ground apart. The photographs showcase the department's graduating classes stretching back to just before the First World War. In the earliest, black-and-white ones, a dozen or so white men stand or sit in rows, the students dressed in suits, the professors and deans donned with gowns or robes. They all look regal and cerebral, serious and studious—enterprising folks who now ready themselves to take their knowledge, their formulas and new devices, to the mines and modernize the practice. As the years pass, the graduating classes grow in size but remain monochrome, with a few white women appearing here and there. Not until the early 1990s do men and women of colour sit and stand in the photographs, beside their white counterparts, and when they begin to gather in greater and greater numbers, it begs the question, especially for unfamiliar viewers, of where they were before.

On the Senate House's first floor sits the African Centre for Migration and Society, Africa's leading research centre for shaping global discourse on human mobility and where I am a student. The centre, focused as it is on past and present and future forms of migration, could not be located in a more appropriate place. For it was migrants, both from within and outside South Africa, the men and women absent from the photographs, who built this university, this city and country. It was they who travelled to the pits of Witwatersrand and pulled from the ground valued rocks and minerals, whose wealth gave birth to roads, homes, and buildings. I pass the centre's entrance, which stands firmly locked and secured with bars and buzzers, walk down a twisting staircase, and enter a hidden seminar room with a blackboard and about a dozen desks. I take my seat next to a group of graduate students from all over the continent, as we prepare to discuss, with the guidance of a white American professor and a Burundian PhD student, what exactly it means to be a migrant and what it exactly means to be a forced one.

"What is a migrant?" the professor asks. "What is a refugee? What is a forced migrant? Is a forced migrant a refugee? Does it matter in which context we use the terms refugee or forced migrant? If I discuss refugees in an analytical context, does it have the same meaning in a legal one? If two Zimbabwean asylum seekers apply for refugee status in Johannesburg and one is accepted and the other is not, does that automatically mean that they have experienced two substantively different experiences? What is the value of these categories? If these categories in which we group people go unchallenged or unquestioned, what processes are we, as social scientists, misidentifying, which experiences are we making invisible, and which assumptions are we presenting as truths?"

The professor sits at a desk across from me, on the other side of the U-shape our desks have formed to facilitate discussion and conversation, and he has a few notes lying in front of him, next to his cellphone, which is not switched off. He looks almost comical sitting there. He displays the typical eruditeness one would expect from a professor, a man obviously well versed in the scholarly and scholastic tradition, yet his sitting in that flimsy and rickety desk, as confined and cramped as he looks, contradicts that learned glow.

"What is the difference between an international and a domestic migrant? Isn't it interesting how much we take these terms for granted?" he asks. "Isn't it interesting how often we use these terms as if their existence were stable and solid? Yet now, in this very room, a room full of people coming from all over the world, we resist defining the word our entire course is predicated upon knowing and debating."

The class is a cosmopolitan one. Young women from Zambia, Kenya, and Cameroon sit across from two white South Africans and another South African with Somalian heritage, whose name is Bihar. I sit between two older refugees from the Democratic Republic of Congo (DRC), Claude and Mary, who have attempted, with varying degrees of success, to create a life for themselves here in the often mean streets of Johannesburg. Claude speaks four languages, works with DRC refugees in the city, and wants to study the discrimination refugees face while trying to access basic social services promised to them under their refugee status. Claude had applied to this program four times previously and now, after his fifth, has finally been accepted. Mary, also a polyglot, walked from the DRC, through Angola and Namibia, to seek asylum in South Africa. She, too, wants to study the experiences of refugees in Johannesburg. She, too, struggles to survive with a young family in a city, in a country, in a world that views refugees as leeches sucking the national breast dry.

"The United Nation defines a migrant as a 'person who lives temporarily or permanently in a country where he or she was not born, and has acquired some significant social ties to this country.' But I would also add that migration involves, as it is often understood, crossing a barrier."

The professor suddenly looks at me.

"For example, Jesse, you are from southern Ontario. If you moved to upstate New York would you feel as if you had crossed a cultural barrier? Would you feel exposed or as an 'other' walking through the streets of Albany? I doubt it. Whereas living and studying as you do now in South Africa, you may feel a little different, perhaps, as if a barrier has been crossed. In both cases, he is a migrant, legally speaking, but his experiences in each place would be very different, in one he may be able to integrate far easier, develop social ties far more seamlessly, than in the other."

Behind me, someone has left the window open to allow air and light into the subterranean room. I hear voices from outside; they are loud and voracious. I imagine shoes scurrying about in the sun.

"Wouldn't you agree with that assessment?"

I wonder why he has asked me. My colleagues to my left and right, who have softly rolled their eyes in my direction, could speak far more articulately and authentically to a migrant's ability to cohere, or fasten, to the body politic.

"I haven't had many difficulties," I say. "I've been able to blend in, as it were. I speak the language. I feel comfortable. I can fit in."

The professor speaks to me through his eyes, and I know he wants more.

"I would say I am a migrant in the legal sense, but I don't feel I have crossed a significant barrier. I possess certain attributes, or characteristics, that have facilitated my integration."

The professor smiles.

"It is because you live in the university. It is because you know how to exist in this particular social milieu, this specific social setting. You speak its language. You breathe its air. You possess its capital. This is why you feel comfortable. This is why you fit in. You belong here. But Johannesburg is not its universities. I invite you to spend an afternoon in Alexandra and see how well you integrate there."

Alexandra. I recognize this name from the literature. Sitting only ten kilometres to the northeast from where I sit now, Alexandra, one of the poorest areas of the entire country, gained international notoriety in May 2008. On the night of the eleventh, violence erupted in the township, as the beleaguered and impoverished targeted and then attacked any person deemed a makwerekwere, or foreigner, who happened to have settled there; settled there among the shacks and corrugated iron roofs, among the cinder blocks and barbed wire; settled there among post-apartheid South Africa's newest Black citizens. The violence then spread to other townships and settlements in the country, engulfing and destroying and ravaging entire communities. By the end of May, when the violence finally ceased, when the ANC government finally decided to intervene, sixty-two people had been killed, hundreds had been injured, many homes and livelihoods had been destroyed. Thousands of foreigners—Malawians, Mozambicans, Zimbabweans, and Congolese—fled back to their countries. For those who could not or would not return, the government erected emergency shelters and within the tents and makeshift structures, the displaced and homeless gathered and waited. And wait they would, for this was a cleansing, not along ethnic lines but national ones. This was a purging of those who did not claim membership to the new, post-apartheid South Africa, purged by those who could, who were now citizens but who had grown tired and weary from not reaping its benefits, fourteen years on and still poor, still marginalized, still forgotten, and they would not have others, others without documents, others who could not claim allegiance, come here and take what was not theirs to take. And these migrants would wait because as the nation becomes stronger and more unified, the more citizenship is enacted through violence, through the scapegoating of the other. Government officials, community leaders, and the exhausted and downtrodden will parade the migrant through the streets and scream "Look, look at how much he takes from you!" Xenophobia, as many scholars have argued, is only the logical conclusion of the national project.

I think about Alexandra when I run through the streets of Johannesburg. I think about the extent to which the more affluent suburbs will protect themselves from the threat of Alexandra, from the thought of its contents sneaking and leaking over and through porous borders. Evidence of this fear is everywhere. I see it in WITS's security checks and tall fences, in its steel bars and gates. And on this early Sunday morning as I push myself through the university's main turnstile, I flash the security guard my identification card to show I do indeed belong here and slowly begin to jog. All around me WITS rises in the early morning light and reminds me of a fortress. I run along Jan Smuts avenue, one of the city's principal arteries, and since I must put in thirty-six kilometres this morning in preparation for an upcoming ultramarathon in Cape Town, I take many detours from Smuts and run through the neighbourhoods of Parkview, Rosebank, and Parkhurst. The streets here curl and coil and circle into nonsensical designs. Roads end unexpectedly. Parks and hills and gardens appear suddenly and prevent further movement. Straight lines are rare. "It is urban planning as designed by a racist," Bihar, tells me one day. "It is the geography of apartheid," she says. "It is the geography of control; it is an example of how space can be crafted to facilitate segregation, to keep people apart and in their appropriate places."

There are few cars this morning, except for a few pickup trucks roaming the roads. One drives slowly by me, and in its cab, two Black men speak on walkie-talkies. The words "private security" grace the truck's side. I keep my eyes focused ahead on some definite marker and avoid unnecessary contact with the patrol truck, for I do not know what right I have to be here in this leafy, quaint suburb, whether I can be here, whether I am permitted to run here. But as they drive on without giving me a second's thought, I realize how silly it was for me to worry.

Each house is its own bastille. Each is protected by steel or electrical fences. Along the fences' tops, many have glued shards of glass, with their sharp ends pointing skywards. They look like little knives. They look like fangs. Many have cameras pointing down towards the street. Many have intercoms. Many have dogs, which I hear bark and snarl. Some untethered ones throw themselves against the gate as I pass; their teeth are bare and ready. Here, dogs do not run; they chase.

Up ahead, I see a Black man sitting on a wooden chair outside a gargantuan home. He wears a uniform and looks bored. A pickup pauses next to him, and he and the driver speak, undoubtedly giving each other updates, vital information. Above them and the truck and the gates, windows covered in lovely vines look out to the world, and I wonder who stands there now, sipping a tea, gazing down on the men and on me. I wonder how much his view has changed in the last thirty years. I wonder how much this corner of Johannesburg has changed, if at all.

On the next street, a minivan stops a hundred or so metres ahead of me. It is a derelict vehicle, well past its prime, with its wipers and tires and windows ready to break and flatten and crack. A Black woman exits the side door. She slides the door shut, and it rattles and creaks under the weight of its history. As the minivan races away, on the lookout for any pedestrians idling by the side of the road the woman, colourfully dressed, ascends the steep road to her right and passes impeccable home after impeccable home. She wears sturdy yet respectable shoes and has her purse slung over her shoulder. She maintains focus and walks with purpose. I do not see which house she enters, but I do see, just up ahead, a large yellow billboard foregrounding the smiling face of Jacob Zuma, president of South Africa. An election looms on the horizon, and the billboard encourages its viewers to vote ANC because "Together we move South Africa forward."

In Sandton, a large shopping complex glitters and its glass reflects the sunlight back onto me. It rises gloriously into the blue sky, a monolith demanding reverence. Its gardens and trees have been tended to. The sidewalks have been cleaned and made spotless. On the mall's exterior hang posters promoting the latest sale or latest style innovation. Exclamation points are everywhere. Attractive, fit bodies, some men, some women, some Black, some white, decorate the modern, slick façade. Brand names also appear in large lettering—Woolworths, Zara, H&M—and entice visitors with their well-earned reputations. As I approach the entrance and see the well-dressed and well-moneyed shoppers using its revolving door, I suddenly become aware of my state: A sweaty, heavy polyester shirt clings to my torso; my shorts ooze perspiration; my hair is a tangled and matted mess. So when I pass the door and momentarily feel the air conditioning on my skin and see the luminous and polished floors guiding the patrons towards the lustrous shops and maybe to the food court or maybe even to the cinemas, I do not pause, nor do I linger, because I know at this moment, only this moment, I would not fit and would not be welcomed. Instead, I run past the Sandton Convention Centre, near the Johannesburg Stock Exchange, and continue through Nelson Mandela Park, where I slow to note the construction equipment and the new apartment complexes underway. And I wonder, standing there in Mandela's park, whether, once the buildings are completed, the residents on the upper floors will see, only two thousand metres to the east, just over the M1 highway, the shacks and stalls of Alexandra.

After over three hours of running, I turn right on Empire Road and see WITS in the distance. Just a few kilometres away to the left sits the neighbourhood of Hillbrow, another reportedly dangerous area, but before Hillbrow, even closer to WITS, lies Constitutional Hill. Once a prison under apartheid jailing some of the most radical freedom fighters of the twentieth century—Nelson Mandela, Mahatma Gandhi, Joe Slovo, and Albertina Sisulu—the hill now hosts the Constitutional Court, the highest legal authority in the country in matters relating to constitutional issues. The South African Bill of Rights, enshrined in Section Two of the Constitution, has been regularly celebrated as one of the most progressive documents ever produced, not only because of the protections it affords South Africans but because it makes no explicit distinction between citizen and non-citizen in terms of accessing them. The end of apartheid was paradigmatic, the last domino to fall in the continent's fight against colonialism and against white supremacy, and I imagine, as I pass through WITS' turnstile and collapse on the green football pitch, the joy and energy of its demise resonated beyond the South African borders and into nearby countries—Zimbabwe, Mozambique, Zambia, Tanzania—for they, too, supported and trained ANC fighters and offered refuge for exiled leaders.

Lying on the soft, dewy grass, high from the fuzzy glow of exhaustion, open to everything and everyone, I imagine the first constitutional meetings, the drafting of the first proposals, and the ANC leaders thinking of how to repay those allies who, too, sacrificed much for this moment, this symbolic rebirth of not only a country but a region and maybe even a continent. I see Mandela and his team high on idealism, envisioning and then implementing, a region of sanctuary, a place of equal distribution of rights and freedoms regardless of status or membership. But as fatigue replaces my exhaustion, and my legs begin to ache under the warm sun, I trace a similar process in South Africa's trajectory, from hope to pragmatism, from human to citizen.

In the classroom, the professor stands at the board holding a marker.

"What is the passive voice?" he asks.

The students stare at him. His cellphone shakes on his desk, and without hesitation, he scoops it his hands, studies it, and then sits it back down.

"In your writing, as far as I can tell, you have developed the habit of writing in the passive voice. You think with it. You write with it. But what exactly is it?"

His cellphone rattles again, but he ignores it.

"Give me an example of a sentence in the passive voice."

I raise my hand.

"The film was watched," I say.

"And what does that sentence lack?"

"A subject."

"A subject," he repeats.

A few students jot down a word or two.

"In this sentence, all we have is an object, 'the film,' which is acted upon, 'was watched.' We know nothing about what? What don't we know?"

Nadia raises her hand. She has worked with refugees in Kenya in the refugee camps of Dadaab and Kakuma, and she has witnessed them wither and wane in the decades of waiting for a solution to the protracted situation and has watched the camp citizens, the children and elderly, entire generations, living in tents and subsisting on rations, try and create a semblance of dignity and a picture of purpose.

"We don't know who watched the film," she answers.

"Precisely. We do not know who watched the film. In our work as social scientists, we are interested in actors. We are interested in identifying actors, in identifying human beings who act, who choose, who decide. We are not interested in assigning agency to inanimate objects."

A few more colleagues scribble down notes.

"When we talk about refugees, for example, we must submit that even individuals suffering through the worst abuses, living through the worst atrocities, make a choice to leave. No matter how circumscribed, no matter how constrained their options, they choose to leave or they choose to stay. And we see how people choosing to leave can, eventually, affect the structure that influenced them to depart in the first place.

Claude raises his hand, but the professor continues.

"When we talk about migrants, and we say, 'Migrants have been denied their rights under the Constitution, under the Immigration Act, under the Refugee Act,' we want to know by whom. Denied by whom?"

"The state," Bihar shouts.

"The state is not an actor," the professor says. "The state does not act. The state is a conglomerate of structures and bodies and agencies. When we say the state did this or the state did that, we are skirting the true issue at stake: Who acts in the state's name? Who sings the state's songs? Who are the state's foot soldiers? And even more importantly, what do we say when state agents operate against the state's wishes? How do we as social scientists respond when the symmetry between what the state says, as in its acts and decrees, and what its representatives do, as in its bureaucrats and officers, no longer align?"

The professor looks at us.

"When you find yourself wanting to say, 'The state discriminates against migrants,' always dig deeper. Always ask yourself 'Who?' Who, who, who, who, who, who?"

In 1950, the Nationalist Party redesigned Johannesburg. Inspired by their 1949 election victory—while the rest of the world reflected on the consequences of racism and hatred—the party passed the Group Areas Act, which designated specific areas of the city for specific racial groups and promoted the Afrikaans cause above all others. This piece of legislation was the progeny of older segregationist laws—the Native Land Act of 1913, Pass Laws, the Native Urban Areas Act of 1923—but what made the post-1949 period particularly nefarious and what separated it from earlier periods was its unabashed desire, its brazen zeal, to choke the life from the majority Black population. The Nationalists systematically attacked the trade unions and political organizations of the non-white majority, brutally controlled the migrant labour system and movement in general, and mercilessly suppressed any dissent or cultural expression. All action advanced the white cause. Apartheid was institutionalized.

On a class trip, we are driving in a minivan from Sophiatown to our next stop, Feitas, and I am sitting beside Claude. A few seats up is our guide for the afternoon, our professor of research methods from Cape Town. She will lead us on our journey into Johannesburg's past. Before 1950, Sophiatown was a cultural treasure, a magnet for Black artists, musicians, dancers, and gangsters. In the museum, we saw old photographs of trumpeters and dancers, the excited and sweaty faces of bodies in motion, the little joys that creativity and spontaneity wrought. In the early 1950s, the Native Resettlement Board drew up plans to raze Sophiatown and relocate its residents to Soweto to make new space for white citizens.

In 1955, the first bulldozers slouched into Sophiatown, followed by two thousand policemen armed with rifles. Before the buildings and homes were sacked, before a thriving community was turned to rubble and debris, the policemen, in the pouring rain, marched the townsfolk out, out of sight and mind, out of their culture, history, and traditions. As the apartheid government systematically removed the non-Afrikaans population from urban centres to native reserves, these areas ballooned in size and density. Eventually, the government transformed these reserves into ten national homelands, or Bantustans, for the majority Black population: 13 per cent of the land for 75 per cent of the population. The government now determined these Black South Africans as citizens only of their respective homelands—the places where they ethnically belonged, as determined by white ethnographers. They had all their political and civil rights stripped and became imprisoned in open-air jails in their own country.

"I have no sympathy for poor white folks," Claude says, as we sit in Johannesburg traffic.

"Then or now. They had every opportunity to succeed. They have every opportunity to succeed. If they find themselves poor or jobless, it must be their fault because they have been given everything."

I nod and watch young Black men move from car to car selling newspapers.

"If the world is handed to you on a plate and you do not take it, then surely, surely, it must be your fault. No? Who else's fault could it be?"

Feitas, today called Pageview, shares a similar history to Sophiatown. Built towards the end of the nineteenth century and known throughout white circles as the city's "Malay location," even though the area housed a predominantly Indian population, Feitas was also famous for its cultural beat, for its bustling shops and street life, for its legendary fourteenth street drawing shoppers from every economic and racial background. In the 1970s, under the Group Areas Act, the apartheid government removed the residents to distant townships and ransacked the buildings and homes. Today, only a few original buildings remain, one of which is the Feitas Museum. And the museum tells the story of the district in a series of photographs from before, during, and after the forced removals.

A resident of Pageview and of Indian descent guides us through the photographs and other mementos, stopping at each to tell its history and significance. She gives us time to inspect the photographs at our leisure, and I inch towards one that has won my attention. It is an aerial shot, slightly overexposed, of Feitas, of what must be fourteenth street, from what must be the 1960s or earlier, predemolition. Dozens of cars—Volkswagen beetles and husky Chevrolets—have parked along the sidewalk and their metalled frames of reds, blues, whites, blacks, and browns shine in the afternoon sun. Light reflects from their windshields. In the above-store apartments clothing hangs over balcony rails to dry. In the distance, the skyscrapers of downtown Johannesburg loom. Despite the evidence of activity, the cars and clothing, there are no people in the photograph, just an empty street and quiet store fronts like Babs Fashions and Subway Grocers. This contrast, this upending of expectation, gives the photograph an eeriness, an almost prelude to what was to come: disappearance.

"It's good to know our history, wouldn't you agree," the guide says as she stands next to me. "Before we can learn from our past, we must first know it."

I nod.

"It's a cliché of course, and like most clichés, the words have become stale and meaningless for most. They are said without much reflection or emotion or passion. It is our job to resurrect those words. It is our job here to infuse the past with greater significance. It is our job to make visitors, whatever their backgrounds, think on the past and then, hopefully, act for the future."

I notice that there is, in fact, a person in the photo, deep in the background, a man I think, and he is crossing the street, and the photographer has captured him in mid-stride. He is stuck in motion.

"I am happy you have come," she says. "This museum is not about assigning blame. It is about building bridges and constructing dialogue. White South Africans need to know this history. To construct the South Africa on paper, we must lay the past bare for all to see."

"I am not South African," I say to her.

I blurt this without thinking. It is only reaction—an instinctual scratching of an inch. I am intrigued by how quickly I relieve myself of responsibility, how quickly I pretend to be outside the fabric of reconciliation, how quickly I distance and detach myself from the phenomenon of whiteness.

"Where are you from," she asks.

"Canada," I reply.

She nods.

"I mean, yes, white Canadians, settler Canadians, non-Indigenous Canadians have much to account for as well in terms of the historical treatment of Indigenous peoples in Canada. So when I say I am not South

African, I am speaking of objective fact, I mean, I am not trying to say I have no work to do."

She nods again, and I examine the photos of destruction and displacement.

"I mean, yes, of course, I have much work to do unpacking my privilege. I have much to consider about how the historical abuse committed against Indigenous peoples has benefited me and my family."

She nods.

"I suppose white Canadians share more with their white South African brethren than they would care to admit."

"Well," she says, "guilt is of no use to anyone."

"I am from Cape Town," the professor, who had been examining the photos along with the rest of the students, says. "So I don't know much about the land issue in Johannesburg, about whether any of the taken land will be returned."

"The courts are still trying to work what belongs to whom," the guide says. "They are trying to bring a semblance of justice to those who were forced to move."

"Interesting," the professor says. "I should know more about this history."

"We all should," the guide replies.

The two women walk side by side and fade further into the museum.

A few weeks later, I am sitting again among the U-shaped desks, and the blonde-haired Capetonian stands at the blackboard. Today, we discuss our research proposals.

"Jesse, what is your research topic?"

"Deportation."

"And what are your research questions again?"

I look down at my white, printed paper.

"I have two. The first relates to identity, the second to sovereignty."

"Go on."

I slowly read.

"How do Zimbabwean deportees negotiate their forced return home? How has the deportation process altered their conception of belonging? What new subjectivities have emerged?"

"Okay. Good," she says. "And the second?"

"What does the increased role of the IOM (International Organization for Migration) in managing deportation processes between South Africa and Zimbabwe say about emerging forms of sovereignty in the Southern African region?"

"Okay. And what are your methods?"

"Well, I am interested in how deportation perpetuates the nation-state, how it tries to solidify a national mode of belonging the world over, wherein every human being belongs to a certain country. But I want to know how deportees themselves react to this, how they understand themselves as deportable, where they see themselves as belonging."

The class is silent; I suddenly feel warm, uncomfortable. I sense the seeds of perspiration forming on my skin, and soon they will grow to sweat.

"I am also interested in the increasing role non-government organizations like the IOM play in managing migration on the behalf of states. What kind of ideologies do they promote in their seemingly neutral political practices and discourses?"

She stops me.

"Ok. But this is not method. What is your principal method of research inquiry?"

"Ethnography."

"Go on."

"I plan to work at or simply observe the IOM office at Beitbridge on the South African and Zimbabwean border."

"Access?"

"Still to be determined."

"Okay. So you are at the office, what are you doing?"

"Observing."

"So, observation. What else?"

"Working, maybe."

"Participatory observation. What else?"

"Interviewing both deportees and IOM officials."

"So, formal and informal interviewing. What else?"

"Collecting IOM documents."

"Ok, so maybe discourse analysis or narrative analysis."

She looks over the class.

"In your research proposals, these are the words you need to use. We have moved passed your theoretical positions and personal ontologies; we have already established your research questions. Now, you need to show me how you plan to answer them. How do you plan to get from point A to point B?"

She looks back at me and smiles.

"I forgot to ask you about reflexivity."

I do not speak.

"Remember to continuously analyze how your personal histories as researchers and writers may affect what you see, how you document, and how you conclude."

She then turns to me.

"Do not simply tell me that your position as a white man affects how your subjects interact with you or see you or that it affects your research. We know that it does. We know that it will. Tell me how. Show me."

She glances down at her notes.

"Oh, and do not forget about ethics. Tell me how you plan to research a vulnerable population in an ethical way, in a reciprocal way, or, even, in a participatory way."

Ethics. We have debated this notion in all our classes. We have debated how much we owe the forced migrants or the refugees or the deportees themselves whose words we take and whose experiences we use. The American professor tells us that we must approach the field and the people we study with a sense of detachment and with an objective rigour. We must not become simple cheerleaders for the downtrodden because such advocacy often creates misleading and simplistic portrayals of them, and poor data collection and skewed representation cause poor policy implementation. If we as researchers, if we as scientists, the American concludes, wish to help migrants we must take large samples, find characteristics generalizable to a larger population, and be neutral, unbiased, and impartial in our research. To be ethical, he says, is to be scientifically rigorous.

Other researchers argue the only ethical research improves the situation of the people researched, and the only way to accomplish this is by centring the voices and wishes of the forced migrants and refugees and deportees themselves. The research should, they say, be participatory and reciprocal. The research should be directed by the researched. The benefits of the research should be felt by those who divulge their information, who disclose their data, who detail their experiences. Better informed policy, they say, often does little for the researched, many of whom live precarious existences, many of whom understand the state and its representatives not as people eager to solve pressing social issues regarding migrants in a humane and dignified way with scientifically sound social research, but as people ready to use such data to expedite their expulsion, to facilitate their removal. If governments, they conclude, care little about improving the lives of forced migrants, of what value is objectivity? Of what value is detachment? Why should migrants speak to researchers at all?

I think about myself at Beitbridge. I imagine what it will be like there. I picture myself among the deportees, people who have just been uprooted and expelled, people who must decide whether they wish to return to a home they may not know or risk another irregular crossing into South Africa. I see myself walking beside deportees asking them about their experiences, probing them about their fears, apprehensions, and sense of belonging, about being back in Zimbabwe, about their new goals, plans, and aspirations. I see myself asking how they feel. How are you feeling? Are you feeling worried? Are you feeling angry? I see myself with printed consent forms asking for their permission to use their stories in my research and in my thesis. I see myself telling them, firmly yet respectfully, that my research will not improve their lot, will not make the South African officials less enthusiastic about deportation, and will not suddenly make them more conscientious about migrant rights.

I see one deportee then turn to me. His eyes are tired and exasperated. He is exhausted from his long train ride from Johannesburg and from his long stay at Lindela Detention Centre. He looks at me hard. He is no longer a statistic in a table or graph. He is no longer an anonymous voice from the literature. He is no longer a quotation. He is real. Alive. Human. And he is standing in front of me. He demands to know what I can do for him. He demands to know if he answers my questions, if he gives me his story, what will I do with it. How will I help him? Will I simply use it to write my thesis, to get my degree and eventually to get a job that involves stealing stories from people like him? And when I see him asking me this, I see myself standing in silence with absolutely nothing to offer him.

I feel inadequate, insufficient, a charlatan. The enormity of what I have proposed to undertake weighs on me. I sense an unbridgeable gulf between what I think and what I must do. I sense an unshakeable feeling that to proceed down this road would be to perpetuate systems of thought I do not care to see prosper. I who may float from country to country with ease because of my passport's authority, I who may give voice to a hitherto neglected population because of my institutional backing, I who may pick and choose which social justice cause to pursue as if sampling from a dessert tray—I cannot begin to fathom how to do this research in an ethical manner.

And one day, reflecting on these issues in my dorm room, surrounded by paper and binders and notepads, I receive an email from Claude addressed to all students saying he must, with great pain, withdraw from the program because he does not have the requisite funds to continue. He writes that he must be realistic and objective. Claude, who had applied to this program four times previously and who is a refugee in Johannesburg, apologizes to us if he had ever caused offense during one of the class's heated discussions—he had a tendency to argue with passion—and he says he has learned much from us. We have been a blessing for him. He wishes and hopes the program rewards our work and investment.

On my second Sunday in Johannesburg, Claude picks me up from campus, and we drive through the congested downtown streets and towards one suburb and its glitzy shopping mall. We talk of his family, his children, as we pass the road on which he lives. He tells me about his work with the Congolese community in Johannesburg, about its tensions and problems, and how he has worked as a leader among them building trust and solidarity and providing them with vital information about how to survive in Johannesburg as an irregular migrant, an asylum seeker, or refugee among the looming threat of violence and expulsion. He says he hopes this degree will further his employment opportunities in Johannesburg, as for now, his income comes mainly from the sporadic work he finds as a French-English translator.

In the mall, we walk side by side past swanky shops and South Africans hurrying about with bags hanging from their fingers. The floors twinkle with bleach and disinfectant. The store windows shine with cleanliness, and I see people trying on shoes, inspecting shirts, and asking for their prices. Everything is quiet. People glide through the light as if on ice, faces full of elation, human joy, since the mall, it seems, provides them great relief from the uncertainty of outside, the dangers of un-airconditioned air, the threat of dirtier windows. Claude asks me if I need any supplies for my room, and I tell him no, and then, without provocation, he leads me to a restaurant, a chain one, possessing the same amount of charm as any of the mall's other soulless stores, and says he will buy me lunch and will not take no for an answer.

Over ribs and a beer, I ask him questions of the DRC, about its recent past and present condition. I ask him about Belgian colonialism, independence, the assassination of Patrice Lumumba, the thirty-year dictatorship of Mobutu, CIA meddling, resource extraction, the Kabilas, the 2006 elections, the persistent and prolonged violence in the eastern provinces. His answers are coy, evasive, and limited. He is cagey about details and is reluctant to give comprehensive answers or at least the ones I have come to expect from the literature on both the DRC and refugees. He only says the DRC remains his country, a home he would like to return to before he dies. He tells me about the large Congolese community in Quebec, and when I tell him I had not heard about such community before, he smiles and says to not expect any information from him. "Trust," he says, "should never be broken; it is the only power the displaced have."

After lunch, he drives us to the edge of Johannesburg to an old warehouse. It looks forlorn and decayed. Near collapse, near extinction. Forklifts move bags and wooden crates. Teenagers unload trucks parked near the entrance. Men stand and chat outside. Claude parks his car, and as we exit, he reminds me to lock my door. We walk up a ramp, past the talking men, through the door, and into the warehouse. The room is of colour and activity. On the floor spread out on mats, or held in crates, or secured in boxes are fruits and vegetables of remarkable shapes, hues, and variety. Men and women move from vendor to vendor touching and feeling the produce, asking for and haggling over prices, and then selecting and dropping pieces of fruit or vegetables into boxes or bags. The room is full of frenzied commerce. Everything is loud; the floor and walls and windows are not spotless. The space is wonderful.

Claude negotiates the price of oranges while I walk through the aisles and reflect on the range of goods on display: apricots and asparagus, bananas and blackberries, peaches and pineapples, radishes and rhubarb. I watch Claude select lemons and limes and finally a box full of mangoes. I help him carry his fruits back to the car and place them in his trunk. But then he hands me a plastic bag and tells me to choose ten mangoes for myself. I tell him I couldn't possibly take any, but he says with a smile he will interpret my refusal as a personal insult. He thinks I am not getting the necessary vitamins to survive our program's grind, living as I do on campus and only among fast-food joints and convenience stores. I reluctantly choose my ten mangoes and thank him, but when I return to my dorm room and bite into one's yellow flesh, the sour and bitter taste brings tears to my eyes.

I often think about Claude's mangoes since he has left the program, but especially on the day I hand in the take-home midterm examination, and my other classmates—Mary, Bihar, and Nadia—pressure me to join them for lunch to celebrate. The exam asked us to argue about the benefits and drawbacks of the categorization of migrants—what are the benefits and risks—and to discuss the relationship between rationality and agency as relating to migration. Economic theories of migration have long centred goal-oriented behaviour in their analysis, a Weberian understanding of what drives people to leave their homelands. Migrants perform cost-benefit analyses, weigh the associated risks with the expected benefits, and then decide whether movement is in the household's best interest. But what interests me are those types of migration that look different to Western eyes—appearing irrational, as the American professor said—and function outside widely accepted theories and paradigms. By expanding our gaze beyond economic rationales for migration, I write in my exam, we can reveal that human rationality does not solely operate within an economic framework. Cultural factors also cause people to move. Cultures of mobility dictate the norms and expectations of movement; cultural understandings define the purpose and the rationale and denote failure. Some people move for the sake of movement. Mobility, for some, whether successful or not, is simply a rite of passage, an act of being in the world, a choice to experience what they had only seen on television or on the computer screen: other cities, different places, strange things.

"Agency is the ability to act" I say when Bihar ironically asks me what it is.

"There is a fine line between celebrating a migrant's resiliency and legitimizing neoliberal ideology, whose economics have been instrumental in propelling migrants to move in the first place," she says.

Bihar's family comes from Somalia, and I can only guess they left in the aftermath of the state's collapse in 1991 and the subsequent exodus of Somalians north, south, east, and west. I can only guess they made their way down Africa's spine—from Somalia, through Kenya and Tanzania, passing over Malawi and Zambia and Zimbabwe—and arrived in Johannesburg to survive, and eventually to live, among the vibrant Somali sanctuaries, home to remarkable entrepreneurship and prone to regular xenophobic attacks. I can only guess what they endured on their journey southwards.

"There is nothing romantic about drowning to death in the Mediterranean Sea or starving to death in the northern Kenyan desert," Bihar says.

I listen while I eat the hamburger Mary bought for me and think about Claude and his mangoes.

"In the camps I worked at," Nadia says, "I saw refugees act every day. Their resiliency does not surprise me. What does surprise me is that generations have existed in these camps without any solution to this protracted emergency. What does surprise me is that the camp is still in existence."

Sometimes Nadia and Bihar switch to Swahili when the mechanics of English prove too limiting. Mary speaks a little Swahili, too. They tell me I must learn Swahili, and I smile. While I wait for them to return to my language, I dip a French fry in a drop of ketchup and think on my shortcomings. I feel wonderfully exhausted, up all night as I was writing the exam, and in those moments of vulnerability, when too tired to lift and prime my defense mechanisms, I trip, fall, and consider difficult thoughts. I listen to the voices of these women—eloquent, authentic, experienced—and realize that a generation of reading, of learning, would never make me their equal in terms of personal, embodied knowledge. Migrancy in one form or another has imprinted itself on these women's bodies and minds, and when they speak about movement, its theory and application, it is so visceral and potent because they have lived the literature and need not dress those experiences, so acute and profound, in the impenetrable fog of academese, in the terse and fat language of higher learning. I think research advocacy, or maybe all social research itself, should not prioritize giving voice because all humans have spoken since time immemorial, but instead ask why some voices have been hushed or hurried away while others have been spotlighted. No one gives voice; one can, however, take it away. One can also listen. And listening, truly listening, requires far more effort than speaking and certainly more than writing.

I consider these thoughts more gravely in the coming weeks but especially when I receive the highest mark in the class on the exam, and the American professor admonishes the rest for being far too descriptive in their essays. "In graduate school," he says, "it is not enough to summarize the readings; you must critique them and use their arguments and data to fashion your own arguments." "Your argument," he repeats. "We are in knowledge production," he says, "not knowledge regurgitation."

My classmates ask to see my exam, to see how I answered the questions, to examine how I took the heaps of articles and chapters and fashioned them into an argument with an opening thesis, a body of supporting evidence, and a conclusion neatly tying everything together in a pleasing and reassuring way. But when they take my exam and thank me, when they elect me class representative and come to me with grievances I should take to the Capetonian, when they email me about questions about the week's readings, I feel no swelling of pride but the anxiety of performance, the duties of perfection, and the mounting sense they soon will see through me and appreciate me for the swindler I am because I know only words, only the language of the academy—I know only that lexicon. I want to tell them this. I want to tell them I did well because I am fluent in the only acceptable language herein. I want to tell them I did well because while they were outside, among people, among the very processes under study, I was in a room reading and reading and reading. You look at me, I want to say, and see someone succeeding but only within WITS's walls, only here in the classroom. Take me outside, walk among the streets with me, see how well I interact with people, and you will see I am nothing. Nothing. You are the future of migrant studies, with your alliances and networks and social capital—the people with the experiences and the knowledge—for whom academics and faux allies wish to speak. You have the stories that scholars, like me, will try to take.

When I tell the Capetonian I am leaving, tears well in her eyes. She sits across from me in her office. While she speaks, I try not to listen. I want to run away. I want to leave her office, the centre, the school, the country as soon as possible. It is May. I have been here only three months, but it has felt like an eternity. I answer her questions in quick succession and give only the faintest of whispers in response. She wants to know whether I have support networks at home; she wants to ensure I correctly withdraw to allow for a possible future return should I choose; she wants to reiterate I am a good student and belong in the program. I thank her for the help, jot down a few notes, but as I rise towards the door, she says, "You know, if it is a matter of money, we will find a way to make it work." I think of Claude. "Money is always a factor," I say. "But in my case, it is not the most pressing one."

On the morning of my departure, I cleanse my room. I dump my binders and notepads and papers and pens in the trashcan. I wipe away the remnants of dead mosquitos from the walls, little bodies and wings I crushed months ago upon my arrival. I remember I heard them buzzing throughout the night, screaming their infuriating sounds, until I rose, switched on the light, and preceded to hunt them down. My half-asleep eyes focused, and I saw them fluttering around the ceiling, near the light. I took the pillow and waved it at them to disturb their tranquility and force them to retreat a little further down the wall to my reach. Feeling enraged, I swung wildly at them, and slapped and pounded the wall until I finally saw them smashed and flattened and destroyed in little puddles of blood. I turned to the window and noticed that I had not properly secured it; in fact, I left a little space exposed, more than enough for a swarm of mosquitos to freely trespass. Imagine, I thought, the amount of rage and blood I could have avoided if I had only shut the window.

A knock lands on my door, and it startles me. I have been watching YouTube videos of David Foster Wallace discussing the importance of fish knowing what water is and of Christopher Hitches from the 1980s discussing the ANC's resistance to apartheid. I reluctantly open the door and there stand Nadia, Bihar, and Mary. Their presence is a punch to my stomach. I strain to say anything at all.

"How did you find me?" I ask.

"Professor told us," Mary says.

"Were you just going to leave without saying goodbye?" Nadia asks.

"I didn't think it was appropriate to make a big fuss," I say.

"Is this why you like to run?" Bihar asks.

"What do you mean?"

"I mean to keep you in shape for when you decide to run away."

"I'm sorry. I can't explain it. It is untenable."

The three stare at me in silence

"I should have told you, but defeat is not something I advertise."

They nod.

"How was class?" I ask.

"Okay. Professor is still telling us to form our own argument. Casual relationships. Analysis," Nadia says.

"Reminding us to avoid normative statements," Mary adds.

"No one in academe wants pure originality from their students," I say. "It is impossible at this stage. And no prof is value free. The trick is to sell them what they're selling in a creative way. Put their arguments in your words and line them up in logical manner. You already have something far more valuable than any method: your experiences. Just survive."

"Surviving is preferable to thriving," Bihar says. "Thriving has a short life expectancy."

"Anything above 50 per cent is vanity," I say.

They smile remembering the favourite statement of another classmate.

"You could have survived, Jesse," Bihar says. "If you had only said something."

"It's fine," I say.

I tighten my grip on the door handle and feel as though I am under many spotlights.

"Would you like my books?" I suddenly ask. "They're too heavy for me to bring home."

I go to my shelf and grab a half-dozen monographs on the Zimbabwean exodus, displacement risks in Africa, international refugee law, global migration patterns, and research methods. I cradle them in my arms, and let Nadia, Mary, and Bihar select two each. They thank me for them, and we share our goodbyes. I watch them descend the staircase and walk over the stony pathway—side by side by side comparing the titles they have acquired—past other residence buildings until they fade from sight. But I imagine them continuing on, strolling under the hundred-year-old tree, past the faculty buildings, the swimming pool, the libraries, and then finally going through security until they are outside WITS among the people, the cars, the noise, the chaos in the heart of the city—Johannesburg, with its many migrants, its meanness, and its undoubtable creativity and energy, Johannesburg, a city I have yet to know.

It's April 21, and I have been in Cape Town for four days, and I have been in Claremont public library for all of them. Tomorrow, I run the fifty-six-kilometre Two Oceans Marathon.

When I arrived at my hostel, I asked the receptionist if there happened to be a library nearby, and she told me I was in luck, as there was one only four blocks away. So the past four mornings, I have woken with the sun, bought a take-away latte, and walked away from Cape Town's attractions and towards a pretty little library, tucked away on a side street, sitting in wonderful view of mountains, which look so lovely in the morning's soft light.

I must prepare for a presentation in a week's time, but first I must write a response paper addressing the week's readings and themes: the politics of asylum in Africa. I need to address each required reading while making a thoughtful and original argument. I must critique and engage the literature. The readings are disjointed and disparate; some are macro in focus and look at global transformations, whereas others look at specific country case studies in more intimate detail.

I have already spent forty hours on this assignment, worth less than 5 per cent of the final mark. I have tried to cobble together an argument, but in every attempt, I find confounding factors to undermine it, so I must dig deeper, read outside the given readings, do my own research, find my own threads, discover my own argument. Hours tick by, people in the library come and go, and all I have is white screen and blinking cursor. I do not know how to begin. I cannot shape it. I cannot form it. Nothing comes. Nothing.

And before I know it, I am completely overwhelmed, drowning in information, choking on dates, schools of thought, articles, and monographs. In desperation, and for the sake of convenience, I choose the simplest of arguments. I choose to blame African governments in relation to the deplorable ways refugees have been treated on the continent.[1] I argue scholars typically view asylum in Africa as falling into two distinct phases concerning refugee reception: the post-independence "Golden Age," wherein states accepted and housed refugees with great enthusiasm; and the period from the 1980s to the present, wherein states viewed them with increased skepticism and mistrust and saw them as a burden to be minimally cared for and used as a bargaining chip for international humanitarian support. I argue this view is incorrect. There was no Golden Age. From the 1960s to the present, African states and their leaders have used refugees to their political advantage. Their reactions to refugee flows in a particular politico-historical context are always informed by how forced migrants may be used to further a government's legitimacy in the eyes of its citizens.

I hear a noise behind me, somewhere in the stacks, maybe a cough or a grunt.

Take the case of Tanzania, I write. At independence, the Tanzanian state was weak in its foundation, fragmented in its means to project power, and had boundaries that did not map onto its cultural and ethnic realities. In the immediate postcolonial moment, the Tanzanian African National Union (TANU), led by the indefatigable Julius Nyere, sought to transmit its power and influence and benevolence into the far reaches of its new territory; people would no longer be discriminated against based on ethnicity or language or custom. A citizen is a citizen is a citizen.

The voice in the stacks sounds angry, but the words crumble into an incoherent snarl—a beast howling at night.

At this moment, refugees served TANU's political wishes and its developmental philosophy of ujamma: the establishment of farming collectives to encourage self-reliance and promote a more egalitarian society as well as to exploit and make productive underused lands in the nation's periphery. Between 1963 and 1979, TANU authorized thirteen refugee settlements to host approximately 182,000 refugees, mostly those fleeing conflict in neighbouring Burundi. Refugees were given land to farm for the production of export crops and, in the process, created valuable foreign currency for Tanzania. Through exploiting refugees' muscle and brawn, TANU not only broadcast their power into previously uncaptured lands but further legitimated their authority in the eyes of the newly formed citizenry.

The voice increases its volume and pitch. Other readers hear it too and turn towards the unseen thing crying and yelping from the corner.

Although scholars laud early Tanzanian refugee policy and its Pan-African spirit and note the transformation to a more punitive one only occurred in the 1980s and 1990s due to the debt crisis and structural adjustment, the introduction of democracy and multipartyism, and the increased influx of refugees stemming from the Rwandan genocide, TANU, it should be remembered, was suspicious of refugees from the very beginning. The 1965 Refugee Act, for example, controlled refugees in a draconian fashion. The Act granted the government sweeping powers to deport refugees and detain any suspected of committing crimes; refugees could not leave their settlements and were under strict control of the commandants. Scholars have also argued these early refugees, unlike their later counterparts, could integrate into the local communities in which they lived; they could, in essence, become Tanzanian. However, in the forty years since the 1972 Burundian genocide, those refugees who fled to Tanzania still find themselves, as well as their descendants, without citizenship and its concomitant civil and political rights.

A word fires from the corner that I recognize. I think I understand it but cannot be sure. But the word comes again, and it suddenly erupts in clarity, becoming so loud and precise that I stop typing. "Fucking kaffir," the voice says.

In the 1980s and 1990s, the political utility of refugees underwent a transformation in Tanzania. In exchange for much needed loans, the International Monetary Fund forced the Mwinyi government to undertake severe austerity measures; severe cuts were made in the areas of education, health, and service delivery. These cutbacks happened alongside the arrival of Burundian and Rwandan refugees fleeing the violence gripping the Great Lakes region in 1993 and 1994. Unable to provide for its citizens or control its borderlands, the Tanzanian government faced a crisis of legitimacy, and in the face of such domestic upheaval, the Mwinyi government cast the refugees as the cause, as a threat to both the physical security and socioeconomic wellbeing of Tanzanians and placed them in tightly controlled camps administered by humanitarian organizations.

A Black security guard moves towards the stacks to confront the growling voice. He walks with authority; his gait is commanding. Among the books, out of sight, I hear the guard's voice: "Sir, sir, you have to leave."

With the introduction of multipartyism in 1995, the sitting government became beholden to their constituents in important ways. Democracy forced all parties to justify themselves in the eyes of voters. During the 1995 elections, each party politicized the refugee issue, and each promised to solve it. The refugee became demonized as the outsider, the usurper seeking to rob Tanzanian citizens of their rightful privileges. As resources became constrained and electorates became increasingly disillusioned over their impoverishment, the Mkapa government attempted to consolidate its power by engendering a nationalist mode of belonging by tying rights and privileges to national citizenship and by casting refugees as illegitimate competitors for scarce resources. The refugee was the cause of every ill, every bad thing. The refugee poisoned the body, the land, the country, and the soul of the nation. The refugee did not belong.

The commotion comes closer, and the voice draws nearer. Out of the stacks emerges a haggard old white man led by the security guard. He wears a dirtied overcoat, and his trousers are torn, ripped. His eyes are wild, bloodshot. He stumbles through the tables and staggers past onlookers. He is as intoxicated as he is enraged. "Kaffir," he says. "Kaffir," he repeats. The security guard trails behind.

Rather than looking at asylum policy in Africa as separated into two distinct periods, I conclude, scholars should examine the postcolonial asylum experiment from the vantage point of continuity. Governments neither apply refugee law nor act altruistically towards refugees without first conducting a political cost-benefit analysis. As the Tanzanian case has shown, African governments manipulate the presence of refugees to legitimize their rule. Whether using the labour of refugees to broadcast their power over peripheral lands or scapegoating the alleged crimes of refugees to mask their own shortcomings, governments maximize the political utility of refugees in a variety of ways.

As he approaches the staircase leading to the first floor and to the exit and to a sunny Cape Town afternoon, the white man spins and faces the security guard. His face is mangled with hatred, his body tense and rigid with mistrust and anguish. The white man raises his finger to the guard's face and screams "You fucking kaffir." The guard does not blink, does not respond. He absorbs the blow. "Sir, you must leave," he says. The white man turns towards the stairs, grabs the handle rail, and gingerly steps down. Before he vanishes, he looks back over his shoulder and sees me sitting at the table with my laptop open, my books and papers scattered everywhere. He says not a thing, but his look unsettles me. And as much as my eyes condemn him, and as much as I deride the old racist caricature, I know there is nothing inherently different between him and me, just chance and circumstance, just plain old luck. I think about Zimbabwe, Black and brown deportees, and asking them to confide in me and my whiteness in the shadow of South Africa, underneath a white world.

I close my laptop and gather my things.
Tomorrow, I run.

Endnote

1. The sources I used to develop this argument are as follows: Chaulia, Sreeram Sundar. "The Politics of Refugee Hosting in Tanzania: From Open Door to Unsustainability, Insecurity and Receding Receptivity." *Journal of Refugee Studies*, vol. 16, no. 2, 2003, pp. 147-166; Manby, Bronwean. "'I Can't Be a Citizen if I am Still a Refugee.' Former Burundian Refugees Struggle to Assert their New Tanzanian Citizenship." *Citizenship and Displacement in the Great Lakes Region Working Paper 8*, 2013; Milner, J. *Refugees, the State and the Politics of Asylum in Africa.* Palgrave Macmillan, 2009; Rutinwa, Bonaventure. "Forced Displacement and Refugee Rights in the Great Lakes Region." *African Journal of International Affairs*, vol. 1, no. 2, 1998, pp. 11-43; Rutinwa, Bonaventure. "The End of Asylum? The Changing Nature of refugee Policies in Africa." *New Issues in Refugee Research*, Working Paper No. 5. Geneva: UNHCR, May 1999.

Part II

6.

Mozambique

It's May 2018, I am thirty-three years old, and I am on my way to Africa. Four years have passed since I left WITS. Four years have passed since I left South Africa, and the African continent, without doing so many of the things I had wanted. When people asked me whether I have been to Africa, I would always pause before answering "Yes, I have." I had walked the streets of Johannesburg and Cape Town, of course, and my passport still contained my South African study visa. I had proof of a visit. Yet I wavered in responding in the affirmative because I knew the libraries and classrooms of Johannesburg and Cape Town better than those cities' actual sites and sounds. Despite my living in Johannesburg, I spent so much time safely ensconced in my dorm room or in a library or in a classroom that Johannesburg, the real and dynamic city, seemed a thousand kilometres away. I had spent so much time reading and studying about migration in Southern African that I associated the word "Africa" with only words on the page, with a problem that needed fixing. I had come to experience South Africa, yet I remained as divorced from it as I had been in Toronto, Montreal, and Busan.

This trip would be different though. I have two months to explore Southern Africa—to put faces and sounds and smells to the words I had spent years reading and analyzing. Finally, I can step outside the book, the classroom, and the school. I can walk amid the people and their histories. I can visit their worlds.

Portugal and Mozambique have shared a long history. Portuguese explorers were the first Europeans to set foot on the country's fabled beaches at the end of the fifteenth century, and they did not leave for almost five hundred years. I have decided to stopover in Lisbon for a few days before travelling to Maputo, Mozambique's capital, because I want to trace that connection between the two disparate cities. I want to see how the Portuguese, or at least their government representatives, remember that connection, how they commemorate those five hundred years of encounter.

Across from Jeronimos Monastery and the verdant Da Gama gardens, over the N6 highway littered with red, open-deck tour buses, and towards the northern banks of the Tagus River, flowing nonchalantly from Old Lisbon to the Atlantic and to the rest of the world, stands the Padrão dos Descobrimentos, or the Monument to Discoveries. Soaring 56 metres high and spreading twenty metres wide, the monument evokes the memory of overseas Portuguese exploration—a glorious and golden time when Portugal was the world's epicentre. Its lantern lighted the earth's darkest corners. Of the monument, I snap a photo.

I had read that in 1940, to celebrate Lisbon's hosting the World Fair, architect Cottinelli Telmo and sculptor Leopoldo de Almeida built the monument, yet unwisely did so with perishable materials, which proved unsuitable for the long life such spectacles demand. Twenty years later, in 1960, to mark the five hundredth year of Infante Dom Henrique's death, better known as Henry the Navigator, patron of voyage and discovery, the monument was reconstructed in cement and limestone to ensure future generations could enjoy an afternoon under the sun and by the sea gazing up at the structure and ruminating on the past victories it summons.

The Padrâo resembles a three-sail-ship preparing to depart the harbour and head out into the ocean. At the bow, Henry holds a miniature ship in his right hand and an old map in his left. His fingers are long and boney, perfect for tearing things open or pulling things apart. He stares with his magnetic eyes and seems to draw the world closer to him. His vision is unfeeling, unrelenting, and unflinching—hard. Around him assemble other explorers from Portugal's Age of Discovery—Vasco da Gama, Ferdinand Magellan, Pedro Álvares Cabral—as well as missionaries—Gonçalo de Carvalho, Fernão Mendes Pinto. Some hold swords, others crucifixes; all wear an expression of haughty determination, an unwavering certitude in both their cause and the outcome. They fear not the unknown because providence has already secured their favour, already written their triumph in the stars, sky, and clouds. Doubt is unbecoming for men of belief and faith. It is fear's handmaiden and has no place in the minds and hearts and bellies of the God-fearing. After all, what does one fear when the world has already been promised?

Under their boots, I watch tourists gather and aim their cameras at the men above. They kneel and bend trying to fit the explorers into their frame, but the monument proves too grandiose for a mere photograph to capture. Eventually the tourists resign themselves to their smallness, their insignificance in the face of this monument to human ingenuity, and simply linger and loiter below. And underneath the weight of remembrance, five hundred years of history, the visitors do look small and humble. They seem unfit to grace the presence of greatness, unworthy to stand next to giants of the Portuguese past, when the kingdom and her explorers were the universe, when their ships lighted the Atlantic's gateway and ignited the corridor to far-flung and dark places, when Portugal was synonymous with superlatives—greatness, magnificence, transcendence—not decay, collapse, or poverty. Indeed, looking at the monument, standing brazen over the Tagus, it is near impossible to think on anything but achievement, the simple beauty of hammering rock or cutting forest.

In front of the monument, towards the highway, a mosaic, donated by the apartheid South African government in 1960, covers the pavement. As I hover above it, I see the mosaic is of a compass and a map of the world, which charts the routes taken by the Portuguese explorers and the years of their discoveries. The continents are painted in an ugly, ruined, and scratched red. Countless shoeprints have dirtied them. A man in white running shoes steps on Brazil. Then, a woman in a grey skirt and brown slip-on shoes wanders across the Sahara. A boy in a red baseball cap licks from his vanilla ice cream cone as he strolls past the Pacific Islands and does not flinch when drops of white splash over Fiji, Vanuatu, and then the Solomon Islands. A young woman sits cross-legged on China, her heels stabbing at the southern Japanese islands of Okinawa, and she turns upward at the May sun as the light lands across her sunglasses and then on her tanned skin—her cheeks, nose, and lips—and she returns the favour with a smile.

From the highway, a tour guide leads his group through the crowds of people amassing on the sidewalk. He deftly manoeuvres through the bodies—stopping and starting, weaving and zigzagging, as if by instinct—and then abruptly halts at the world's edge. He points his finger at the oceans and the continents and barks in quick bursts information about the mosaic, about the monument, about the historical importance of Belem, the district in which they stand. He speaks his simple and punchy sentences in a robotic, mechanical manner; his voice is monotonous, his tone flat, his demeanour uninterested. He behaves and acts as if he were showing his apartment to a group of friends—this is the bathroom, here is the kitchen, welcome to the living room—and his words, and their meaning, have lost all significance, merely uttered in repetition, until they are just sounds strung together in a language that could be any. And when he smiles at his practiced jokes or admits that he bought his sofa on sale, his mind roams elsewhere—on the dish in the oven, the beers in the fridge, the salad on the counter—and his mannerisms come to resemble those of a salesperson.

I closely study the guide.

From Lisbon, he steps to the Azores. "1427," he says.

He leaps to Cape Verde: "1458."

He lunges south to São Tomé and Principe, "1471," and then tiptoes north to Elmina on the Ghanaian coast, "1482." He steps south to the Congo River, "1482," and further south again to the Cape of Good Hope, "1488." He pivots, turning north, and stretches across South Africa, Zimbabwe, and Malawi, until his heal lands on Mozambique Island, "1497." He glides over the East African Coast, landing at Zanzibar, Mombasa, and Mogadishu, and sashays across the Indian Ocean, anchoring at Mumbai, Goa, and Sri Lanka. He navigates through the islands of Southeast Asia, pausing at Malacca, Sumatra, and Timor, before he raises his foot, extends it in the air, over the Philippines, and drops it on Guangzhou, China. "1517," he says.

Shielding their eyes from the sun, the tourists nod and listen as they watch him move over the world. In the background, sailboats are tied to the harbour's docks. People eat leafy salads and drink white wine on the patios. Along the boardwalk, people jog and ride bikes. Families stroll and laugh together. A father picks up his daughter, places her on his shoulders, and then points to something in the distance, maybe the 25 April bridge spanning the Tagus, maybe the flock of seagulls rising and falling with each gust of wind, or maybe to the two cracked, sun-hardened gentlemen sitting and chatting by their fishing poles. Or maybe despite the activity, the motion and buzz, the man points to nothing at all. Maybe despite the histories and stories, the plaques, statues, and landmarks, Belem resides perpetually in her locked chest. Maybe despite everything the sun reveals, each fissure and fracture, Lisbon lives perpetually in the dark.

By the river's edge, underneath Henry the Navigator's big boots, a man in a black cowboy hat and blue jeans strums a guitar and sings into a microphone.

I listen.

Like a bridge over troubled water
I will lay me down

Like a bridge over troubled water
I will lay me down

More and more tourists descend the red tour buses and walk over the world towards the monument. Some notice what they step over and stop to take a photograph of the earth from above, as if a bird or a god, trying desperately to fit the known world into a single shot. The man still sings.

Like a bridge over troubled water
I will lay me down
Like a bridge over troubled water
I will lay me down

Few tourists, however, stop to listen. They are too fascinated with the monument, the river, the sun. They are too eager to see and experience what they have long associated only with book pages, only with legend. They pay no attention to places and things of this world, of now. They have no time for yesterday and certainly none for tomorrow.

Like a bridge over troubled water
I will ease your mind
Like a bridge over troubled water
I will ease your mind

So the man sings on, invisible in the light.

On the drive downtown from the Maputo airport, I watch a mosquito hunt. From the windshield, it drifts to the dashboard, pausing there momentarily before its thin wings flutter again and carry the insect past the radio, seatbelt, and indicator, floating and sailing in the air, and towards the steering wheel, where it lands, a mere inch away from my driver's hand. She twitches and readies. Her smooth antenna must smell him, those receptive proteins picking up his scent, his fatty acids wafting and rising from his skin, his carbon dioxide, too, emanating from his mouth and permeating her proximity and drawing her closer and closer and closer. She is thirsty as much as she is hungry. She lifts clumsily into the air again and goes to him, as fast her abdomen allows, oblivious to the obvious danger, the certain death, blinded and controlled as she is by appetite, the need to fertilize her eggs through a simple injection of blood, which flows so close, just under a layer of skin, just a prick and a bite away. She lands on his wrist, and her six legs nestle into his skin, securing her body and allowing it to move and manoeuvre more freely. She raises her proboscis into the air—her spear-shaped mouth comprising six separate needlelike parts skilled at piercing the skin, finding vessels, and sucking blood—dips her body, and drops her weapon towards the unknowing victim. Before she may drink and satiate each and every part of herself, she senses it coming and moves before the hand can crush her frame. She reacts swiftly, bouncing and bobbing in the air, and manages to avoid each angry blow. The window rolls down, and she flies to the safety of the outside world, towards a white pickup truck filled with standing young men in t-shirts, exposed to the air, wind, and sun. As we drive from Maputo airport to the central business district, along Lenin Avenue, stopping frequently in the mid-morning traffic, I lose sight of the mosquito among the men and the hubbub of city activity. To where she may hunt next, I cannot say, but hunt she will.

In Canada, mosquitos are notorious for the delight they take in ruining a summer evening. It was a lovely time at the cottage, we say, except the bugs were dreadful, especially the mosquitos; I got bit a hundred times, we exaggerate. Around candlelight or the fire, we hear them buzzing and threatening, preparing to sully an engaging or a merry conversation, readying to destroy a drunken, spirited moment. They ruin walks in the woods; they make enjoying an evening's fish impossible. We are always slapping at ourselves—our legs, arms, faces—and crushing their little bodies and then flicking and wiping their remains from our skin. We curse God and question how a loving being could create such a vindictive creature. Yes, a real nuisance, a real pain. I remember as a kid, we would take revenge on mosquitoes whenever given the opportunity. One of my friends would let the insect settle on his arm and actually suck his blood, but once the menace had firmly secured her mouth and had begun to drink, my friend would pinch his skin just above the pest to increase the blood flow so that the little mosquito could no longer control the amount, so that she would fatten and balloon, so that what she craved and stole punished her, beaten and killed by her own needs, and so that she would eventually burst and splatter amid our laughter.

"The traffic is bad this morning," the driver says.

"Yes, it is," I say.

Such a game would not be advisable here. In Mozambique, malaria kills thousands each year.

Formerly called Lourenço Marques, named for the Portuguese trader who landed here in 1545, the city grew as a trading place for ivory and slaves. The Portuguese erected a fort in 1787, then inaugurated a city council in 1887, and finally made the southern city its capital of Portuguese East Africa in 1907, replacing the fabled island of Mozambique, founded by Da Gama in 1498 and lying 2,500 kilometres from Maputo. The morning I explore the Mozambican capital seems a morning like any other. Along the city's main thoroughfares named for both international and local communist luminaries—Karl Marx, Ho Chi Minh, Patrice Lumumba, Samora Machel—people queue in long, twisting lines outside of banks—Barclays, Standard, First National, Millennium Bim. At their feet, sheets spread over the sidewalk showcasing a spectrum of products and goods. Men and women peruse the goods—the shoes, handbags, and clothing—while a solitary man sells single roses to anyone drawn enough to the red petals. A man pulls a cart piled with pineapples onto the road to avoid the melee on the sidewalk, and when he returns to the concrete, directing his cart over the curb, he pauses to inspect a game of checkers played by two old men who have replaced the standard pieces with bottle caps. In the distance, towards the Espirito Santo Estuary of Delagoa Bay and the city's port, cranes reach towards the sky followed by black billowing smoke. With the help of Chinese investment and expertise, construction workers are building a bridge spanning the bay to shred a typical two-hour commute time to mere minutes. Maputo is open for business, as the FRELIMO government eagerly proclaims, to show foreign suitors how it has forsaken its red, hammer and sickle past—its skepticism and outright hostility towards capital, privatization, and foreign investment—and now welcomes the world to its beaches and cities, to marvel at the potential, the untapped markets, the unexplored, underutilized resources. Near Independence Square and close to the tourist information centre, where I will meet my guide for the morning, I notice a teenager sitting in an alleyway next to a pile of empty Coke cans. He reaches for one and sits it in front of him. He takes the rock lying nearby, raises it high in the air, and smashes it against the lid again and again until the can has collapsed and flattened into a metal pancake. He throws it among the others in a pile and reaches for another Coke can.

At tourist information, hidden just to the northwest of Tunduru Botanical Gardens—a cool and shady and pleasant respite from the sun and home to thousands of fruit bats, who hang from branches and squawk and holler in cacophonous delight—Ercilo takes my hand and welcomes me to his city. He is young, barely twenty it seems, diminutive, and slight, the perfect size for a city subjected to a ruthless sun all year long. His gait resembles a breeze, languid and leisurely, and when I ask him why he is wearing two t-shirts in a morning already approaching the high twenties, he simply says that it is winter and graciously does not remark on the beads of sweat forming on my forehead. He speaks softly, his English is perfect, and his voice travels in such a pleasant and reflective way that I follow it and concentrate on its flow and tone and rhythm, instead of my surroundings, which almost proves deadly.

We walk towards Independence Square, Machel's statue and Maputo Cathedral both rise in the distance, and I am chatting about my first impressions of the city, my love of the crumbling, Portuguese art-deco architecture and its haunting ambience, and as we prepare to cross a roundabout, I look left, see plenty of space, and step to cross, only to be blocked by Ercillo's slender arm and the blur of a passing truck, whose body passes less than a metre from my face and whose breeze rustles my hair. "Careful" is all Ercilo says and again is courteous enough not to remind me of what I already know: Here, they drive on the left.

In Maputo, cars, along with their drivers, are like the Old Testament God: unpredictable, impetuous, violent. To cross them is to flirt with death. In Canada, pedestrians possess an almost haughty personality—a cavalier and contemptuous attitude towards drivers and the weapons they direct. They expect the speeding hunk of metal to stop on a dime for them. And they usually do. In Maputo, however, pedestrians yield to the motorists as an observant man yields to his God: He submits to their ominous, omniscient power, crossing only when safety, as well as salvation, is secured by providence. Traffic lights are Maputo's endangered species, and those that do exist exude an authority relegated to something extinct: quaint and wonderful to look at but holding no real power in this particular cultural milieu. Ercilo, then, becomes my priest in navigating the whims of Maputo's angry gods, possessing as he does an almost innate knowledge of cars' patterns and speeds, as if he can predict their movements and determine the time we need to not only cross the street but also manoeuvre through an endless stream of vehicles: stop, go, wait, go, stop, wait. When Ercilo says stop, I stop; when he says go, I go, zealously.

On the Cathedral's steps, he asks me why I have chosen to visit Maputo. I tell him I studied Mozambican history at university—the Portuguese colonial era, the war of independence, the civil war, the impoverished postcolonial reality—and the long country has always intrigued me. I don't tell him my interest in Mozambique was part of a failed PhD project, a convoluted and contradictory tale that still hangs a powerful pall over my sense of self. I spare him the boredom and myself the chore of dredging the familiar narrative up and noticing whether any profound changes have happened in this retelling. He smiles and swiftly laughs to himself, as if my sentences confirm something about Canada he has always thought.

"This is why I want to go to Canada," he suddenly says. "The people are interested in the world."

Underneath the steeple of the Cathedral of Our Lady of the Immaculate Conception and its white, imposing exterior, so white in fact it seems crafted from ice and snow, I am thrust into a familiar position that I loathe: a representative of Canada. I resent being a personification of Canada whenever abroad, an ambassador of its values and morals, an embodiment of the nation who must metaphorically wear the flag and peddle the narrative Canadians, particularly white ones, love to tell about ourselves—how good we are. Yet I remember while performing this internal diatribe that the only reason I am here visiting Maputo is because I was born in Canada and, as a result, possess the one article separating me from Ercilio, my birthright, the gift bestowed on me for the simple accident of being born in a Western country with a long history of colonization, dispossession, and discrimination: a widely recognized passport. I tell him Canada is not always what he sees on the internet or hears on the news. I tell him about the ongoing deplorable treatment of Indigenous peoples, racialized poverty, police brutality, Islamophobia, environmental degradation, violence against women, the disgusting detainment of undocumented migrants, and so on. At the end of my reappraisal of Canada's image, a sort of reckoning I feel is my duty to give if I become the voice of Canada abroad, Ercilio merely smiles and says every country has such a dark past: Having skeletons in the closet is a prerequisite of becoming a nation-state.

"So who are the Canadians?" he then asks.

His question unsettles me, and I stumble over a brief and haphazard overview of Canadian history—Indigenous culture, the arrival of French and English explorers and settlers, fur trade, mass European immigration, mass assimilation of the First Peoples and their struggle for self-determination, language politics, and the advent of multiculturalism as official doctrine—yet my story sounds superficial and bookish, divorced from feeling and personality, impersonal. I tell him my ancestors left Ireland for Canada in the nineteenth century during the Great Famine and settled in eastern Ontario, but beyond that official family history, I tell him, I have not given my roots much pause or contemplation.

"Maybe you should," he says. Yes, I probably should, but my mind still lingers on the question of what Canada is and what it is not. I think for Canada to redeem itself from its past, for it to reconcile the image of what it is with what it wants to be, then Canada, as an identity marker or as a symbolic gesture, must come to mean nothing at all. Canada must become a vase in which residents can fill it with whatever they choose. Canada must become so diverse and complicated in scope and in meaning that to try and label it, to articulate it in coherent sentences, would be as ambitious and foolhardy as trying to label and name every bluster of wind.

"So where would you like to go in Canada?" I ask.

He glances at me in polite disbelief, his shrewd and prescient eyes searching my face for any meaning hidden there, as if the question and its intent do not register in any rational sense.

"What do you mean?" he asks.

"Well, would you prefer to visit Vancouver, Montreal, Toronto?"

He shrugs his shoulders in well-mannered indifference to a question that astutely demonstrates the difference between me and him.

"It doesn't matter," he says. "The important thing is just to get there."

"But would you like to study while you are there?"

"Of course, university is the goal. But travel itself is a form of education, or at least it should be. Good travel is an exchange of cultures. Wouldn't you agree?"

"I would," I say. "Have you seen many other places?"

"No," he answers. "I have never left Maputo."

A woman in a red dress sashays across the church courtyard as the sun shines and then erupts over her body, before she passes through the shadows of tree branches and their green leaves, which in the mid-morning stillness, register not a rustle in the blue, empty sky.

"Shall we go in?" Ercilio asks and motions to the church's open doors.

I follow him inside, and I am struck again by the building's whiteness: the ceiling, walls, and floor. The cathedral is an austere, serious place, perfect for a didactic voice to grip a congregation in a doubtless, unquestioning fervour of belief. The interior is oblong shaped, a rounded rectangle, a whale's belly, and rows of wooden pews dissect the space. It is empty this Friday morning, eerily quiet, and remarkably still. On each wall hang a half-dozen fans, whose blades remain still, and just above, the stained-glass windows refract sunlight as it falls on the benches to remind the practitioners that the heavens are always watching. In between the windows are some paintings adorned with crucifixes and telling the story of white men in black robes coming ashore along picturesque Indian Ocean beaches to teach the word of God to Black men adorned in grey chains.

"The Portuguese came here to spread Christianity," Ercilio says. "And in the process, they destroyed our culture."

He walks among the pews and lets his hand wash over the cool wood.

"Construction on the church started in the 1930s," he says, motioning to the ceiling. "But it was not completed until 1944." He waves his hands and summons the air, as if a conductor and the church his orchestra, as if wanting to pull the church towards him. "Planners had a limited budget from the beginning, so only very simple materials were used." He pauses. "And forced labour was used. Do you know about forced labour?" I nod.

Chibalo.

Since the beginning of the Mozambican colonial era in the late nineteenth century, Portuguese officials had relied on unpaid labour to facilitate the exploitation of the country's resources.[1] As the international community became less tolerant of slavery and more encouraging of freer forms of labour, colonial officials throughout Africa became craftier and more flexible in how they reaped the benefits of unpaid labour without it actually falling under slavery's definition. By the turn of the century, the South African mining and agricultural economies to the west had grown exponentially, and Portuguese East Africa, possessing as it did a long yet undeveloped coastline, sought to become the port of call for South African gold, sisal, and sugarcane—their gateway to a voracious world. Officials needed ports and railroads—infrastructure—and men to build them. In response, the Portuguese government introduced the first native labour code, which tied labour to moral and social betterment as well as to freedom. Indeed, Black Africans would have the opportunity to choose whichever job they wanted, yet if they refused, if they remained idle and truant, if they succumbed to vagrancy, the devil's workshop, then public authorities, in cahoots with local African collaborators, could compel them to work. Overnight, entire rural areas transformed into labour reserves, where farmers, merchants, or factory owners could arrive one day, slip a gift to a local administrator, and leave with an untold number of labourers the next. When the state required bodies to plant cotton or tea, when they needed muscle to lay railroad or blast through rock to make roads, anyone who did not subscribe to European conceptions of work or possess European chalky skin tones were called idle, were bound and tied, and were sent to distant areas to work on projects for years on end under the most gruelling and abusive of conditions. But they were not slaves. Chibalo workers earned a salary, sometimes ten per cent of what their non-Chibalo colleagues received for the same work. Sometimes merchants and farmers simply refused to pay their Chibalo workers, turning them into debt peons and bounding them forever to the land. Chibalo ruthlessly compelled Africans to enter the labour market while it kept wages down and undercut the bargaining power of free African labour. But they were not slaves.

In 1932, the authoritarian Estado Novo, headed by Antonio de Oliveira Salazar, came to power in Lisbon, which revolutionized the relationship between Portugal and her colonies. From Mozambique to Angola and from Cape Verde to Guinea Bissau, the African colonials existed for the betterment of the metropole. As a result, the manner in which Lisbon extracted material benefit from her colonies had to become more efficiently rendered, and to placate international concerns over forced labour, colonial officials had to become more discrete and ruthless. Though ostensibly abolished in 1928, Chibalo remained an integral part of colonial life. Africans who could not pay their taxes were forced to work. Africans who could not show they had worked in South Africa or Southern Rhodesia as migrant labourers in the previous six months were forced to work. Anyone, anywhere, could be compelled to work. Salazar also allied his colonial project with the Catholic Church to give colonialism a civilizing quality, a way to bring Africans out of the shadow, to raise them up from the muck, through the guiding hand, the loving touch, of both Christianity and Portuguese culture. The desire to Europeanize the African was reflected in the Regime do Indigenato, a cultural ladder rising from depravity to virtue, from backwardness to uprightness, and upon the ladder, the Africans would climb and climb, rung to rung to rung, mimicking the Portuguese and adopting their mannerisms, their ticks and tricks, as they stepped higher and higher, until they reached cultural whiteness themselves. And for those Africans who climbed the highest and reached the heavens, who could now take a pen and scribble their name as Jose or Ferdinando, who could bark out orders in breathless Portuguese, who could easily forsake and forget their past tribal ways, and who could sell their labour on the open marketplace in dignity and self-reliance, these men became assimilados and enjoyed all the rights and responsibilities of Portuguese citizenship, except the colour white. Those who failed the test, the 99 per cent who slipped and fell from the ladder, back into the mud and dirt of their customs, the superstitions and barbaric practices, were called indígenas and were requested to carry identity cards explaining such a failure: They were Africans through and through, and they were never to become citizens, forever subject to their customary law and the whims of Portuguese officials, forever fodder for public work projects.

The Catholic Church helped construct this ladder to heaven. Under Salazar's tutelage, the Church reaffirmed its commitment to saving African souls from Africa and to fastening Lusophone Africa to the Portuguese Empire. And for those Africans who could not, or would not, succumb to the light, they would serve God in a more tangible way: They would break the rocks from the quarry and drag them to the heart of Lourenço Marques under watchful European eyes. In the heat, they would mix cement and mortar and would secure one block to another, up and up, until the steeples touched the sky. And for those Africans who fell from the ladder, who had their bones break and shatter over those very same rocks, who had their dead bodies covered in dirt and concrete, who had their memories forgotten under a beautiful, white cathedral, they could rest peacefully knowing that their deaths contributed to something larger than themselves: a crucifix on African soil. The Church Fathers must have seen something recognizable in Salazar; they must have understood that powerful desire to spread from the centre and to douse the world in familiar scents and fragrances so that wherever they went, they were already there.

"Are you Christian?" Ercilio asks me as we leave the church. I take a cloth from my pocket and wipe the sweat from my forehead. In the short time inside the church, the temperature has risen.

"I believe Christianity has done more harm than good in its history," I say. "I have trouble believing the Christian God is a loving one."

"So you're an atheist?" he asks.

I swallow.

"Yes, I am."

I expect a rebuttal or surprise, but Ercilio remains silent while we both watch Maputo roar to life from the church steps.

"What about you?" I ask. "Are you a Christian?"

"I am not a Christian," he says. "But I believe in God."

In the distance, Samora Machel's bronze statue rises nine metres from a three-metre-high marble slab. His back faces us, but Machel stares across his city, down the avenue of his namesake, past the high rises and chipping Portuguese architecture, to the old fort, and finally to the ocean.

"I don't go to church, and I don't pray. But I believe in God," Ercilio says. "I believe in the duality of things. I believe that in this world both good and evil exist, and they reinforce each other. I've seen the devil in many things. I've seen horrible, evil things. So I believe the opposite must exist. The good. A god. The devil cannot exist without a god."

He does not elaborate on the evil things he has seen, and I do not ask.

He points to the roundabout below.

"Here is the heart of Maputo, Independence Square, and its competing sources of power. Behind us you have the church, and to the right is the city council. And in front of us stands Machel's statue. Secular and religious—each competing for devotees."

"Is the Catholic Church still powerful?" I ask.

Ercilio smiles his subtle smile as if hoping I would ask such a question.

"Anywhere there is poverty, the Church is powerful."

We descend towards Machel, and Ercilio speaks while guiding me across traffic lanes, in between cars and motorbikes.

"Samora Machel became leader of the Mozambican Liberation Front (FRELMO) in 1969, helped win independence from Portugal in 1975, and fought the South-African-backed RENAMO during the country's long civil war until he died in a plane crash in South Africa in 1986. He never saw Mozambique at peace."

President Machel, I remember him from my books. The Portuguese forced his parents to grow cotton after settlers forced them from their land. Mission schools educated him—the only source of schooling for many Black Mozambicans—and he became a nurse in Maputo. After ten years of saving lives, he decided to join FRELIMO to help save his country. He said watching his parents disgraced by colonialism's mechanics, the system's preference for a certain kind of people, radicalized him far more than reading Marx or Engels or Lenin. Experience is the ultimate radicalizer. No book can tell you what you already know and feel.

He oversaw Mozambique's post-independence espousal of Marxist-Leninist principals, including nationalization and collectivization; he strove to deracialize the country and to nullify the odious legal distinction between citizen and subject, between whites and assimlados and the native majority; and he sought to detribalize the land and extinguish ethnic-based distinctions that had divided colonial subjects and left them to the mercy of native authorities and chiefs who often worked as colonial agents and as puppets for the Portuguese. Machel worked towards a pan-Mozambican identity—one transcending the disparate and hostile ethnic pieces promoted by the Portuguese and underwriting the indirect rule system—and tried to extinguish traditional holdovers, alternative sources of power hostile to FRELIMO and secular, scientific socialism. In the countryside, away from learned circles discussing the parameters and shape of African socialism, FRELIMO officials eagerly denounced and sometimes proscribed various antiquated cultural rites: bridewealth, polygyny, initiation rites, rainmaking ceremonies, and witchcraft. Chiefs were ridiculed, repressed, and were branded as colonial holdovers susceptible to foreign influence and vulnerable to alien, perhaps even supernatural, political swaying.

The early FRELIMO leaders understood that Western imperialism was not only a brute instrument, full of bombs and machine-gun fire, but also a seductive whisper enchanting local actors with promises of power. When RENAMO, backed by apartheid Rhodesia and South Africa, arrived on the scene in the 1970s as a rebel force hostile to the socialist nation, FRELIMO could easily dismiss them as a proxy for white Western interests, oppositional to the will of the majority, and as colonial reactionaries aggressive to the new egalitarian order. Yet in 1994, after peace between the warring factions finally arrived, the country's first general elections showed RENAMO had popular support that FRELIMO could no longer ignore: 33 per cent of the presidential vote and majorities in five of Mozambique's eleven provinces. RENAMO had become a legitimate political party, and the picture of Mozambique as Africa's last-standing socialist project, epitomized by FRELIMO, was forever shattered.

In the following years, when the post-civil-war players put the pieces back together, glued and affixed all the little shards, the image reflecting back bore little resemblance to what stood there before. Mozambique, a name once synonymous with African socialism, had undergone a neoliberal revolution, an abrupt and tumultuous transition to capitalism and a market economy.[2] A posterchild for the World Bank and the International Monetary Fund, FRELIMO abandoned direct state management of factories and farms and relied more on private sector actors, foreign investment, and international loans. Privatization schemes have been absolute and far reaching, as FRELIMO has courted companies with rich tax incentives the world over. Gone are the idealistic Marxist slogans, replaced by technocratic language extolling the virtues of good governance, capacity building, and partnerships. Beyond the glean and shine, however, as with all neoliberal success stories, beats a disillusioned drum, sounding the downtrodden lines and rhythms of people who have followed the rules, listened to the experts, and did what they were told to do yet still struggle for sustenance while they watch Portuguese tourists and expatriates shop and eat along July 24 Avenue, the day of independence, and descend from the hotels and apartments along Engels Avenue to play near the water.

So I stare at Machel staring at his city and wonder if the great revolutionary would recognize either his city or country if he returned resurrected from the remains of his Tupolev Tu-134 Soviet jetliner—the broken metal and ruined engine parts littering farmlands—that suspiciously fell from the sky over South Africa in 1986. The North Koreans, who designed and built the statue in 2011, have dressed him in standard army wear—a thick coat emblazoned with medals and decorated lapels, an average army cap, and long, heavy trousers. He looks like an ordinary soldier, a man who simply does his duty without pretense or celebration. He has no hint of ostentation or pretension, no ceremonial pomp, no luxurious regalia. He does what is necessary, humbly, and nothing more. Yet what separates Machel from the commonplace are his eyes, which the North Korean sculptors must have laboured over for weeks. They are intense and decisive, almost fanatical, captivating. I see him standing in front of a crowd, amid the flashing camera lights, and electrifying his listeners, not with words, which can grow so stale and rotten, but with those eyes, resolute and determined, eyes befitting a man who sees beyond his contemporaries to a future dreamed only by him, a visionary, a prophet. Machel, the statue, has his right arm raised and has his index finger pointed skywards. We will persevere, he says. We will prevail.

Yet statues hide more than they reveal. Statues take historical and individual complexities and encase them in unyielding bronze. Statues do not speak. Statues do not move. Statues justify. They become what whatever power needs them to be. In eastern Europe, after communism's fall, the new democracies removed all Lenin and Marx statues, all references to the hammer and sickle, all mention of the glorious workers' struggle and hid them in dark rooms. The new governments understood a symbol's ability to metamorphose, its malleability, how hands, any hands, could take an old statue, wash it clean, freed from the cobwebs and grime, and present it as something new, daring, and exceptional. Machel's statue does not remember the man for who or what he was, good and bad, the complexity of living and leading in times of turmoil and violence—as a statue, he has become a hero, and nothing more. For the powerful, heroes are wonderful, unthinking things. And as I watch young Mozambicans come to have their picture taken next to Machel, Mozambicans born after his death, I sense the beauty of bronze: Machel's presence in Maputo, his eyes watching over both decay and development, his magnificent aura, may be used to legitimize whatever FRELIMO wishes. Machel's eyes validate what once was unfathomable.

Ercilio rehashes the standard Machel narrative. He has memorized all the important dates and events; he has well honoured the first president's legacy, even if he was born well after Machel fell from the sky. And after he finishes, he gives me a few more moments to stare at the statue while he checks his cellphone.

"Aren't there many conspiracy theories surrounding his death and plane crash?" I ask. "Isn't it true that the truth isn't yet known?"

Ercilio looks up from his cellphone and then shoots a cautious glance around his surroundings.

"I get nervous talking about politics," he says. "But, yes, you are right."

Sensing the illicit nature of the topic, I ask no further questions and merely follow Ercilio through his city while he guides me to both well-known sites and hidden gems known only to locals, like an old theatre whose interior, the stage and seating area, seems neglected, with its unkempt floors, bent and broken chairs, but the venue still hosts plays and concerts, Ercilio assures me, as we sit and sweat in the poorly lit and poorly ventilated room. Still fans are plugged into the walls yet represent only a cruel hint at what the room could be, but my guide does not seem to mind, as I see the room and its potential, what transpires here, the music, magic, and memory, still sway and affect him in wonderful, subtle ways.

We pass a concrete building, whose colourful façade reminds me of a child's Lego tower, bright and playful, and Ercilio says the Portuguese built the structure in the late 1950s, and it once served as the offices for Portuguese airlines. Ercilio cannot explain his fascination with the old TAP building, but it remains his favourite in Maputo, and he hopes they never demolish it because somehow, as I sense, the edificio has become an enduring piece of the varied urban landscape. At the market, Ercilio smiles while he negotiates with a market woman over the price of her Bull's Heart fruits, a pear-like item, but pricklier and messier, he advises me I must try, and I sense my anxiety grow as she selects four Bull's Hearts from her fruit mountain—a table so full of colour and shapes and variety that I can only identity a handful of them—drops them into a bag, and hands it to Ercilio, who promptly reaches into the bag and tosses me a Heart before he himself grabs one, into which he sinks his teeth. And when we have finished and have wiped the juices from our mouths and licked the sweetness from our fingers, Ercilio hands the remaining contents to a homeless man sitting at the foot of a table loaded with vegetables, fruit, cashews, peanuts, and almonds.

At the railway station, designed by an associate of Eiffel, of Parisian fame, Ercilio says the tracks laid here connected Africa to the world, as the goods from South Africa offloaded in Maputo—the sugarcane and gold and diamonds—and found their way onto ships bound for ports in various oceans, and, the tracks symbolize not only economic connections but cultural ones, since people here, he says, are connected beyond borders, beyond the artificial lines these tracks try to delineate, yet the railway no longer goes to South Africa, as Maputo trains do not fit on their tracks, and nowadays they are used primarily as commuter trains by locals travelling to the capital for work from the outlying communities. Through the old Red Light District, along Rua de Bagamoyo, we then trod, past bars and other debauched establishments, and I keep my eyes looking forwards and try to ignore the sex workers who sit huddled outside of seedy doorways yet talk to one another in the most convivial of ways. But when one woman grabs my arm and asks whether I would like a memorable time, I simply respond "No thank you" and think how ludicrous it was for me to even think I had the necessary skills to study the social lives of Mozambican sex workers under apartheid in South Africa.

From tight Bagamayo street, and its colonial pastel-coloured buildings with balconies and air conditioners, Ercilio expertly manoeuvres me through cars blocking the sidewalk, drooping electrical wires, and the men of women of suspicious, undefinable morals congregating near steel-barred shops. We emerge unscathed in 25 June Park and amble towards the old Maputo Fort, built by the Portuguese in the mid-nineteenth century and symbol of Portugal's eventual pacification of the Mozambican interior. Inside the square-shaped complex, there is a garden and a plethora of trees sprouting from the grounds, under which rest benches providing shade, a lovely respite from the sun. There are also more artefacts typical of a museum fort: cannons and statues of famous men. Many cannons decorate the fort's lower level, encircling a cactus patch and aiming towards the yellow walls. Ercilio leads me up a ramp to the fort's second story, upon which stand more old cannons perched on wheels point beyond the fort to the water and to the skyscrapers and apartment blocks and trees rising far above the little Portuguese fort. The sun momentarily drifts behind the business towers along Karl Marx Avenue and its clean, symmetrical art-deco buildings, and in the shade, I experience the wonderful sense of Maputo's juxtaposition, of unbridgeable contrasts bleeding and coalescing into something with no right angles or smooth corners, something that cannot fit inside squares or ideologies or dogmas.

Below, Ercilio guides me past a statue of Portuguese officer Joaquim Augusto Mouzinho de Albuquerque on horseback adorned with a sword and a lush mustache, the man responsible for conquering the great Gaza Empire,[3] just north of Lourenço Marques, and for capturing the great King Ngungunyane, the Lion of Gaza, and exiling him to Azores where he died. But his remains were returned many years later, Ercilio tells me as we enter a small chamber, and were deposited here, he says, gesturing to a wooden coffin. The defeat and exile of the Lion encapsulates the story of Portugal vanquishing Mozambique's original kingdoms.

At the Berlin Conference of 1894 and 1895, where Europeans leaders carved up Africa and decided which country would get which piece, Portugal—the sick man of Europe as the country was unceremoniously called at the time—had its historical claims to Mozambique resolutely rejected by Europe's healthier men and was informed that to demonstrate its claims over this vast land, Portugal must pacify it with her brawn. Such disrespect initiated a mass of nationalist sentiment within Portugal itself and encouraged greater military expenditure and a more hostile relationship with the African polities within Mozambique itself. Indeed, some colonials went to sleep at night dreaming of connecting Maputo in Mozambique to Luanda in Angola, and controlling Southern Africa's vast bountiful belly, just as Cecil Rhodes dreamed of joining Cape Town and Cairo under the Union Jack.

Towards the end of the nineteenth century, Ercilio says, Portugal directed most of its subversive activities to undermining Africans to the north, yet its hold on its southern position, the area around Marques, was growing increasingly tenuous, as the Kingdom of Gaza was growing increasingly recalcitrant. Gaza traced its origins back to the 1830s when General Soshangange fled Zululand to the west after he had suffered defeat from Shaka during the Zulu-Nguni wars known as the Mfecane, yet in retreat, he seized the lands between the Komati and Zambezi Rivers, incorporated the local Tsonga and Shona peoples into his emerging state, and created a new ethnic identity—Shangaan. Gaza had never signed any treaties with the Portuguese during its seventy-plus years of existence and understood the white man as simply another actor in the Southern African network of competing actors. And as the white man's equal, as a sovereign state equal to European ones, Gaza acted and negotiated for its own benefit and survival, as any independent polity would. Under King Ngungunyane, Gaza quelled various internal rebellions, negotiated a treaty with Cecil Rhodes's agents for one thousand rifles and two thousand cartridges, and entered into a cross-border agreement with the Ndebele and Swazi. These activities rattled Portuguese colonials, who despite Ngungunyane's deft diplomacy and strong hand still saw his kingdom as under Portuguese suzerainty, as an entity to be tamed or cajoled into submission with promises of European treats. So when in 1894 Ronga chiefs rebelled against increased Portuguese taxation, they took refuge in Gaza, and the Portuguese colonels presented Nungunyane with an ultimatum: Hand over the chiefs or face war. The king chose war.

"Excuse me," Ercilio suddenly says standing by Nungunyane's coffin. "Are you recording this?"

I follow Ercilio's eyes and turn to see a man and a woman behind me; the woman has her iPhone pointed at Ercilio and is recording his lesson.

"Yes, I am," she says. "Do you mind?"

"I do actually. I don't think it's polite to record someone without his permission."

"I am sorry," she says. "I just found your talk interesting."

"Thank you, but I am conducting a tour for a paying client. If you would like to join one of our tours, we can be found online at Maputo a Pe or Maputo by Foot."

"No, thank you. That's okay," the woman says as she tucks her iPhone into her pocket, as she and the man step towards the exit.

"Where are you from?" Ercilio asks.

"South Africa," the man says.

"Do you speak Shengaan?"

"We understand it, but do not speak it so well ourselves."

"See," Ercilio says smiling at me. "No border can make us forget we are family."

Turning back to the couple, Ercilio says, "Enjoy your time in Maputo."

After they leave, Ercilio tells me the Shengaan worked the Witwatersrand gold mines during apartheid and helped make South Africa rich. They were labour migrants who sacrificed their home life in order to earn a wage for their family's survival.

Outside the fort, Ercilio watches as I struggle to buy an oil painting from a local artist. The painting is of an African woman carrying a child on her back.

After I pay and we walk to the tourist information, the tour effectively over, I ask Ercilio if I overpaid for the painting.

"Yes," he says. "You paid double. But I wasn't going to come to your rescue."

There is a scar on my thumb I once thought resembled Mozambique's coastline. The coarse and rough skin, the remnant of an accident that never properly healed, represented failure in my mind. It symbolized every opportunity I squandered, every road I should have taken. Mozambique and its history and its people transformed into a measuring stick for my life, and it always revealed my shortcomings. And whenever

I had enough courage to look at it, to face my thumb's scar, and to imagine my distorted skin and each mangled edge as Maputo, Inhambabe, Beira, Quelimane, Nacala, Pemba, I would always imagine what might have been if I had simply endured those Montreal days with a measure of strength and grace, if I had known what a gift it was simply to open a book on Mozambique and want to know more, and if I had whispered to myself in my darkest moments, you are not the voices deriding you.

But now, walking Maputo's streets, I realize my scar is just a scar, a product of a cut that should have been stitched, the skin should have been better aligned, the flesh pulled tight and held together, for better, straighter, healing. I realize I cannot simply take a place and use it as metaphor, no matter how personally profound, because Mozambique is bigger and more complex than that. As much as Mozambique as an idea and a symbol has tantalized and frustrated me for years, I can only approach the place in humble awe of its grandeur. A place is always greater than its literature. A book captures a place in the same way a bucket captures a lake. Yet a place's intricateness—its dizzying blend of cultures and stories, its episodes of bloodshed and its smaller overlooked moments of triumph—never dissuades me from walking down the street, from engaging with my own shortcomings and misunderstandings. Expectation is learning's death knell, just as arrogance is the bane of knowledge. Whatever I might have learned about Maputo, a city born from cataclysm and creativity, can only be shown in fragments and shards, in half-light and half-ignorance. And if I am asked to describe Mozambique in any specific way, I think not on the dozens of books I've read, but on the two images standing quickly in my mind.

On Hoi Chi Minh Avenue stands the modest National Museum of Art, which showcases the best contemporary art from Mozambique and Africa. On the first floor and on the southern wall hangs a painting done in ink by the Mozambican artist Gemuse. A rowboat sits still in the sky among grey clouds; the boat does not seem to move. There are no paddles or oars. In the stern, around ten figures huddle together; their faces and bodies are smudged. They have no distinguishing features: no mouths, no teeth, no lips, no faces. Some sit on the boat's edge; others appear to be fleeing. In the bow stands Lenin whose broad shoulders, fine moustache, pointy chin, and balding scalp are unmistakeable. His body has turned from the faceless figures, and he stares towards the horizon in his customary confidence befitting the man, legend, revolutionary. His body is stiff and tight with certitude. He embodies the boldness necessary to peer into the future and then drag the world into it. He personifies the conviction and power required to sacrifice a few underlings for the movement, a couple of soldiers to the cause, which is why Lenin, in the painting, does not look back to see a few faceless figures fall through a widening hole in the boat's bottom, does not flinch when his comrades drop from the vessel and fall through the sky to the ground. Yet the bodies descending through the clouds do not appear frenzied or wild. Their movements are controlled and relaxed, and as they approach the ground, they steady themselves—arms outstretched, knees bent, face down—for impact. The figures may be escaping because the land, below Lenin's boat, is empty, devoid of people, signs, and symbols; only a few blades of grass bend away from the people dropping from the sky. And there among the space, they may build whatever they see fit, a new beginning, another opportunity to try again for utopia. Yet how affected they remain from the boat ride, from rubbing shoulders with Lenin, from such an inspiring failure, how such an experience stays, burrows, and hibernates within, until the strange and foreign become intrinsic, for wherever there is sunlight, there is also shadow.

In a garden near the Mozambique-France cultural centre, there is a bush that does not look like any other bush. Instead of greenery or flowers, this particular shrub is comprised of old gun parts and spent bullets. Since the civil war's end in 1992, and the country's instigating of programs to disarm its thousands of combatants, Mozambican artists have been transforming weapons into art, transforming something ugly into something creative and beautiful. In Maputo's galleries and cultural centres, these artworks appear as faces with rocket canisters for heads or bullet casings for hair. They appear as an assortment of animals: a horse with a gun handle for a head or a goose with a rifle tail. They appear as a variety of furniture: chairs and benches of machine guns. They are all elaborate and detailed. They speak to both the pursuit of peace and the reality that violence remains an ever-present threat. Yet the garden piece possesses none of that artistic wizardry; it is humble, withdrawn, unpretentious. The parts, in fact, coalesce into a crude ship. The artist has tethered three handguns together in a rough circle resembling a sail. A belt of bullets appears to be the boom. An assortment of barrels and scopes and triggers and muzzles create the hull. The artist has placed the ship in recently broken earth, as if someone has just tilled the dirt, as if someone has just dug a garden and is about to plant something full of colour or nutrients and wait for it to blossom into life. And it would be wonderful to watch green wrap itself around rusted and twisted metal, strangling and killing death, until it rises triumphant through the ship's hull, up and around the poles and beams, past the sails, up and up and up, reaching and grasping and then touching the blue sky.

I am wandering through Lisbon's old town, a cluster of winding lanes and alleyways that seduce with their old-world charm. I walk with no aim or purpose, only to soak in the atmosphere and the silences, as tourists are relatively scarce on this May afternoon. Without much effort, I exit the maze and find myself standing at Commerce Plaza, the heart of Lisbon's old empire, and staring into the water. Lying on the banks of the Tagus River, the plaza once served as Lisbon's principal entryway. In the fifteenth century, King Manuel built his palace—Riberia—here and soon government buildings sprung along the riverside like willows, especially those administrative offices that regulated trade between Portugal, Europe, and her newly inaugurated colonies and southern entrepots. In 1755, however, an earthquake destroyed Riberia Palace and the custom houses, but King Dom Jose and his ministers led a massive rebuilding effort, including architect Eugénio dos Satnos's design of a new square reflecting Lisbon's status as global centre for trade. Commerce Plaza, as it was called, was rectangular shaped with the southern end opening to the river, ocean, and world. Ships would dock on the Plaza's port and merchants would haul their goods up the ramp, which dropped into the water like a thirsty tongue, and would then walk them across the wide-open square to the government and custom houses circling the square. After paying the requisite custom fees—Lisbon was fanatical about controlling trade and benefitting from its special place as Europe's mouth to the world—and having their property physically inspected, the merchants would lead their products through Baixa's tight streets to another smaller square. There, the traders would pull their chattels upon the auction block by their chains and would field offers from the prospective buyers below shouting out numbers based on the perceived value, the going market rate, for black biceps, black deltoids, black quadriceps.

On this fine afternoon, however, I notice no ships docked on the Tagus and no men sauntering across the Plaza; in fact, metal fences cordon off the square and people have gathered at the entrance to have their tickets checked by security personnel. Beyond the fences, a large stage stands under lights; signs have large lettering reading "Eurovision Song Contest." Over the coming days, singers from all over the continent will sing their hearts out on that stage and will be cheered on by their fellow citizens—waving the appropriate flag, chanting the appropriate language, mingling with the appropriate people—in hopes they will be crowned Europe's champion crooner, in hopes they will bring a measure of pride to their homeland. Here, at Commerce Plaza, in just a few hours, each contestant will walk upon that stage, above the stares of both adoring fans and Lisbon's history, approach the microphone, and sing and sing, sing until their voices are hoarse, until their lungs burst, until all the tension and pressure from preparing and practicing are released, and their bodies and muscles go limp from the sheer joy of creative release. And how the audience will clap and shout and scream.

I see a woman sitting on a ramp descending into the Tagus with her hands wrapped around her knees. The river ends just below her sandals yet slowly creeps closer to her toes. She wears headphones and stares at the blue water and sky. I wish to whisper something into her ear but dare not. She does not hear the commotion behind her. She does not acknowledge Lisbon glowing in celebration and festivities. She does not care for all that silent noise. She focuses on the river, the ocean, and the Portuguese ships that returned here from discovering the word, their sailors full of stories of excitement and daring, their cargo including women and men who, despite their shackles and chains, would form an indelible, unbreakable part of this city—a city that despite the sun shining on the wonderful hills and terracotta roofs, despite the sounds of songs and merriment, prefers to live in shadows and in silences.

Endnotes

1. Information about Portuguese forced labour practices in Mozambique was taken from Penvenne, Jeanne Marie. *African Workers and Colonial Racism: Mozambique Strategies and Struggles in Lourenco Marques, 1877-1962:* Heinemann Publishers, 1995.
2. This transition is explored in Pitcher, Anne. *Transforming Mozambique: The Politics of Privatization, 1975-2000.* Oxford, 2002.
3. The following history of Gaza is taken from Harries, Patrick. *Work, Culture and Identity: Migrant Laborers in Mozambique and South Africa, 1860-1910.* Heinemann Publishers, 1994.

7.

South Africa

Ngoyi is a long street and a principal artery of downtown Johannesburg. Starting in Burghersdorp District in the west, Ngoyi bisects the Central Business District (CBD) and terminates almost at Ellis Park in the east. It passes, or passes close to, various important Johannesburg landmarks and administrative buildings: the Museum of Africa, the Workers Museum, the Department of Home Affairs, Park Station, Gauteng Local Division of the High Court, and the Fashion District. Locals often frequent Ngoyi—sidewalks are often crammed with pedestrians and informal traders—as beyond administrative and historical sites, the street also supports numerous malls and shopping centres: SPAR, PEP, Newtown Mall, and Bree City Mall. Urban designers designed Johannesburg's CBD as a grid—tidy and neat, with a right angle at every corner—yet people and things often spill from the sidewalk into the street, especially on busy days, so that if you were to look at downtown from above, maybe from the Ponte City Apartments or Carleton Centre, you would see lines dissolve and then disappear in a sea of people.

And on this May 2018 morning, the CBD is hopping. Dozens of deals are shouted in a dozen different languages. Bodies jump in and out of buildings, buses, and taxis. Vendors lay out their wares, open their steel doors, and announce their products to the city. Normal. This is normal. What isn't normal is the white man wearing an orange backpack walking north on Troye Street. He wears shorts, and from one pocket stretches a cord, undoubtedly leading from his cellphone, hidden so well there in his nylon pocket, to the earphones squished into his ears. He is listening to music. But every now and then, he retrieves his cellphone to glance at the GPS map to confirm he is walking in the right direction. He darts into a Reavaya bus station—a red, white, and blue enclosure with a waiting area only accessible for those who have bought a ticket—but he does not proceed through the turnstiles to the spacious platform where other passengers wait for their bus to arrive and for the glass partition to magically open. No, he wants to buy a smartcard on which he can load money at his leisure. The employee working behind a smudged window informs him that they do not sell such cards and that he must go to Park Station, a few blocks north, to buy one. She waves in its general direction, and he thanks her before skipping from the station to rejoin the exciting melee outside. He has a boastful air about him, not arrogant per se, but a haughty, oblivious demeanour attributable to those raised on books and good intentions. He is one of those kind-hearted souls who believe they may saunter into any milieu and be welcomed with open arms because on paper, and in his heart of hearts, he is on their side, an ally, a friend, someone not like the rest, someone who does not subscribe to fear or reputation or stereotype, someone whose white skin does not automatically make him oppressor but self-reflective and aware, cognizant of the privileges such soft pigmentation affords him and in his efforts to confront and destroy them.

At the corner of Troye and Ngoyi, the traffic lights change, and he waits as packed buses and cars drift pass him. The scene—the movement, activity, and energy—amazes him, and he cannot believe he is alone in the once-notorious CBD, for when he was here not four years ago, tucked safely within the walls of the University of Witwatersrand, he never would have dreamed of venturing downtown alone. But things change, he knows, and situations improve, and now he looks forward to experiencing Johannesburg as the real and somatic—corporeal, fleshy, and human—not ink on a page, not a noun in a policy report, not merely a name on a travel advisory. Yet when a Black middle-aged man in a sweater and a cap passes by him, less than an arm's length away, and whispers, without stopping, in a pleasant but serious tone that "This is a dangerous place, and you should leave," the white man turns his music off, shoves the earphones into his pocket, and decides he does not need the smartcard. It is not worth the effort to buy it, as he can simply pay the bus fares as he goes. So he decides to turn right along Ngoyi and towards the general direction of his hotel, not too far away, in the Maboneng neighbourhood. Maboneng is the posterchild for a rebirthed and regenerated Johannesburg; it is a space full of restaurants, art galleries, and museums blossoming in old buildings that were once dedicated to industry and manufacturing but are now visited and photographed by tourists. Yet hotel staff are quick to remind visitors not to venture too far from the designated and patrolled two or three streets and to ignore the dozens of nearby homeless people sleeping in thick blankets under a highway ramp. The white man thinks of his upcoming days in Johannesburg—a trip to Soweto, Alex, and the Apartheid Museum—and remains thankful for the opportunity to revisit a city whose sites he had missed when he was here four years ago.

"Where are you from?" a middle-aged Black man asks the white man. He smiles and has a confident, strong stride, whereas the white man's gait resembles a tourist's relishing and savouring ramble. The white man knows this routine and the role the man plays: the polite and charismatic tout who promises the world in exchange for a few coins or bills. The tout knows the best places and the hidden gems; he has the best deals and the most extensive networks. He can take you anywhere and show you everything for half the price other tourist companies charge. In each of the eighty or so countries the white man has visited, he has met and interacted with a variety of touts, and he has learned the most effective strategy is civility plus movement. The white man answers "Canada," and the Black man nods and transforms his hand into a fist, extends it forwards, and his flexed knuckles hang in the air and wait for the white man's fist to touch and bump his in mutual recognition. The white man grins and recognizes the familiar sales patter, the friendly routine to endear the foreigner to the rhythms and mannerisms of the local population, a welcoming gesture to disarm the man's defensives, to allay his suspicions, and to dissuade him from embracing fear. So the white man touches the other's fist, while quickening his pace, and prepares to say a long and steady harangue of no thank you, no I am not interested, I don't want to go, thank you but no, thank you but no, no thank you, no thank you. Firm but polite.

Yet before the white man utters a word, he feels something behind him, some force tugging on his backpack, and he turns to see another Black man inspecting his bag for its weight, and he senses yet another person nearby. The man yanks his bag free, but before he can run, before he can instruct his legs to move, to sprint and to flee, an arm wraps itself around his neck and other hands secure and hold his arms, and there on Ngoyi street, in the heart of Johannesburg, on a sunny May afternoon, the white man, for once in his life, is rendered immobile and is instructed to stay still.

The white man goes limp; he does not struggle. He raises his fingers skywards and opens his palms to indicate his surrender. He has difficulty breathing and tears well in his eyes, as the forearm tightens around his throat. He cannot shout for help, for he cannot make a sound. The arms and hands slowly pull him down, like an animal ensnared in rope and wires, hunted for its fat and meat, not for pleasure but for sustenance and survival. He is a big white beast, almost two hundred pounds, so they take no chances and work as a team. Their actions are coordinated and well rehearsed. They bring the white man to his knees, the cement and its coarseness digging into his exposed flesh, and they pull again and again until the white man collapses on his back. The men search his body for hidden treasures, and the leader, the tout, shouts instructions for where to probe and hunt, where their fingers should linger. He knows how tourists hide their valuables under their shirts, in their pants, close to their privates. The white man feels them searching everywhere.

As the white man remains immobilized on Ngoyi Street, awaiting his fate and completely at the mercy of these hunters, he does not expect anyone, any passerby, to come to his rescue. And people are around. This is not some back alleyway or darkened street in the early-morning hours. No, this is downtown Johannesburg on a bright and beautiful May morning. Yet he expects no hero to intervene on his behalf and anticipates zero clarion calls, no sirens, no shouts. So even as he bleeds from his knees and tears trickle down his cheeks, his body limp and relaxed in total and complete surrender, he congratulates himself, however slightly, however subconsciously, for thinking that no Black person struggling to survive in the CBD would risk their neck for some stupid white man foolish enough to go for a little stroll through their rough streets. No, let the hunters have him. Let them feed on his white skin. Let them sever the horn from that big, fat rhino. Let him taste what we must swallow every day. Let him savour the world he only knows from his expensive books.

The hunters have released the white man. They have left him his emptied wallet and identification cards. His credit card, cash, backpack, and cellphone are gone. He grabs his blue wallet, cards, and struggles to his feet. His cellphone gone, he only has a vague sense of where he is going. East, he tells himself, go east. And he does, stumbling past pedestrians and crossing intersections. He pauses only once to inspect himself, his reflection, in a store window. His hair has loosened from its ponytail. His shorts and jacket are a bit dusty. He runs his fingers over his sore neck, checking and feeling, down his chest and stomach, checking and feeling, and across his legs, checking and feeling. He approaches his reflection and looks deeply at himself. "You are okay," he whispers. "You are fucking okay." And he moves east again, towards a building he knows is on the CBD's border, close to safety. He quickens his pace, but does not run, no, he does not run. He jumps a puddle, dodges a car, then a cyclist. But he does not run. "You are okay," he says. He passes more people. "You are fucking okay." Long strides, he moves in long strides. But he does not run.

"You are okay," he whispers. He sees his hotel and the security guard standing outside the big, glass doors. "You are fucking okay."

"I am sorry you were robbed," Patrick says seated next to me on the Veavaya Bus heading east along Commissioner Street past the abandoned and neglected buildings of the CBD—many of which now host an array of squatters and the ghosts of gold barons and white supremacists—and towards Soweto.

"I should have told you certain areas of the CBD are still unsafe even in the day. Even as a white South African, I still feel exposed here."

"I am thankful you offered to guide me to Soweto," I say and look out the bus window at the hundreds of people walking the streets, at the informal traders and the parents with children and the elderly and the young.

"Pleasure," Patrick says. "Although I must say the real reason is I did not want to rob the local guide of a day's work. Work can be sporadic."

Patrick is a well-built white man and has trouble squishing into the bus seat next to me. He wears a colourfully knitted vest and functional khaki trousers. He has a white beard fronting a well-weathered face along with well-aged eyes. He was born in 1947, one year before the official inauguration of the apartheid regime, but Patrick is walking proof that age is only a number. He speaks incessantly and has an encyclopedic knowledge of South African history, which does not come as a surprise. Patrick is a unique white South African, as he likes to say. He considers himself African, a white African. He says it is a cultural thing, a way of looking at the world. I look around the bus and notice we are the only two white people.

"It took me a long time to overcome my own racism," Patrick says. "I lived with it and was taught it every day under apartheid. It was an eleven-year journey to divorce myself from that thinking. I thank Mandela for that. Mandela freed white South Africans; he did not free the Black ones."

The bus stops, and more Black passengers get on.

"Apartheid is not over. They only took the signs down," Patrick says.

The passengers take the seats behind us.

"I first visited Soweto in 1994, and I was struck by the magic and warmness of the place—how hospitable the people were, how they welcomed my wife and me with open arms. The only requirement was that you introduce yourself. I was impressed by the well-constructed houses and the clean streets. The experience contradicted everything I had learned about Black Africans."

"Is that why you started this company, to unsettle stereotypes and assumptions?" I ask.

He smiles.

Patrick organizes walking tours of the less-visited communities of Johannesburg—those where even the locals tend not to venture.

"People should experience Soweto, especially white South Africans—but not from a bus, not like at a zoo. Tourism must empower the local people."

"Do none of the tour operators who visit Soweto support the local company?"

He laughs, as if I just asked the most ludicrous of questions.

"They give back to the community in terms of improved security. In other words, they spend money to keep Vilakazi Street—the main tourist street with Mandela's and Tutu's houses—free of crime. They contribute nothing else."

"The level of private security in South Arica has always shocked me."

"It's our fastest growing industry," Patrick says with a chuckle.

I remember the broken bottles glued to the tops of walls like shark teeth. I remember the dogs with exposed fangs prowling behind electrical fences. I remember the private security trucks roaming the rich northern suburbs looking for anything or anyone that did not belong.

"I hope to throw rocks at them one day," Patrick says looking out the window as we turn onto the Soweto Highway and leave the CBD.

"Who?"

"The tour buses. Eighty per cent of the tourists don't even leave the buses. They just snap photos from their seats."

He pauses.

"But it should be me, as a white man, throwing the rocks."

"Why?" I ask, even though I know the answer.

"Think about it. If a white man had stood with those strikers at Marikana, do you think the authorities would have fired a shot?"

I try to imagine Patrick's face among the strikers at the Lonmin platinum mine on that August 2012 day when thirty-four of them were shot dead by the police. I try to decide whether it would have made a difference to have him there among the leaders and negotiators, those men demanding dignity and a living wage in return for working in hell and lining the pockets of richer and more powerful men. And I try to imagine what police officers might have done if they had seen Patrick sitting atop Wonderkop hill with his Black allies in a symbol of solidarity. Would they have opened fire? Would they have?

"I am an African," Patrick says. "I go to places no white South African would ever dream of going. I go to the hostels of Alex and Soweto, and I talk to the people. I give them copies of my book, which they share among themselves. Then we talk. We talk."

Soweto approaches.

"I ask them to challenge me. Challenge my claim that I can be African and white. Challenge me. I am African, and I am white."

Soweto is the largest Black African city in South Africa, and its history begins in a piece of legislation called the Native Authority Act passed in 1923 by the Smuts government. The South African government had become uneasy about the number of Black South Africans living in the cities, especially Johannesburg, and they feared these people would become detribalized and transform into a restless, unruly proletariat force in the heart of Witwatersrand—the land of never-ending gold. Smuts spoke in terms of parallel lives: separate institutions for Blacks and separate institutions for whites. This act, then, determined where Black South Africans could reside and gave the government the power to remove them to wherever they saw fit, even if no housing existed to shelter them or jobs to sustain them. By the 1930s, more and more Black people were relocated to Orlando, to the southwest of Johannesburg, to what would become Soweto. Into the 1940s and 1950s, the Native Affairs Department launched a robust slum-clearing scheme and removed the communities lying on Johannesburg's edges, a little too close to the white suburbs with all the white families.

Charlotte, my guide, has lived in Soweto her entire life, she tells me, after we say farewell to Patrick, who has meetings planned in the city, and cross Mooki Street and into Orlando East. Behind us rises Orlando football stadium, and underneath its rickety frame, groups of uniformed schoolchildren laugh and kick a ball around.

Charlotte wears a white skirt and purple jacket with a scarf wrapped around her waist and a warm black hat around her head, and her strappy sandals carry her in an unhurried manner. She knows everyone we encounter on the street, always greeting them in Zulu, and asking how they get on.

"Sawubona."

"Unjani?"

And the passersby reciprocate in kind, and then they smile at me, trailing slightly behind her, tucked away in her shadow. I am the shy child, and she is my fierce protector.

The morning sky is an immaculate blue, the breeze languid, unobtrusive, perfect. The scene is lucid, so clear and transparent that I feel as if I am strolling through a mirage, and if I were to touch one of those cacti or lampposts the whole spectacle would crack and then collapse. The residential streets with their low-lying houses and the occasional palm tree and satellite dish are quiet. Some have fences; others have gates and walls. Some houses are nicer than others. A car rumbles past us to break the silence. And the setting's tranquillity does unnerve me slightly, as it betrays every image I have associated with Soweto—all that volatility.

"That is not safe," she says pointing at a house whose owners have built a second story atop the first. The addition does look unsturdy and unsteady.

"Not too long ago, in a nearby house, the ceiling collapsed and a boy was killed."

Charlotte further inspects the brick and cement of the house.

"People take too many shortcuts."

Charlotte says very little, only detailing the important dates and figures in the city's history, as if the Sowetan experience is more experiential than didactic, more exploratory than prescriptive. She talks about how Soweto's early houses were mostly made of brick and were very basic; she mentions how Mandela used to box at the local YMCA; she says very few white people have lived in Soweto since 1976.

She spots a child pushing open a gate and stumbling onto the front lawn.

"Hey, what are you doing," she says in mock outrage.

The child's eyes explode in surprise before a grin forms on his lips.

He speaks.

"He says he's looking for his grandmother, but I know his grandmother, and I know she is not home. How did you open that gate?"

He speaks.

"Naughty child," Charlotte says, hiding her smile. "He now says he's looking for his grandfather."

The house door then swings open, and the boy scurries inside. At the door, a man waves, and Charlotte returns the gesture. Everything returns to how it should be.

"So what do you do in Canada, Jesse?" Charlotte asks.

"I edit books."

"A doctor of words."

"I like that. Yes, I am a doctor of words."

"And you're staying in Johannesburg."

"Maboneng."

"The new, trendy area. And how do you like it?"

I hesitate. Do I tell her? A part of me says no; it is of little importance. I have no need to inform her of yet another violent incident in her country. I have no desire to reaffirm every travel warning, every advisory, about walking alone in downtown Johannesburg, about how scary, crime ridden, and lawless the CBD is. I do not need to sensationalize the commonplace, as the threat of violence looms over every resident, as the manager of my hotel said he had been mugged two months previous, after I told him about my experience and after he had chastised me for venturing into the CBD alone—"I do not even go there," he had said. And I have no wish to give greater salience to the event because of my skin colour.

Yet around forty-eight hours ago, I had an arm around my throat and hands all over my body. A part of me does wish to articulate the passing because it becomes more real and transparent. I can see it and I can touch it and I can speak it. The more I talk of it, the more I understand it in a broader sense, the more I can place it in the realm of history, the tangible and concrete. I do not condone, but I do contextualize.

"I was mugged," I say and tell her the entire episode.

"You're lucky. It could have been a lot worse," Charlotte says.

I nod and remember how fast I went limp and surrendered to their hands.

"I do not often go to Johannesburg. Most of everything I need is here in Soweto," she says as we approach a make shift hardware store assembled on someone's lawn. The proprietor has laid out bathtubs, bicycles, pieces of lumber, and storage units along the grass for any prospective patron to inspect, and he instantly recognizes Charlotte when we approach, and the two share a spirited conversation in Zulu.

"This is Jesse from Canada," Charlotte says, and the man extends his hand. I falter for a second longer than normal etiquette dictates before I interlock my fingers with his. We shake in the customary fashion, once, twice, and then once more, but he does not release his grip. I gently try to pull mine away, but he holds firm and simply smiles.

"He wants to show you a special handshake," Charlotte says.

He knots and twists his hand against and into mine in a series of fast and blurry actions that I cannot follow, until, somehow, our fists are clenched and touching.

"You are now blood brothers," Charlotte says.

The man laughs and then returns to Charlotte, and the two resume their animated conversation.

"He says there are few opportunities for employment. Companies want experience, but there are no paid internships. How can someone get experience then?"

The man motions for me to look at one of his storage units and then speaks.

"Imagine all the things you could fit in there and transport."

"That's not my area of speciality," I say to Charlotte.

Charlotte laughs and tells the man.

"Yes, you are only a doctor of words."

There is no shortage of words along Vilakazi Street: plaques and memorials describing Tutu's and Mandela's houses, the sales patter of merchants selling their crafts and paintings, the robotic voices of waiters taking breakfast orders within the numerous sidewalk cafes, and the lofty declarations of tourists, mostly white ones, extolling how Mandela's house was such a spiritual experience.

Charlotte asks me if I want to visit his museum, but I decline, suddenly remembering Patrick's axiom that museum's present history as dead and gone, only a foreign curiosity to ponder or sigh over.

We climb Vilakazi and pass traditional dancers playing traditional music in traditional clothing for enthralled visitors, a few of whom drop a few rand at their feet. More and more tourists exit their cars or descend from their tour buses and stroll towards Mandela's house. As we ascend the hill, I turn to see Soweto lying before me, and I marvel at its expanse. Over a million people live here, Charlotte estimates, speaking dozens of languages and originating from dozens of places. From this vantage point, high atop a hill, I am, again, struck by the seeming restfulness of the place, its languid and lazy essence, a cat stretched out in the sun.

"The Soweto Uprising," Charlotte suddenly says, "was a response to making Afrikaans the language of instruction in schools, but its roots go much further back."

In 1953, the apartheid government had become frustrated with the mission schools teaching African children and their propensity to produce anti-apartheid intellectuals and crusaders—such as Mandela, Tutu, and Tambo—and outlawed them; instead, Black schoolchildren were subjected to the Bantu Education Act, which in the words of Prime Minister Verwoerd, the personification of apartheid ideology itself, would ensure Black people were "the hewers of wood and drawers of water." In the 1960s, for every 644 rand the government spent on educating a white child, it spent 42 rand on a Black child; a single Black teacher could be responsible for up to sixty students. Between 1962 and 1971, the government built no schools in Soweto, despite its ballooning population.

I remember Patrick saying how post-apartheid politics forgets this history of educational disenfranchisement and forgets how in 1994, there were not two parallel and equal education systems but one superior one and one inferior one. And little has been done in the intervening years to address this inequity in schooling. "No," Patrick says. "Today South Africa suffers from the rhetoric of equality, the discourse that says all schools are equal and shall receive the same funding. And if you're poor, it's your fault. It's your choice. But equality has no sense of history."

At the Hector Pieterson memorial, there is a sign reading "To honour the youth who gave their lives in the struggle for freedom and democracy," and above it, there is the iconic photograph of a student carrying a shot and bleeding Hector, only twelve years old, through Soweto's streets—the first student to die in the rebellion.

"The students did not want to fight that day," Charlotte says. "They marched through the streets singing songs and waving signs."

On June 16, 1976, thousands of students filled Soweto's streets singing "Moreno Boloko Sechaba," a plea for divine protection, waving signs reading, in big, black letters, "Afrikaans Must Be Abolished," "To Hell with Afrikaans," "Afrikaans Is Terrorism," and "If We Must Do Afrikaans, Vorster Must Do Zulu." They marched, and they shouted, "Power, Power!" raising their hands high to the sky as if trying to summon its power.[1]

The students had arrived from different Soweto neighbourhoods, some alone, others as a group, but as each arrived to the street and was sucked into the trembling force coalescing and growing and strengthening around a hatred of apartheid and its symbols, they transformed into a power. They were undeniable. They were there. They could no longer be ignored.

The police noticed this, too—the incipient threat of simply being. They noticed the threat lurking in the tens of thousands amassing and shouting and marching, no longer willing to be stilled by the mere presence of whiteness, no longer willing to be cowed by the mere spectre of apartheid's foot soldiers. So the officers launched tear gas canisters into the crowd of children singing and demonstrating near Orlando West High School, and when the stinging fog and fumes dispersed the schoolchildren, some picked up stones and hurled them at the officers; in return, the officers fired bullets.

"White Soweto residents were then targeted, and after that day, no whites lived in Soweto," Charlotte says.

Oppression had finally extinguished nuance. White was white. White was nameless. White was threat. White was oppression. White had had centuries to show otherwise, to show more compassion, even empathy. No more. Time was up. White was enemy.

A reporter from the *Rand Daily Mail* watched as the protestors dragged a white man from his car and clubbed him to death with sticks. They then took his lifeless body and threw it into a rubbish bin while one student said, "That is where he belongs." Another group beat a man down, until they realized he was Chinese, not white, and released him. More protestors hurled stones at cars with white drivers and passengers as they fled the township. But as newspapers focused on Black-on-white violence, they remarked little on the legions of Black bodies littering the Soweto streets, the hundreds dead or injured. Was it because white-on-Black violence was so expected and commonplace that it deserved no comment? Or was it because reporting Black violence was guaranteed to sell more papers among a terrified white readership?

In the pool underneath Hector's photo, I catch a glimpse of myself, and think I would have probably thrown rocks, too. Maybe.

"How did you cope during the uprising?" I ask Charlotte.

"It was scary," she says. And nothing more. I do not press her and wonder how much she censors herself as a tour guide.

Away from the museums and memorials, away from Vilakazi Street and the tourists and their buses, we return to the unfrequented Soweto and walk towards the railway station. We pass women pushing shopping carts filled with recyclable goods. We pass men sitting on stools having their hair trimmed. We walk alongside the railway tracks and watch a yellow-and-blue train crawl by, stopping and then starting, bumping and bumbling along, and we stare at the passengers looking out the windows or peering from the doors, commuters resigned to the slow and painful journey between here and there. As we move closer to the train station, the orderly streets and their pavement give way to long grasses, and the compact houses of brick and mortar transform into informal settlements, the homes built from whatever is available—corrugated metal, tarps, rocks. And as a gust of wind elevates and then blows a few yellow plastic bags down the road and they twirl and circle and dance among the telephone poles and scattered clouds so effortlessly, I think how easily a stronger wind could steal the walls and roofs of those shacks and lift them into the sky and then toss them far away. I think how difficult it must be to live in vulnerability writ large.

"They come from other countries or from the South African countryside," Charlotte says, waving at the settlements. "They come to make money in the cities. They come with dreams."

A young man turns from the road into the maze of shacks and quietly disappears.

"They buy the materials for their homes when they can. They build in stages. But they hope the government will eventually build them sturdy houses," Charlottes says in a neutral and objective tone, only reporting and not editorializing.

At the train station, we climb the overpass and see people sitting on the ledges with their legs dangling over the tracks, waiting for the next train.

"Sometimes they must wait for hours," Charlotte says.

In the distance, close to a highway, more informal settlements sparkle under the sun. Makeshift wired fences try to demarcate space and separate the grounds, and from some, vegetables sprout and grow.

"On the other side of the highway, there is a shopping mall," Charlotte says. And I see a trail cut through the field, passed the settlements, and towards the highway. Many different worlds coexist here in such an intimate space.

As we stand and chat on the overpass, a little girl with her hair in cornrows and wearing a pink knapsack sneaks past us.

"Can the children of the informal settlements go to school?" I ask.

"Yes, it is free," Charlotte says, watching the girl stroll away.

At a safe distance, though, the girl with the pink knapsack stops, turns, and stares at me.

Charlotte notices her shoelaces are untied and playfully screams at the child to tie them, which she does, and then returns her eyes to me. Charlotte thinks she is intrigued by me.

"Come and say hello then," she says to the girl in English.

The girl shuffles closer, unsure in her step, skeptical and hesitant in her thinking. She looks at me as if I am the first of my kind she has ever seen in the flesh—a white man. She has undoubtedly read about me in her books, talked about me with her family and friends, seen pictures of me in newspapers and on television, but, maybe, this moment is the first time she has put actual eyes to the words and pictures.

"Don't be shy," Charlotte says. "Say hello."

She inches closer, hand on rail, black shoe over black shoe, still reluctant, still cautious, her eyes dancing and darting across my skin.

"I think she's afraid of you."

I must seem like a ghost to her, or a figment of some deranged imagination, and she must inspect, no matter how terrifying the prospect, whether I am in fact real, of actual skin and bone. Could those books and her parents' stories be real after all? Could someone like me actually exist in the world?

"Come and say something to him," Charlotte says.

She steps closer, only a metre or so away, but then halts, turns, and sprints to the other end of the overpass. At a comfortable distance, she stops, faces us, and then screams: "SEE YOU TOMORROW!" Her little body shakes and rattles with confidence, full of strength and smiles, and then she is gone again, in flash, racing down the ramp, running through the field and the long grass, sprinting towards the shacks, whose metals glitter in the sun and are easily mistakable for precious stones. Charlotte and I laugh before going in the other direction.

After lunch, after watching men and women socialize and mingle over plates of porridge and meat, and cans of Soweto Gold beer or bottles of Coke, after viewing piles of beef, chicken, and sausage carried to the barbeque where the master roaster lays the pieces across the grill and flips and turns them periodically, under the patrons' hungry eyes, until they cook and sizzle perfectly, to the customers' satisfaction, and after witnessing all of this conviviality, a scene debunking every image of township life, the big smiles under clouds of smoke and the distinct smell of meat under fire, among the laughter and the fingers tearing apart flesh, Charlotte asks me if I am ready to meet Patrick and return to Johannesburg.

On the way, though, Charlotte stops at a shop to buy minutes for her phone to arrange a meeting with Patrick. I stay outside and watch groups of teenagers return from high school and drift along the sidewalk, the larger groups slowly splintering as individuals break from the cluster to go their separate ways. From inside, I hear voices rise and an argument ensue, and I swing my head to see Charlotte standing at the store's back and yelling at the proprietor who hides behind metal bars. She accuses him of not properly inserting the minutes onto her phone; she says she knows what he is trying to do, and she will not be cheated. Minutes pass, and soon a line has formed behind Charlotte. A small boy waves at me, and I wave back. One woman tires of waiting, returns her fruit, grabs her children, and exits the store while Charlotte keeps pointing to her phone and blames the man for not satisfying his end of this transaction. Eventually, Charlotte storms from the store saying she will never shop there again.

Outside, we walk towards the bus station.

"These foreigners think they are very clever. They think they're smarter than us. They think they can trick us."

Cars and vehicles now clutter the roads. People want to get home. The tranquillity has devolved into the quiet chaos of day-to-day living. Things can quickly change.

"Well," I say, not knowing what to say, "You know you will never shop there again. He has lost a customer."

"Yes, he has," Charlotte says. "He has lost a customer, and he should be careful."

I think Charlotte is overreacting, but I stop myself from pursuing this line of logic. Instead, I focus on the bus stop and the people who keep entering and exiting. I think about the ride back to the city and the walk to my hotel. I remember what Patrick said about the importance of white people greeting Black people on the street with a little touch to the head or a slight nod. "It's important to acknowledge the other," Patrick said. And I wonder if I will.

North along the M1 highway, a dozen or so kilometres from the CBD, drivers may look to their left and see Sandton's sparkling towers reaching towards the sky, or they may look to their right, fewer do, and see, or maybe sense, Alexandra's low-lying shanties and the millions of people fitting into them. Although the motorway offers a better view of Sandton than Alex Township, drivers do not necessarily feel cheated because they know Alex without having to see it, and the sooner the township rests in their rear-view mirror the better. They know the crime statistics. They have the numbers drilled into their minds as if they were their own conscience. In one August 2017 week, for example, the Alex police reported eighty-nine crimes:

- one murder
- three rapes
- seven thefts out of motor vehicles
- seven residential burglaries
- one business burglary
- five motor vehicle hijackings
- one house robbery
- four robberies with a firearm.
- one attempted murder
- four assaults with intent to cause grievous bodily harm
- twenty-right common assaults
- one robbery with another form of weapon
- three common robberies
- four thefts out of motor vehicles
- seven malicious damages to property
- eight general thefts
- three fraud cases

On a map of northern Johannesburg, Alex almost looks like a prison itself, tucked away in a seldom visited corner. Its streets are straight, running along a grid pattern, and are confined and compact. They appear squished and stuck as if two big hands pushed and squeezed the lanes together until they were as tightly packed as possible. Its body lies trapped between two motorways with no room to grow except inwardly as if a suitcase overflowing with t-shirts, trousers, and dresses.

Sandton, in contrast, looks incredibly fluid and flexible. Airy. Its streets meander and curve and circle almost at will. They have room to breathe and improvise. The space is more generously allotted. There are expansive sidewalks, more room to stroll. Cars and pedestrians coexist peacefully; each has plenty of space, plenty of freedom to roam and relax.

Yet Alex did not always sit so incarcerated, so stilted. Around the turn of the twentieth century, or so the story goes, Papenfus, a wealthy famer, purchased farmland in the area; he brought his wife and his cook, along with her family, with him to start a new life in the north of Johannesburg. His wife's name was Alexandra and his cook's name was Hey Nxele Mbanjwa. They established themselves on the land; they built huts, acquired livestock, and Papenfus started transporting his cows' milk to Johannesburg. Mbanjwa's daughter, Annie, married a man named Phumuza, and together they had ten children.

Around the Mbanjwas came more Black families, attracted by the exploding mining economy and the jobs it afforded. Towards the end of the century's first decade, Papenfus further divided his land into plots and sold them to Black families—one of the only places where Black South Africans could buy land. On his dusty and barren property, he erected a large sign reading "Alexandra Township: Freehold Township For Sale To Natives and Coloured Persons Only. Easy Monthly Payments. For Terms, Apply To S. Papenfus, 36 Exploration Building, Commissioner St. Johannesburg." Thus, on Johannesburg's northern edge, hidden from the more unscrupulous white land barons, grew a self-sustaining landholding Black community called Alexandra.

And grew it did. By 1916, thirty thousand residents lived in the township. Yet the City of Johannesburg wanted nothing to do with the burgeoning Black city to its north and provided no resources, no funding, and certainly no infrastructure. No paved roads. No drainage or sewerage systems. No housing. And no street lighting. While Johannesburg glittered in electricity and modernity, the big, bright lights of city life, Alexandra, only a few kilometres to the northeast, became infamously known as "The Dark City." After the National Party officially established apartheid in

1948, government officials attempted to control the influx of people into the township. They abolished the residents' freeholding land rights and expropriated their property. They controlled residents' movements. They raided homes and rounded up people. They checked and inspected passes and expelled anyone who did not belong, and between 1958 and 1973 that included the fifty-six thousand people forcibly removed from Alex to Soweto and the fifteen thousand people forcibly removed from Alex to Tembisa.

Beyond the bruising poverty and the uncertainties of day-to-day life, however, Alex was also a place of culture, politics, and activism. In the 1940s, residents boycotted the buses after the fare was raised, and for six months, they walked from Alex to Johannesburg and then back again, close to thirty kilometres in total. The fare increase was eventually dropped. In the 1950s, students and teachers resisted Bantu education policies, eventually submitting to them, but then twenty years later, they joined in the Sowetan rebellion against them. And despite the long, racist shadow of apartheid, and its policies of dispossession and debasement, despite the crime and impoverishment, and despite the attempts to bulldoze the township and its residents to the ground, an independent Black community—people who wrote, sang, and danced—emerged in Alex's sprawling shanties and among the derelict homes, which sit so close to Sandton's malls and pretty gardens.

I think about this divide between the northern Johannesburg neighbours while I ride the escalator from the Gauteng train, and its lovely efficiency and modern opulence, up through the multi-floor Sandton station, and walk out the swinging glass doors. Around me, buildings compete for my attention as do the handful of Black taxi drivers congregating outside. Around me, still, somewhere close by, is Nelson Mandela Square, which houses the Hard Rock Café, the Renaissance Day Spa, the Intercontinental, Emirates Airlines offices, Citibank, and the Sandton library.

"Are you Jesse?" a man asks, and when I nod and smile, he gives me his hand. "Hello," he says, "I am Michael." He is dressed in a long well-worn overcoat, which appears to conceal several more clothing layers. He wears an old hat and shoes that have walked many kilometres. His attire, clothing worn for its functionality and performance, contrasts with the clothing of the men and women buzzing through the station. Among the tailored suits and elegant dresses, the loafers and high-heel shoes, the briefcases and manicured nails, Michael appears conspicuous, out of place, maybe a little suspicious. Thirty years ago, a police officer might have asked to see his papers, might have demanded Michael prove his right to stand here in Sandton.

"It's a lovely morning," Michael says. "Do you mind if we walk to Alex?"

"Not at all," I say, and we cross an intersection and turn left on Katherine Street. Cars wait patiently at the traffic lights; painted white lines along the asphalt organize them into neat rows. The sidewalks are clearly delineated and spacious, and Michael and I can stroll side by side without any difficulty. A weekday morning, more and more vehicles speed by us and their exteriors shine in the Sandton sun.

When I tell Michael I am from Canada, he launches into a lively autobiography about the time he lived in Edmonton in the 1980s and 1990s. Canada is one of his favourite conversation topics, he tells me.

"The ANC sent me to the University of Alberta to study politics, but I fell out of favour with them when I changed my major and never did finish my degree. I lived underground, doing odd jobs, and travelled around. In the mid-1990s, I decided it was time to go home. I presented myself to border control and they arranged my flight to South Africa."

"I think you may be one of the few people who have actually asked to be deported," I say.

He shrugs.

"I walked up to the desk and said, 'Please send me home.' Apartheid was over. South Africa needed to be rebuilt. I wanted to go home."

We descend a steep hill, and the M85 barks in the distance.

"I miss Canada," he says. "I met a woman while I was there, and we had a child, a son. He's Canadian. But his mother had a drinking problem, and we separated, so I decided to return to South Africa with him. You'll meet him. He has fetal alcohol syndrome, and I worry I am not doing enough for him. I worry he's losing his English-speaking skills. I worry he could have a better life in Canada. More opportunities. More services."

"He's entitled to Canadian citizenship," I say.

"I know he is," Michael says. "I keep all his documentation safely stored. Maybe one day he'll go back."

We cross the bridge spanning the M85 and pause to note the traffic heading south to the CBD and north to Pretoria, the nation's capital. I see the high rises and cranes of Sandton in the distance.

"How are my Oilers doing?" he asks.

"The hockey team?"

"Yeah, I am huge Oilers fan. What a team they had in the 1980s, winning the Stanley Cup in 84, 85, 87, and 88. I loved watching them play. Gretzky was traded to LA twenty years ago this year, wasn't he? 1988? Yeah, I remember that. I liked Gretzky, but people underestimated Messier. I don't think he got the respect he deserved. Gretzky never won a cup again after he left; Messier did, though, with New York. Messier won another cup. What a great leader he was. I hope to afford cable one day, so I can watch hockey again. I miss it. What a great game."

He laughs.

"I never get to talk hockey in Alex. My wife and sons get so sick of it."

"I would imagine hockey isn't the most popular sport in South Africa."

"No, but it is in Canada. I am guessing you are a Leafs fan."

"I was until they lost to Gretzky and the Kings in the 1993 playoffs. I was too hurt to ever emotionally invest in them again. Gretzky was not popular in Toronto after that."

"I remember that series and that game. I was living in Toronto then. Gretzky highsticked a player in game six but was never called for the penalty, and the Kings won in overtime. Who was the player?"

"Doug Gilmour."

"That's right. What a good player. So much heart."

I find it surreal to be talking about the Toronto Maple Leafs with a former ANC party member on the doorstep of Alexandra Township. I find it bizarre to think that when I was sobbing uncontrollably over the Leafs' loss in our family's laundry room, completely inconsolable, Michael was somewhere in Toronto, just an hour south on Highway 400 from where I was, in some bar, maybe, watching the same Maple Leafs team as I was but under very different circumstances—an exile from his own country while paperless and estranged in mine. I find it extraordinary that on the eve of apartheid's demise in June 1993, Michael had one eye on Gilmour and Gretzky and the other on Mandela, de Klerk, and the violence and fear choking South African communities. The Maple Leafs had been my entire world, and what a small and comfortable world it was.

"Welcome to Alex," Michael says, and all I can see is movement. Sandton's sedate and solemn streets have disappeared, and in their wake, roar the township's skinnier and fuller ones. People are everywhere. People on their feet. People in their cars. People on their bikes. Thousands of people, it seems, try to fit onto slender slabs of asphalt or concrete. Privacy appears endangered, threatened by the residents' proximity to one another, their living and loving so close to one another, or so are my impressions as a man who came of age among rolling green hills, forty-acre farms, forests and trails and lakes and streams a plenty, a child spoiled by space. Yet as Michael guides me through the streets, I appreciate their energy and vitality more than their confinement, the bustle and bristle of the place, its well-orchestrated chaos and addictive flow.

I watch Michael greet and socialize with several people, and then follow his hand as he points to his modest home tucked away among other modest homes. From his laneway, narrow paths dart to the left and right, and I can hear voices down them and can see flashes of children chasing a ball or running to a parent's call.

Michael lays his hand on his wall.

"It used to be corrugated iron, but over time and with more money, we changed to concrete and brick. It is sturdier."

He catches me glance at an opened electrical box with dozens of red and black wires that curl and twist into one big knot or bird's nest. He laughs.

"In Alex, we are all electricians."

He motions to a doorway.

"I'd like you to meet my son Andrew, the one born in South Africa."

The room is tiny. Two mattresses lie beside the east and west wall and on one sit a young man and woman playing a video game, and on the other sits Andrew, who stands upon seeing me and extends his hand. He is slim and already taller than his father and displays a confidence and swagger that I immediately recognize and like.

"So," he says, "have you heard anything good about Alex?"

I think for a second.

"Honestly, no I haven't."

They all laugh. Michael says he needs to check on something in the house and will return in a second, and Andrew offers for me to relax on the mattress, which I do reluctantly. Andrew introduces me to his friends sitting on the other mattress and says they are a couple.

"I am letting them use my honeymoon suite for the afternoon," Andrew says and waves his hands around the room. "What do you think? Could you live here?"

I both admire and fear his directness. I glance around the tight, intimate space and the cardboard pieces reinforcing the worn roof and wonder how I should respond. Do I respond in the affirmative and thereby acknowledge his family's effort to carve a dignified life for themselves here in the so-called Dark City with little institutional support and thereby validate his existence by saying that I as a white foreigner could indeed live here and call myself happy? Or do I respond in the negative and thereby admit that his situation is indeed dire and difficult and that I could not even imagine living in such an impoverished setting?

I stammer. "For a little a bit, I think, I could live here, but not for very long."

He seems satisfied with that non-answer, perhaps content with only making me think, however briefly, what it may be like.

"What kind of music do you like?"

"Everything."

"Hip hop?"

"Some."

"You're from Toronto?"

"Yes."

"Do you like Drake?"

"He's my neighbour."

Everyone in the room looks at me with mouths slightly ajar, faces frozen in a tableau of disbelief.

"I'm joking," I say.

Andrew smiles.

"I want to show you a music video my friend and I made," he says, pointing to the young man on the mattress and then rearranging a few cables on the television.

On the screen, the two men stand on an Alex street at a distance from the camera. It is night, and the men's faces and bodies are blurry and unfocused as the camera moves and shakes and bounces, purposely, to create a sense of intoxication, maybe, to create a buzz, a drunken flow—the sensation that everything is moving and swaying so effortlessly. Over a beat, the teenagers rap and rhyme about getting drunk and getting high, about girls, about partying, about life as a teenager. I recognize, to an extent, the same longing, the same desire to punch the roof off my house, to kick the door down, bust a window or two, and then to swagger out into the world and get drunk, high, shit-faced on experience, on life. I was a teenager once, and I, too, felt an insatiable desire to taste and try and do everything now, right now, away from the safety and confines of bedrooms and bedtimes and the terrible, crushing boredom accompanying someone just discovering himself and then finding himself trapped in some laneway, in some house, in some town or city. Coming of age is certainly a universal rite of passage; self-discovery is experienced the world over. Yet as I watch the teenagers rap the same lines over and over, as if a chant or a prayer, and as I identify more and more things marking Alex as Alex, the specificities of a culture and place coalescing and cementing on celluloid, I understand the particularities of getting drunk in Alex as a Black South African teenager precludes my claiming allegiance to an alluring and simple universality, regardless of how much I may want to locate and celebrate those similarities imagined between him and me across time and place.

"Next time you should visit Alex at night; it's one big party, "Andrew says. "We are like vampires."

Michael, Andrew, and I are walking Alex's streets, swerving around people and cars, hopping from road to sidewalk then back again, passing impromptu vendors and residents enthralled in the art of conversation. The vehicles are unrelenting, and the streets seem perpetually clogged, and minivans and cabs—or "cockroaches" as they are lovingly called in Alex—slam their horns every few seconds to attract patrons as someone somewhere in Alex is always looking for a ride.

"Alex is one big driving school," Andrew says. "Because if you can drive in Alex, you can drive anywhere."

He points out the Alexandra Health Committee established in 1916 still standing in quiet defiance despite its peeling façade and the drooping electrical wires sweeping around the building as if a team of hunting boas. We pass a painted mural depicting early farm life at Alex—a Black man unloading large jugs from a donkey-pulled cart, a Black woman balancing a jar on her head, a younger Black man drawing a pail of water from a well, his forearms flexed, his face caught in exertion, all of them working in the shadow of ascending whiteness, building a life together in its shade. We spot a factory-sized building functioning as a church, and Michael says the preacher man does very well convincing his followers that salvation lies in his financial betterment, but Michael pauses, reflects, and says, "Even where there is poverty, there is money to be made."

Michael motions towards the new three-story homes with windows and blinds standing above the shacks and rows of portable toilets—blue, green, and yellow—pushed together as if Lego blocks. The ANC has built these homes for Alex's residents, Michael says, but they cannot keep up with the demand, and all these new homes do is foster resentment among people who do not have indoor plumbing or sturdy walls. We duck under clotheslines extended from pieces of metal and watch as white dress shirts and red tank tops sway in the wind, and we step through mazes of alleyways, each holding dozens of homes with families squished together tightly. And when Andrew spots me inspecting a piece of corrugated iron, which I think resembles a tank tread, he tells me how, reportedly, Michael Jackson once flew over Alex, looked down on its miles of sparkling metals, and said, "That's the biggest scrapyard I've ever seen."

Andrew thinks this rather funny, and I ask him whether any white

South Africans ever visit Alex.

"No, they think they'll get robbed. They think whatever they bring into Alex they will lose. One white friend of mine did visit once, and he loved it."

"I was mugged in the CBD," I say.

Michael is sombre and expresses his condolences while Andrew, too, says he is sorry but then throws a few air punches, grins wide, and says, "I would like to see them try something like that on me. I would handle them." I don't believe him, but I admire his bravado nonetheless.

Then along Roosevelt Street, I see it, the structure representing all of Alex's sorrowful history and internal contradictions and tensions, the five-story, red-bricked building housing hundreds of unemployed Zulus, the scene of much violence over its decades-long existence—Madala or Alexandra Men's Hostel.

"Do you want to go in?" Michael asks.

"Is it a good idea?"

"Not always," Michael says.

The hostel looms over us like a prison.

"I am a Zulu myself," Michael says. "But the Zulus who live there are more traditional. They demand respect and honour. And they take offense quickly if you accidently deny them that respect, even if you are not familiar with those customs."

Andrew quickly converses with his father in Zulu and then disappears into the hostel.

"He will ask for permission," Michael says.

I can tell Michael is nervous. I am his responsibility, and he knows Madala's history. He knows how in the 1960s, the apartheid state, frustrated as it was from Alex's insatiable desire for protest and demonstration, declared a state of emergency and decided to dismantle the township completely and redesign it as a hostel city to accommodate Black migrant workers who came to work the mines. He knows that when Madala was built in 1971, it was a cosmopolitan, if impoverished, place, housing representatives from the Zulu, Shangaan, Venda, Xhosa, Sotho, and Tswana communities and hosting friendly, maybe a little contentious, competitions between the groups like when they played soccer on grounds to decide the best clan. He knows how in the late 1980s and early 1990s, during apartheid's deadly decline, Madala transformed into an epicentre of violence, a hot hell, in which the Zulu-nationalist Inkatha Freedom Party (IFF) fought the ANC for supremacy in the hostels and in the townships. He knows how Madala's carnage its images of Black-on-Black violence—terrified white South African audiences and scored a victory for the apartheid propagandists, as if it were clear proof that a machete is post-apartheid South Africa's fate if Black South Africans were better integrated. He knows how the IFF took the hostels and drove non-Zulus from their homes and displaced them further afield; he knows twenty-five years later, no property has been returned. He knows, more recently, how Madala has become known for its xenophobia, how much of the violence destroying the homes and shops of African migrants originated from those brick walls. He knows three years ago, in 2015, after another xenophobic wave of violence, police raided the hostel searching for suspects and weapons. But Michael also knows that if residents were asked their opinion on xenophobia, most might say those incidences stem from government inaction, most might say they were a message to the ANC saying we are here; after twenty-four years, we are still here with no jobs, no education, no services, no opportunities, and little hope.

Michael leads us to the property manager's office, and the manager himself sits at a desk behind stacks of papers. He wears glasses; he has the aura of authority.

Michael speaks to him in polite, deferential Zulu, undoubtedly aware of the respect this man commands.

The manager turns to me.

"What is your purpose here?"

"I am a tourist, a visitor. I only want to see the hostel." I say, raising my hands, instinctively, as if to say I have nothing to hide. I come unarmed.

The manager inspects me further, trying to gauge my intentions.

"He just wants to see," Michael repeats in English, pointing to me. "We will be quick."

The manager's eyes search me; he makes his internal calculations. What worries him, I wonder. Does he worry the consequences that would befall him if something were to happen to a white foreigner, however unlikely, on his watch, in his hostel? Or does he worry about what I may say about Madala, what I may report back to wherever I have come from? Does he worry about the privacy and dignity of his tenants? Does he worry that outsiders only treat them as photographic specimens, an exotic flamingo or platypus, firing cameras and their flashes at them, asking families to sit but not to smile, asking them to sit stoic and prideful, asking them about their feelings and whether they hate foreigners and whether they are frustrated by South Africa in 2018 and then leaving and never coming back? Or is he simply wary of white people and their expectations and entitlements?

He grants us access, and as we stand, we thank him and then thank him again.

We walk through the darkened narrow hallways and past the little rooms sheltering families, who talk and laugh and who occasionally glance in my direction with a proud indifference, as if tired of seeing these visitors who only come to note the decrepitude in which they are forced to live. We pass moments of intimacy—a child washed with a sponge, hair cut with scissors—on display because there are few places to hide in Madala without meeting other people trying to find a quiet place. We pause in the large communal kitchen with its rows of tables and gas stoves and watch the few people there preparing foods in oiled pots and stirring them with wooden spoons in wonderful rhythm and routine. I look with deep respect, or at least what I consider to be respectful. I walk, nod, and smile at the residents I pass. I walk with my hands behind my back. I walk with my mouth shut and my eyes open. But there is something unsavoury about my presence here as an outsider, as someone who will leave Alex in a few hours and may never return. As much as I play the empathy game, I conclude that if I lived here, I would resent a tourist walking through my home and inspecting and photographing the way I live, the way I wash my child, the way I cut their hair, the way I prepare their food. Yet this hypothetical exchanging of places rings false, rings again of privilege, because I cannot imagine it, cannot know it, cannot fathom what it may mean to be Black in Alex in post-apartheid South Africa.

A breeze floats through an opened window. Outside, I see the burned and rusted cars. I see clothing hanging and drying in the wind. I see Alex spread into the blue horizon, and I cannot say where it ends. It grows and survives, despite the numerous attempts to strangle and kill it. It grows and survives despite apartheid's end.

Michael stands next to me and takes a photo of his city with his cellphone as if he has never seen Alex from above. Maybe he hasn't. He points somewhere among the collection of homes glittering in the sun.

"There is a river running through that part of Alex," Andrew says. "And newly arrived people build their shacks there, and when the rains come, they are washed away. And people have died."

He gazes at Alex.

"But they rebuild," he says. "They rebuild."

The following day, Along Empire Street, my driver and I sit in traffic. He is driving me to the Apartheid Museum.

"How long have you been in Johannesburg?" he asks.

"Not long. Four days or so."

"Have you enjoyed it?"

"Yes, I have."

The light ahead turns green, and we crawl ahead. Beside us is the entrance to the University of Witwatersrand and the fences and checkpoints surrounding it.

"I studied here four years ago," I say suddenly.

"Studied what?"

"Forced migration."

"How was it?"

"Fine. It was fine."

I remember all the times I ran this street, never once really stopping to savour it. I remember all the times from my desk when I pined to experience Johannesburg instead of simply reading about it. I remember the shame I felt when I left. I remember the shame.

But now as WITS fades into the rear-view mirror, those memories do not feel nearly as debilitating. The sense of shame has lifted, and I can understand that time not as failure but as a teachable moment. Life is rarely defined by a single moment, and there are forever opportunities to right wrongs or to reimagine perceived dogmas or to reinvent traditions or to rewrite better myths. It is the arrogance of the living that says life has always been like this and it will never change.

In the Apartheid Museum, I follow a group of Black schoolchildren on a guided tour as they learn about apartheid's birth, its flowering, its decline, its death, and its lingering and lasting effects. They are young, born after 1994. I wonder if they see apartheid's legacy in their day-to-day lives, or do they understand the violent photos and discriminatory signs as only as evidence of some nightmarish past, forever and completely gone? I wonder what they think when they hear the words Soweto or Alex. I wonder what they think when they see me, a white man, walking through this museum of white violence.

The museum itself is vivid and animated. The exhibitions, with their photos and narratives and audiovisual materials, grab and shake viewers and demand of them their full attention and demand of them to reckon with this past. Yet by far the most anemic part of the museum is the post-apartheid period and contemporary South Africa, and I suddenly remember Patrick's antipathy towards this museum because of its desire to present apartheid as only something past and done. The museum does have a celebratory atmosphere and follows the upwards arc of a standard narrative: injustice, conflict, rising action, and positive resolution. Yet as I watch testimony from the Truth and Reconciliation Commission, in which a white officer admits to the extrajudicial killing of a Black protestor, confesses to shooting her in the head and burying her in the ground in exchange for immunity and freedom, I wonder what exactly South Africa has resolved, what exactly it has reconciled.

In one of the museum's final rooms hangs a framed, blown-up political cartoon drawn in the early years of the post-apartheid era. Two cliff edges face each other but are separated by a deadly void; one side reads "Truth", the other "Reconciliation". On the Truth side are Tutu, other architects of the Commission, and the South African media watching and reporting with their cameras, microphones, and notepads. Tutu stands right at the cliff's edge looking at a blank map; the two men behind him peer across the chasm to Reconciliation with no idea of how to get there. The speech bubble emanating from Tutu's mouth reads, "Oops." The hopeful words and sentiments echoing from apartheid's demise have failed to materialize in the lives of those most affected by the brutal, segregationist policies of the past. Twenty-four years on, a large gulf still exists between words and reality, between feelings and the actual.

Outside, I watch the schoolchildren exit the museum, walk across the parking lot in long lines, and enter the Gold Reef City Theme Park sitting across from the Apartheid Museum. The park has rollercoasters and other rides; nearby are also a casino and theatre. The boys and girls in their uniforms disappear into the park as does the sound of their voices and laughter. The sun shines on the quiet parking lot; a half-dozen tour buses rest in the distance. Behind me, more visitors queue for the museum, and depending on the card given, they either enter through the white or non-white entrance. They can see what it was like to be treated solely according to the colour of their skin. It is an enlightening experience, an exercise in empathy. Visitors may imagine how bad it was back then.

Back then.

Endnote

1. Information about the Soweto Uprising as well as about Alexandra's history was taken from Crais, Clifton, and Thomas V. McClendon, editors. *The South Africa Reader: History, Culture, Politics.* Duke University Press, 2013.

8.

Zimbabwe

During my time at WITS, I read copious accounts of Zimbabwe's destitution—a decade-long economic and political catastrophe so widespread that it had forced millions of Zimbabweans to flee into South Africa. I read countless stories of Zimbabwean migrants having their claim of refugee status or humanitarian protection denied, who were then detained, whisked away on a train to the border, and deposited back in Zimbabwe like pieces of trash. I even crafted a proposal to explore the stories and experiences of those deportees and how they negotiated their forced return to their country of birth.

Now I am sitting on a City Link bus on my way to Harare and watching farmland stretch into the horizon. It's a pleasant June 2018 evening. I think about my past project, and the shame does not feel as acute. I no longer necessarily regret abandoning it. I did not have the tools then to faithfully complete the work; everything was rushed and thrown together haphazardly. I did not have the necessary experience. I did not have the necessary connections. I had no real knowledge of the land or its people. My project was a path to another master's degree, not a sustained push to genuine reform and change. I would have returned to Canada at the project's end, still leaving my research subjects in legal and existential limbo.

My knowledge of Zimbabwe had centred on the country's lack—of food, security, wealth, and democracy. But on this trip, I want to focus on the country as it exists beyond the bleak and damning headlines about human rights abuses and approaching economic ruin. I want to focus on how people continue to live and survive despite these social and political ills.

My bus rolls to a stop right across the street from the brightly lit Cresta Jameson Hotel, my hotel for my stay in Harare and one of the few buildings in the city illuminated. I am not one for flashy, lavish things, and I booked the hotel not for its luxuries but because it accepted credit cards and included breakfast in its rate, although those certainly are kinds of luxuries. But I was still taken by its appearance, as the hotel resembled an island of wealth floating amid a sea of hardship and discontent, a lone lightbulb in a dark room. So well known is the hotel that City Link had made it one of two principal stops in the city, which proved a great relief to me, as I had no desire to find a taxi and negotiate a fare from the other, more out of the way stop. Indeed, the greatest obstacle to my arrival to Harare and the Cresta Jameson that night was crossing the street, but once I managed to bypass the cars flying by in the dark, their headlights appearing as some kind of ravenous monster, I checked in without any effort and fell asleep on a nice, soft bed.

The Cresta Jameson Hotel stands guard over Samora Machel Avenue, principal thoroughfare of Harare's Central Business District, and glares over the barking cars and chatting pedestrians passing through the city. The hotel advertises itself as a "grand old dame" who has been etched into Harare's social and cultural scene since its birth in 1959. Yet despite its well-worn exterior—the windows, ledges, and façade—the interior exudes a modernity one would expect from a centrally located hotel catering to a refined and upstanding clientele. The hotel has undergone a recent renovation, updating many of its amenities for twenty-first-century standards without losing its historical feel.

"This is the Jameson Hotel, which was inter-racial years before liberation, and has always been a good-natured place" writes Doris Lessing—an exiled white daughter of white-ruled Rhodesia who returned in 1982 to experience Black-ruled Zimbabwe.[1] She recounts a scene at the hotel's restaurant in which a Black husband and wife sit and try to decide what to eat from the extensive menu, but the husband becomes disappointed when he hears his wife order sadza, a cornmeal porridge, and admonishes that she cannot only eat sadza and must try something new. A cheese dish arrives, and she scrunches her face in disgust. Another plate comes, and she pokes at it with her fingers, and her husband playfully berates her for not using a fork. The wait staff and manager also become amused at the sight of this woman discovering the world's buffet and then deriding each item. Yet when the porridge comes, and the woman sinks her fork into the softness and then brings it to her tongue, a look of ecstasy seizes her, and she gobbles the remaining portion in a few forkfuls.

The Jameson is still celebrated for its food. Tiffany's Restaurant serves a wide variety of dishes from both the buffet and à la carte, although buffets are typically reserved for breakfasts and lunches. The morning buffets are intimidating and are ideally suited for people with big appetites. Heated trays hold a bevy of meats and scrambled eggs and beans, and patrons stand in line while chefs in their typical white hats serve each man and woman by scooping eggs or beans or lifting sausage or bacon and plopping them down the white, warm plate. There are also cereals, pastries, breads, and coffees and teas, and ample space to sit, eat, and savour the early morning and watch Harare rise.

Yet the morning after my arrival, the restaurant is filled with people, which I find annoying. I haven't eaten since lunch the day before because I must use my American dollars sparingly, as I only have enough for a few more days and no ATMs presently work in the country. Thankfully, Jameson includes breakfast in its rates, so I plan to eat liberally. Standing in line, though, plate in hand, I realize that most of the people are dressed in yellow, green, red, and black—the colours of the Zimbabwean flag and also of ZANU PF, the ruling party since independence, and the party that just removed Robert Mugabe as party leader last November, an event I have heard wonderfully described as "not-a-coup coup." They are a boisterous and cheery bunch, as they talk, laugh, and plan over their large breakfasts. There must be a rally somewhere in Harare today, I think, what with the election only six weeks away. Some wear pins of the new ZANU PF leader Emmerson Mnangagwa, a self-described "Man of Action," a man who has gone to great lengths to distance himself from his predecessor, who has declared on commercials and in newspapers that Zimbabwe is open for business, open to foreign investment, foreign partnership, and, especially, foreign currency—and a man, it should not be forgotten, who was a central figure in Mugabe's descent into unbridled violence and oppression, so central they called him "the Crocodile" for the efficiently brutal way he dealt with dissent.

I do not see members of the Movement for Democratic Change (MDC), ZANU's main opposition, or photos of its leader Danial Chamisa. I wonder if MDC supporters are also holding a rally today, and if so, whether their members are too preparing with a hearty breakfast. Since its inception in 1999, the MDC has been the proverbial thorn in ZANU's side; MDC supporters sacrificed body and health to challenge Mugabe's authoritarian rule for the cause of democratic reform. And the face of the challenge had always been Morgan Tsvangirai, MDC's founder; his fearless visage absorbed each and every of one of Mugabe's blows. He was beaten and imprisoned several times, perpetually threatened with death. And then this past February, at only sixty-five years old, he did die in a hospital in South Africa from colon cancer, just three months after Mugabe was ousted and four months before he would have challenged ZANU PF for

Zimbabwe's future. He knew personally how volatile election time in Zimbabwe can be and how violence, or its implicit threat, has marred many of the elections in the 2000s.

Outside, the sun shines. Harare is known as "Sunshine City," as the sun blesses Zimbabwe with many cloudless days and a lot of blue sky. The light reflects from the bumper-to-bumper traffic and pedestrians snake through its openings expertly. I cross the intersection of Machel and Nyerere, perhaps the most anticolonial intersection in all of Africa, but stop at a traffic island, as the lights change, and the vehicles now crawl south to north and vice versa. Behind me, I watch people queue at Baker's Inn and wait for the perfect loaf of bread, warm and soft on the tongue. Every Zimbabwean has a degree in the craft of queuing. Every Zimbabwean who has survived the 2000s knows the experience of lining up for money, for services, for paperwork, for food, as the economy shrunk, dwindled, and almost disappeared completely. Above Baker's Inn rises an eleven-storey, brown-brick apartment building, and on its east side and running the length of the building is pasted Mnangagwa's smiling face. His grin reveals his prominent cheekbones and encourages, at least for me, mistrust. For me, nothing inspires derision like a politician's headshot.

Few white people grace the sidewalks. I watch one cross the street, hands in pockets, shirt untucked, trousers loose. He looks a little haggard and dishevelled and unkempt. He looks conspicuous on the street, his white face among black ones, exposed and bare. He looks vulnerable—a wildebeest cut from his herd. And when he passes me, his head hangs towards the pavement, his eyes only on his feet and those in front of him, and he quickly turns down a side street and is gone. I remember the photos I had seen online of Harare, then Salisbury, from the 1950s and 1960s of white people in their Sunday best—men in fine, dapper suits, women in flowery dresses and heels, and the children in cute hats holding their parents hands—shopping at Haddon and Sly Department Store, of white Rhodesian women dancing and drinking at a Salisbury night club, of Ian Smith, in 1966 Salisbury, standing in front of his white office building and fielding questions from white reporters about, undoubtedly, his country's unilateral declaration of independence from Great Britain to prevent the emergence of an independent Rhodesia under Black majority rule. I remember few Black people in the photos, in the Salisbury streets, since the Rhodesian state curtailed Black people's movement through the imposition of pass laws which stipulated nothing short of how and where African men and women could live. Every pass revealed in detail where they worked, for whom they worked, and what kind of person they were—

their character, work record, past violations. If an African found him- or herself in the presence of whiteness, they could expect to be asked for their pass to ensure they were allowed to be where they were. The passes controlled each and every African, boxed them into corners, and rendered them only as a blunt instrument of labour.

Now, in Harare, and in Zimbabwe, Black people move without hindrance. They flow freely on Machel Avenue through the skyscraper's shadow. Yet when I turn south and meander along Harare's smaller and narrower side streets, the sidewalks become more crowded, the people grow thicker, the roads fuller. And when I pause at the fruit vendors stationed just outside an OK Supermarket and see its security guards checking the bags of each and every exiting shopper, I remember history has no end and the past is never done with the present. I remember how easily Mugabe and his cohorts wielded the apparatus of the colonial state and how easily Mugabe and his paramilitaries produced terror and controlled lives just as effectively as his Rhodesian predecessors and how all governments view unorganized movement as a threat to their existence. And I remember in the aftermath of the ZANU's 2005 election win, Mugabe declared war on the city of Harare. Softly referred to as only an urban "cleanup program," Operation Murambatsvina was more militaristic than municipal. In spring 2005, armed police patrolled the more impoverished townships of Harare and destroyed all informal infrastructure and targeted informal businesses, anything existing outside the state's grasp, anything challenging its authority. Communities were obliterated, and hundreds of thousands of people were displaced. In her novel *We Need New Names*, NoViolet Bulawayo has her child narrator describe the clean-up program and the bulldozers coming and bulldozing homes and the drivers laughing and the residents screaming "why" and the lorries then arriving with more men carrying guns and baton sticks and those sticks landing on pleading bodies and the women yelling for their children to come while they grab whatever they can from their homes before the metal and brick crumble, before everything comes down. And after everything is gone, a barefoot man kicks bits of brick, rips his shirt, and points at a long scar. "I got this from the liberation war," he says. "We put them in power, and today they turn on us like a snake."[2]

At the National Gallery, a man of trash stares at a sapling of wire. The artist has assembled him from garbage, people's waste, and refuse and has fastened him together with cement and wires. He is made from cans, plastic rings, metal bits, old children's toys, wrappers, and various kinds of colourful containers. The man of trash sits on a cement bench with his elbow resting on his knee and his chin resting in his cupped hand. Between his legs grows the little tree and how he stares at it with such focus and concentration, as if he cannot believe something can grow here among the waste, garbage, and shit. It is one of the most spellbinding and hopeful pieces of art I have ever seen because it reminds me that wherever there is power, wherever there are forces trying to reduce people to trash, there is resistance, there is intelligence, and there is a sapling in need of watering.

In a nearby painting, a team of African men on horseback have pulled the Coliseum—that symbol of Western civilization—from Rome all the way to Southern Africa, and men from different ethnic groups dance and celebrate its arrival. At first, the Coliseum strikes me as out of place among the landscape, but as I stare longer and my eyes grow accustomed to seeing it among the brown earth and patches of green trees, it no longer seems so outrageous a concept. For me, it speaks of the connections that forever link Africa and Europe, Italy and Zimbabwe; no cultural treasure grows in isolation. I wonder if on a gallery wall in Rome, a painting hangs in which a team of European men on horseback arrive on the banks of the Tiber pulling the ruins of Great Zimbabwe, the great stone city that early Portuguese explorers could not believe was built by African hands.

At night, Harare wraps itself in darkness; electricity is scarce, and only a few buildings and lampposts flicker with light. Cars and their headlights illuminate the most space. In my hotel room on the Jameson's eastern side, I am watching *Orphan Black* on my laptop when I hear screaming from outside. I go to my window and below at a taxi rank, four men stand over another man curled in the shape of a half-moon. One of the standing men has a belt or a rod or a switch in hand—it is difficult to see in the night—and he brings it high and then whips it across the body of the quivering man, and when it makes contact on his arm or leg or midsection, when that sting and pain explode along his skin and nerves, the man lets loose a horrible, barking wail. I watch as each passing car brightens the scene, momentarily, and brightens the man writhing in agony and humiliation. I watch in disbelief. I debate screaming from my window and then worry about the consequences for my own wellbeing. I imagine giving details to the police: I saw a group of men, maybe four or five, a weapon, maybe a belt, and a man on the ground, maybe middle aged. But as the cries grow in intensity, I decide to call reception and let them know what I see, just as if I were ordering room service or asking for another complimentary bottle of shampoo or for another packet of instant coffee, and I would breathe a sigh of relief knowing I did everything I could, everything in my power to do as a visitor—that even as a visitor I recognized the humanity of a fallen man. Yet as I reach for the phone, the cries go silent, and I return to the window to see only a few men milling around the taxi rank. The victim and his perpetrators are gone, vanishing into the night. I put the phone back on its receiver, return to my bed, and watch *Orphan Black*. I try not to think of the man and where he is now.

The Bulawayo Club is a Zimbabwean landmark. Sitting on the northeast corner of Fort Street and Eighth Avenue in downtown Bulawayo, the City of Kings, the place of slaughter in the Ndebele language, this guesthouse slash gentlemen's club has dominated the city's cultural and political imagination since its founding in 1895. The architecture is pure colonial: tasteful ostentation, imposing yet subtle. Standing at the gated entranceway and waiting for the receptionist to open the bars, visitors have a hard time judging the club's size and scope. It is only when walking to the opposite side of Eighth Avenue—after passing the manic traffic flows, the street vendors, the taxi touts, the families walking together, the men chatting together, Bulawayo's frantic bustle—that visitors can appreciate the building's grandeur: its neo-classical style, its white walls and pillars and verandas, and its clay tile roof. Its ambience is one of charitable power, paternalist benevolence. It dominates the city in the name of goodness.

Inside, I am struck by the elegant and tasteful interior and immediately sense that my shorts, backpack, and general unkempt appearance put me at odds with the dignified atmosphere. The wooden floors creak under my weight. There are couches and busks of white men. There is a chandelier. Ahead, just past the entrance area, there is an atrium with tables, and at one, a white man smokes a cigarette and sips a coffee under rays of sunlight. The Black man at reception has my reservation printed in a big book, and when I ask if he has noted that my room is prepaid, he waves away my concern and says he is sure everything is in order, as if talking about costs and money were unbecoming in such a locale. While the man puts my reservation in order and checks to see if my room is ready, I am seduced by the silence of the place. It feels as a museum does. The quietness is intense and made more so when juxtaposed with the outside's commotion, the energy of the street. I watch the white man suck on his cigarette and watch the smoke disappear into the light, and I admire how peaceful he looks, how at ease inside these walls, among the expensive and nice things, and how it appears he has sought sanctuary here in Bulawayo Club.

The receptionist notices my staring and says that area is the Lobengula Cocktail lounge, but breakfast and dinner are served on the second floor.

He hands me my room's key and a young Black man takes my bag and motions me to follow him up the grand, carpeted staircase, up past paintings and photos of more white men in suits and army wear, and past lounging areas with reclining chairs and a table with two ashtrays and a Bible, past the large windows through which endless sunshine flows, and past the doors leading to the verandas, on which visitors can see Bulawayo's wide streets.

The young man unlocks my door, sits my bag on the narrow bed, and checks to make sure all the amenities are accounted for. I hand him a dollar coin—Zimbabwe is a country that runs on coins—and he thanks me and departs. I unpack a few items myself before I open the door and walk into this museum of Rhodesian ghosts.

The silence is unsettling. I feel as if I am the only one in the hotel. With every step, the wooden floors creak and crack underneath. The only other sounds come from the streets outside. The walls are an immaculate white, so clean and pure; everywhere, it seems, there are comfy chairs with no bodies in them. The club must have functions, I think, some reason to justify these bars and restaurants and seating areas, some reason to need these signs of exclusivity, these firm reminders that the club is an elite place for only elite people. I pass a wooden sign reading "Presidents Room. Members Only." I pass another sign warning members that anyone not adhering to the dress code will not be served in the cocktail bar. The dress code I learn, from a nearby picture, demands that gentlemen be in long trousers, a collared shirt, and closed shoes and forbids the following items: leather jackets, jeans, shorts, golf shirts, t-shirts, sandals, joggers, trainers, and bush boots. I read further, much to my relief, since I am adorned in forbidden attire—shorts, t-shirt, and trainers—that these rules do not necessarily apply to hotel guests, but they are still expected to conform to accepted norms of good taste and decency. I wonder what those are.

I also assume the club still has members because of all the photos displayed and the historic items behind glass casings and the dead antelope heads on the white walls. The central motif of all these items is the outdoors, the bush. There are paintings of men on horseback in colourful and stylish outfits jumping over a water trap or an obstacle and showcasing all their equestrian talent. There are photos of old rugby teams seated together in rows. Behind a glass casing, there are trophies and banners and plaques and old pieces of sportswear and a rugby ball. There are photographs of hunters or soldiers, seated white men in green camouflage with rifles lying across their knees. And there are the old black-and-white photos of the early white settlers traversing and taming the bush, the symbolic home of the white Rhodesian, with its endless miles of grass and shrubs and trees, and the animals, birds, and insects who call it home. There are old photos of Bulawayo showing how it had grown over the decades. In one photo, there is a big wagon with big round wheels stopped in front of balancing granite boulders, the future Matobo National Park, and there are some Black people sitting around the brush. The photo is of the Pioneer Column, a settler expedition financed by Cecil B. Rhodes, the most famous British imperialist, whose portrait hangs nearby, and in it, he leans on a shovel. Rhodes liked nothing more than to dig.

In the imperial heyday of nineteenth-century Europe, when Western Europeans were competing with one another over who could carve out the biggest chunk of Africa, Cecil B. Rhodes humbly stated that the British were the finest race in the world, the most honourable, and it would behoove the world, especially the uncivilized bits, to succumb to Anglo-Saxon benevolence and rule. He believed, then, in a sense, that British imperialism, and its physical manifestation of cobbling up land and creating colonies, was a form of altruism, another example of British charity and patronage, simply lending a helping hand so that savages could, maybe, become men one day. So Rhodes set to work acquiring as much African land as he could, dreaming of linking the lands between Cape Town and Cairo under British rule, but because he worked with larger, loftier, and, even, utopian ideals in mind, he cared not for the manner in which he seized the land, for its inhabitants were children, and adults know better than children. To claim such land, however, Rhodes still required British authorization, and the British required Rhodes to show he had entered into a treaty of friendship with the local people—in the case of southwestern Zimbabwe, this was the Ndebele people led by Lobengula from his capital of Bulawayo. Rhodes dispatched his business partner, Charles Rudd, to Bulawayo armed with a document promising Lobengula weapons—"one thousand Martini-Henry breech-loading rifles, together with one hundred thousand rounds of suitable ball cartridge"—a steamboat loaded with guns capable of defending the winding and treacherous Zambezi River, and "one hundred pounds sterling [paid] on the first day of every lunar month." In return, Rudd sought nothing less than complete control of all minerals and metals found not only in Matabeleland but in Mashonaland to the north—an area that Lobengula had no control over—and demanded that Lobengula assist Rudd and his men in repelling any parties seeking similar fortunes in these lands, assist them by any means necessary, in all their power, to guarantee that it would be the British, and the British alone, who would enjoy the profits and revenues found deep in the ground. When Rudd presented Lobengula the document, its incomprehensible scribbles, written in a turgid, bloated, and opaque language, a purposely dense British legalese must have confused the king. Skeptical as to what the document actually contained, Lobengula turned to Reverend Helm of the London Missionary Society for advice. And when Helm—a man of God, a man the king had allowed to live in Bulawayo among his people—said the document was harmless, Lobengula marked an X next to his name.

The concession satisfied the British government, and they granted Rhodes and his British South Africa Company (BSAC) rights to colonize Zimbabwe on Britain's behalf. Rhodes assembled the Pioneer Column, a ragtag group of white adventurers and their African servants and ordered them to march to the lands north of Limpopo and claim them for Britain, and in exchange for their bravery and their determination, each man would receive three thousand acres of land and mining concessions. Wary of Lobengula's anger over the duplicity of the Rudd Concession, Rhodes advised the Pioneers to skirt Matabeleland, travel northwest, and to occupy Mashonaland, and if Lobengula were to attack, he would receive no mercy and should expect "the disappearance forever of the Matebele as a power." But the Ndebele did not attack, and by 1890, the Pioneers had occupied Mashonaland and had risen the British flag at Fort Salisbury, one day to be renamed Harare.

The BSAC still desired the Ndebele lands to the south, which they believed held greater treasures, but they needed a pretext to invade the kingdom. Thus, when the Ndebele attacked a Shona-speaking community around Masvingo, Leander Starr Jameson raised a volunteer settler army, coaxing each man to raise arms through promises of more acreage, mining rights, and other spoils from Lobengula's fallen kingdom. In 1893, the settlers attacked and destroyed Bulawayo, and the king was chased northwards, where he perished. Matabeleland was destroyed, and its beautiful bush was carved and sliced and passed around like cake to the ravenous settlers who eagerly and shamelessly swallowed it.

After only three years of nascent colonial rule, the Shona and Ndebele could already see its consequences—the violence European civilization entailed. They saw how the British undermined and disregarded their traditional leaders and social systems and then imposed alien British ones. They saw the British dispossess them of their land and cattle and turned them overnight into squatters and labourers, now dependent on the jobs settlers could provide as well as their good graces. They saw the British demand of them an assortment of taxes—a hut tax, a dog tax, a head tax—

and to collect these taxes the British created the Native Department in 1895. They saw the British resort to violence and coercion when the tax load did not meet their demand for farm or mine labour or when the African (no longer a Shona or a Ndebele) simply did something unpleasing to them, as the white settlers, it was remarked once by a reverend, "think less of shooting a Mashona than they do of shooting their dog."[3]

But on March 20, 1896, the Shona and Ndebele united and took a final stand. And although the British eventually defeated them—resorting to a scorched earth policy they would use on the Afrikaans a few years later during the South African War—and the Ndebele negotiated peace with Rhodes at Matopos, and the Shona, too, eventually succumbed, the uprising's significance, known as the Chimurenga and Umvukela in Shona and Ndebele, respectively, would far outlive the actual event. Zimbabweans would invoke the rebellion during the liberation wars of the 1960s and 1970s and in the early 2000s, when they invaded white farms and expelled the great-grandchildren of the men who had expelled their great-grandparents.

I look at Rhodes again, the great imperialist, this man of untold ambition, and note how his modest frame does not really befit a man of empire, does not really speak to conquest. I look at his eyes, those pupils that saw the Union Jack draped across the African continent. Yet I wonder if those powerful eyes could have predicted this: His portrait tucked away in some ghostly club in Black-ruled Zimbabwe. I wonder if he could have predicted that today in Southern Africa his name is largely said with venom and vehemence, layered in thick vitriol. I wonder if he could have foreseen the students gathering on campuses around his statue and shouting for its destruction and demanding "Rhodes Must Fall!" I look again at this little man with his tie and suit, his hat in hand, and his shovel and conclude of course he couldn't have seen the future. And it is a curious shortcoming of the powerful, drunk perhaps on their own sense of ubiquity, that they cannot see their own fate. The past is not done with them. Every action has an equally strong reaction. Maybe not today and maybe not tomorrow and maybe not in fifty years. But the reckoning is coming. The present is merely a prologue.

The next day, I ride in the back of open-air safari vehicle surrounded by a group of Europeans, as we drive along a slim piece of asphalt under another cloudless sky and pass bendy acacias and light-brown grasses—the bush of Matabeleland—and creep ever closer to Matobo National Park, home to both Cecil B. Rhodes's final resting place and one of the largest concentrations of white and black rhinos in the world. Yet behind the idyllic, pastoral setting, the miles of unfettered and unspoiled forest, a war brews between conservationists and poachers over the fate of the primordial rhinoceros. When white settlers first came to Zimbabwe, they noted what a nuisance rhinos were, how pedestrian a sighting was, like spotting a chipmunk. There were millions of them. In 2016, poachers killed over 1,100 rhinos across Africa leaving roughly twenty thousand white rhinos and only five thousand black rhinos; some predict the black rhino could become extinct within five years. The demand for rhino horn rests primarily in East Asian countries, whose citizens, particularly the men, believe the horn possesses medicinal and aphrodisiacal qualities. Once grinded to powder and consumed, rhino horn, it is believed, will turn even the most perfunctory and uninteresting of men into the most dashing and enticing of lovers. Male sexual insecurity has literally driven a species to the edge of extinction.

In the front of the vehicle sit our three guides, representatives of the conservationist community who do their utmost the save the rhino from poachers. The guides themselves, like the rhinos they track and protect, have become something of a rarity in Zimbabwe: All three of them are white. At the conclusion of the liberation war in 1980, the white population had dropped from 350,000 to 270,000, as most fled fearing reprisals from the new Mugabe government. Twenty years later, the white population further dropped as the landless invaded white-owned, commercial farms to protest the failed promises of independent Zimbabwe, causing whites to flee to neighbouring countries or further abroad to North America, the United Kingdom, and Australia.

Todd, our driver and principal guide, has lived through it all, and he is a man that bleeds bush. He is tall and lanky, standing well over six feet, and unceasingly gregarious. He talks. He talks a lot. And when he isn't talking, he's smoking. He's a consummate smoker, Marlboro Reds, and if there isn't cigarette hanging from his lips, one isn't far behind. He adorns the typical safari ware: a beige nylon vest with shorts that stop well short of the knees. He is tanned, very tanned. His body seems to loathe shade. He speaks Ndebele and knows everything about every species of tree and plant. He knows each's medical and psychedelic properties. He knows what to eat and what not to eat. As he is fond of saying, everything you need to survive is in the bush.

Todd's greatest passion, though, is the rhinoceros. He has lived with rhinos his entire life. He knows their behaviour; he knows how to follow their tracks. He knows how to rescue them. When we finally arrive to Matobo Park, he walks us over to a display area with signs explaining the history of the park and detailing its rhino population. Below the signs, attached to wooden posts, are two giant rhino skulls: one white and black. Above the mouth of each is a gaping hole where a horn should point towards the sky. Todd drops his left hand on the black rhino's skull and tells us about the sad state of the rhino in Africa. Whenever he asks us a question about the difference between the black and white rhino—black rhinos have a pointed lip for grazing while white rhinos have a wide lip for grazing—or about Western intransience in refusing to try unorthodox conservationist methods or about the fact that if a rhino's horn breaks off, it can eventually grow back, he is shocked at our ignorance.

"How many of you have heard about Cecil the bloody Lion?" he asks.

A few hands rise.

"Of course, you have."

He smiles at the other guides.

"An American dentist comes to Zimbabwe in 2015, pays fifty thousand dollars, kills a lion, and the world goes mad."

I do remember the outrage. I do remember feeling repulsed by that man or by any person who would spend that kind of money to hunt a living creature—the trophy hunters who kill for pleasure, not sustenance or survival.

"I was that hunter's guide," Todd says. "And let me tell you something: Cecil the Lion was already a dead lion. He had been banished from his pride. He was alone. He was vulnerable. He was dead already."

Todd lights a cigarette.

"And do you know how we spent that money? We hired more rangers, paid for more facilities. We protected and saved animals."

He exhales a cloud of smoke.

"Cecil the bloody Lion," he says again, shaking his head. "Not too long ago, the lion numbers in Southern Africa were dwindling. They were being poached. So we set up a farm that bred lions to be explicitly hunted. And the poaching numbers dropped, and the lion has thrived ever since. We took control of the market."

He looks at the black's rhino skull.

"The West talks about education. We need to educate East Asian countries about the fraudulent claims associated with the rhino horn. With enough education, the demand for rhino horn will drop. Maybe so. But a group of people doesn't change its thinking overnight. It could take a generation. And by then, the rhino will be gone."

He takes another drag.

"We know the rhino. We know how to tranquilize the animal without hurting it. We could cut the animal's horn in a painless way and in such a way that it would grow back.

Todd looks at us tense and desperate.

"We need to regulate the trade. We need to remove its illicit nature. We need to remove the financial incentive for poachers. Imagine what we could do with that money. Imagine how much good it would do for our conservationist efforts. Think of how many rhinos it would save."

I sense my face twitch and then harden into skepticism, a not so subtle glare of incredulity, and Todd must feel it, the collective disbelief among us about his proposed plan, as if he has already had to justify this course of action, because he launches into a rebuke of the very thoughts circulating in my mind.

"I know what you're thinking. Isn't it cruel to tranquilize a rhino and then saw off its horn? Doesn't supplying the product only legitimize and, in fact, prolong the trade? Of course. But I ask you, which is more important: saving rhinos or how we save rhinos? Pragmatism or idealism? Which is more important? Because we are losing this battle. Idealism is literally killing rhinos by the hundreds. So ask your governments in the West—the same governments who block our conservationist efforts at the international level in the name of curbing cruelty against animals—which do they desire: a hornless dead rhino or a hornless living one?"

Todd stuffs his cigarette out on the ground and puts the butt in the packet.

"Let's go find some rhinos," he says. "I left a group tied to a tree this morning just for us."

"Kidding," he says. "Just kidding."

Todd has stopped the vehicle by a patch of bush that seems indistinguishable from any other. He glances down to the ground and interprets dirt markings—footprints, maybe—in a way that is incomprehensible to me.

"Okay," he says. "Everybody out."

He tells us the rules of rhino tracking. He tells us we must walk in single file, and we must keep quiet at all times. He tells us when we spot a rhino, we must squat low to the ground, and we must respect its space and keep a safe distance. He tells us he will first go and judge the rhinos' temperament, whether they are in a socializing mood or whether they wish to be left alone. He tells us not to make the dangerous assumption that because of the rhino's hefty and thick build they are slow. He tells us that rhinos can accelerate to 55 km/h in just three seconds, so if a rhino charges, you have three seconds to step aside, not turn and run, find a sturdy tree, and climb and climb and climb. And finally he tells us we may take pictures but not to enable the GPS function on either our phone or camera because if we then post those pictures to social media, poachers can use those coordinates to locate and then kill the rhinos.

We follow Todd single file through the bush, and I am amazed at just how nimbly and deftly he moves through the branches, thickets, long grasses, just how easily he commands the ground. I am in shorts and struggle to keep up through the terrain, and once I feel the grasses and shrubs, and their unknown chemical properties, rub again my exposed skin, I immediately regret my decision not to don pants and immediately fear what this vegetation could do my lower legs. But as I see Todd up ahead, ducking and weaving through trees and clamouring over rocks, his calves receiving the caress of many grasses, seemingly without incident, I forego my anxiety and align my behaviour so to match his.

Todd raises his hand, and we stop in the thick bush. He seems to sense something and then darts into the bush and disappears. We stay silent in single file and watch as the late afternoon sun slowly falls and more shadows creep along the ground. Todd then reemerges and motions for us to follow him, and we do softly and carefully, desiring not to disturb whatever it is we cannot yet see. Pushing past branches, I follow the body of the person ahead of me, until I see him crouch to the ground, which I then do, and in seconds, we are all kneeling in the bush. Todd points to a small clearing, and there among the feathery grass, three rhinos graze. Their size and grandeur are spectacles to behold. Their bodies resemble miniature tanks, and I find it hard to believe that something appearing so cumbersome and awkward could move so swiftly if provoked. Todd seems so at ease and relaxed around the animals, as if he has grown up with them and came of age with them, and in many ways, he has. The relationship, though, has had its hardships, misunderstandings, and flares of pugilism, as Todd has told us stories of his being chased up trees or his dodging of charging rhinos. But that history does not seem to bother him because he now knows how to better act in their presence and how to change his behaviour when he walks on their territory. I watch him gently move closer to the animals while making rhino sounds by cupping his hands to his mouth. He tries to calm them and tries to convince them to approve of our presence here among them. He asks them if we may ingratiate ourselves in their little herd for just a few minutes, not more than ten. But as Todd steps towards the rhinos, one small step following another, they mirror his actions in the opposite direction, slowly ambling away from us, faces and horns towards the ground, jaws and teeth ripping and tearing the grasses.

Todd turns to us and whispers, "They are not feeling very sociable today" and advises us that it's best if we leave them be. We do not want to overstay our welcome. And we don't.

Later in the afternoon, we stop at a small market where the local people who live in the park can sell homemade crafts and jewelry to tourists. Todd assures us that the money we spend here goes a long way to helping the locals and to making sure they derive some benefit from tourism. As a few members from our tour group go and peruse the items on display, Todd cracks open a bottle of Coca Cola and lights a cigarette. He offers me a bottle, but I politely decline.

"You're staying at the Bulawayo Club," he says. "How are you finding it?"

"It's a veritable museum of Rhodesian history," I say.

He smiles in agreement.

"There's a lot of history there."

The Europeans glance over the objects for sale, but none seriously consider buying any.

"What happens to poachers if they're caught?" I ask.

"Twenty-five years in prison for the first offence," Todd says.

The sun has begun to set and has washed the afternoon in a cool glow.

"It's basically a death sentence," Todd says. "Zimbabwean prisons are unpleasant places. The HIV rates there are catastrophic."

The long shadows across the paved roads appear as prison bars broken only by retreating light.

"I agree with the law," Todd says. "But I also understand the poacher. I understand the desire. Unemployment in Zimbabwe is 90 per cent. He kills one rhino, just one, and he's won the lottery. The money from one horn is more than he could make in his entire life."

Dusk in Zimbabwe is a wonderful time of the day. The cool night air descends fast. After the sun, the cold is an unexpected guest. Temperatures move quickly here. Nothing much changes, though, in terms of sunlight. Whether in January or July, you get twelve hours of sun and twelve hours of night.

"The poacher knows the risks," Todd says. "He knows he might be shot and killed in the grass. He knows he might be captured and might die in prison. But for him, it's worth the risk. What exactly does he have to lose?"

Todd kills another cigarette, and we all board the vehicle and drive into encroaching darkness. We pass more locals who wave, and we wave back.

And Todd turns the lights on, and everything is much colder, darker, and quieter than it just was.

I think about Todd's love for the rhino, just as I think about my fondness for every animal I've seen so far on my trip, just as I think about my fondness for every animal I've seen on my trip and my worry for every mistreated animal I've seen throughout my travels. I remember shaking my head in disappointment about the number of stray dogs in Santiago, Chile. I remember being concerned about the teams of donkeys carrying heavy loads through steep, narrow, and winding Himalayan Mountain passes in Nepal. I remember feeling anxious over the fate of the whale shark in the Philippines, the sloth in Costa Rica, or the hippo in Botswana. Yet how little do I remember about my feelings of empathy for the people who lived and died there. I remember being driven along rural roads in Moldova and watching an oncoming car strike and kill a stray puppy that had been crossing the road with his sibling. I remember turning back to see the pup lying dead on the road and the sibling returning to check on him. The scene broke my heart, broke my heart so much that when my driver later told me about the lack of opportunities in Moldova, the unemployment and poverty, about how he would have to go abroad to seek meaningful work, all I could think about was the puppy dead on the road.

The youngest of three guides is driving me back to Bulawayo Club, but she tells me that we have to pick up her father because she does not know the way to return to the Club. She hardly ever drives in the city.

"Don't worry," she says. "I am not going to traffic you into forced labour."

We turn down a residential street hidden in darkness; the streetlamps are purely decorative, it seems—a vestige of what was. Our car lights illuminate bodies only at the last instance—bodies walking on the dark streets, bodies riding on lightless bikes—and the young guide swerves each one with only centimetres to spare.

"Christ," I whisper as I brace against the dashboard and watch a body of a cyclist quickly vanish in the rear-view mirror.

The young guide smiles.

"Welcome to Zimbabwe," she says.

She parks the car in front of a mechanized gate and a wall protecting a modest house with electricity. She honks the horn, and the gate shudders to life. A middle-aged man appears and takes the driver's seat, which the young guide has vacated; she now sits in the backseat.

Through the night, we drive.

"How are things in Canada?" the father asks after I tell him from where I come. He strikes me as paternal: protective and wise and patient. He seems prepared to extend advice even when none is sought. He drives with the desirable blend of caution and confidence, the grace coming from years of experience navigating this wild terrain. But even the hardiest of souls can find some ground too shifting.

"Not as volatile as they are here," I say, and the father smiles.

"Yes. Things are not easy here. Everything is difficult—the limitations, the obstacles. Running a business here is impossible."

The struggling Bulawayo lights flicker in the distance.

"Elections next month, though," I say. "Is this the end of ZANU-PF?"

The father laughs.

"I doubt it. The MDC, the main opposition, is too splintered, too fractured. There is no unity. And with Tsvangirai's death, there's no recognizable face. There's no experienced leader. There's no unity."

"So you're not optimistic?"

"No, I am beginning to lose hope. And I think if ZANU-PF wins, we will leave. We will migrate. My family and I, we are running out of time. I am fifty-five, and I am almost too old to start over, but I feel that's the risk we must take for hope of a better future. There's no future here."

He looks at me and smiles, one of fading resolution, but when he turns his attention back to the road and traffic, I think about how even in exile, or on the eve of exile, certain people are inoculated against the perils and pitfalls of migration, the anxieties over the threat of looming violence, more so than others. I think of my time studying the great Zimbabwean exodus of the 2000s, when the white commercial farms were invaded by the landless, when white owners and their Black workforce were expelled, when the economy collapsed, when unemployment and inflation skyrocketed, and when Zimbabweans fled in the millions. I remember reading about the Black Zimbabweans who moved to South Africa, who sought refuge from the chaos, who sought sanctuary from the violence and deprivation and were greeted only by further poverty and discrimination and hardship. I remember reading how they were denied refugee status and were instead vilified as economic migrants, usurpers of the national South African pie, vile cockroaches who bled the social system dry, who would spread disease, violence, and vice. But I also remember reading how the exiled white Zimbabwean farmers eventually found work in Zambia and Mozambique and Angola and Nigeria and Australia and North America, prized as they were for their extensive experience and know-how, praised as they were for their work ethic and no-nonsense approach to farming. I remember watching *Blood Diamond* and sighing on cue when

Leonardo DiCaprio's Zimbabwean character disclosed, over firelight, how his family had been maimed and dismembered during the war of liberation, and then cheering when the character overcame his own cynicism, shed his selfishness, and saved the life of a Black West African man, and in essence, restored his own humanity. I remember reading Peter Godwin's memoirs on white Zimbabwean suffering and how he devoted chapters to Mugabe's violence yet spent only a paragraph or two on pre-1980 history, on Rhodesian history, and the white fondness for violence.

"I am not a racialist," the father says. "But the African has trouble disinvesting himself of power once he has it."

I nod, stay silent, and again marvel at the phenomenon of white historic myopia. If African leaders have had difficulty handing over power once they have finally felt it in their fingers and have held it in their hands, what then do you call European colonialism? What do you call settlers dispossessing an entire population and then forcing them to live under their thumb? What do you call the installation of an entire mechanism of governance designed to suck the vitality and knowledge of one population to enrich another? What do you call a white-minority-ruled British colony unilaterally declaring independence when the inevitably of Black-majority rule became too terrifying to consider? What do you call Ian Smith?

I remember hearing about white Zimbabweans during my adolescence. Oh so and so is from Zimbabwe, my parents would say. And I never really understood why if Zimbabwe was a country in Africa, then how come all the Zimbabweans I was hearing about were white. I did not know the history and did not bother to learn it, so their presence and identity seemed so wildly at odds with my limited worldview. At university, I learned a bit more and became intoxicated on that knowledge, as I used every fact I swallowed as ammunition for the drunken arguments I would get into about this and that, some world issue I would conveniently forget the importance of the following afternoon hungover and in bed. My masculinity at that time was not centred on brute force. I had no desire to destroy a man physically because it was cliché and undignified. But what I did crave was to intellectually humiliate another, especially someone foolish enough to argue a point I found distasteful.

There was a boy I went to high school with. He was intelligent, athletic, and good looking. His family had some connection to Zimbabwe, some linkage of which I had never discovered the specifics. But for me, the word "Zimbabwe" hung over him, and I thought about him the more I learned about the country and its history. And the more I learned, the more I wondered about his relationship to it, how he or his family fit into that tale of white domination and then white exile. It was his weakness, the one vulnerability in his perfected exterior. Then on Christmas break during my fourth year of undergraduate studies, I saw him at the local Bradford bar with a young woman who was not his girlfriend, watched him talk to her close and then dance with her closer, until they were almost indistinguishable, blending into one on the dancefloor. I examined him with a profound repugnance, as if he were sack of carrots gone bad, turned to mush and slime and blackness under an August sun. I questioned why he deserved such attention, why he was entitled to such an experience given the long history of events that led him from Zimbabwe to here, in southern Ontario, on the cusp of finishing an engineering degree, on the threshold of money and love and independence and freedom, on the dancefloor with a beer in one hand and her in the other, dancing and dancing and dancing.

When the bar closed, we all stumbled outside into an unseasonably mild December night. I lit a cigarette and watched the crowd slowly disperse and wondered if any men would feel the need to end the night with a punch or two, a somewhat common Bradford experience. The dancing man with the hazy Zimbabwean connection smiled at me, and we shook hands. I offered him a cigarette, which he skilfully removed from the packet and slid between his lips. He took my lighter and subdued the bouncing flame with his hand and then exhaled his smoke into the night. And as I watched him enjoy my cigarette, revelling in something else that he neither bought nor worked towards, I felt myself overcome by an acute animosity; something stirred within me, with a momentum I could not control—the lump in the gut that eventually transforms into vomit. I despised this man. I despised his good looks and his intelligence. I despised how the world just fell at his feet and begged his attention. I despised how he plucked an apple from its branch and never felt compelled to reflect on how his fingers were able to caress the fruit in the first place.

I asked him about the woman he danced with, and he grinned. I asked him whether he knew she had a boyfriend, and he nodded. I asked him whether he would have danced with her if the boyfriend had been in the bar, and he shrugged. I laughed at his cocky indifference, and he smiled, too, tapping some ash onto the pavement, laughed at his ambivalence towards any sense of responsibility, laughed at his meagre attempt to hide his own arrogance, to shield his presumption that everything on this earth is owed to him.

I felt good in my hatred. I felt alive and purposeful and strong. I played the fool and laughed at all his misadventures and all his witty jokes. We giggled like a couple of schoolboys laughing at a naughty joke or reaching for a cookie in its jar. And then I asked him, maybe, about his family's Southern African progeny, or, maybe, about his Rhodesian ancestry. And, maybe, I asked him about what had motivated his family to leave Zimbabwe, or was it even Zimbabwe, and about whether he felt guilty about leaving or about whether he felt shame about contributing to the ruinous mess Zimbabwe found itself in. I felt good. I felt good releasing my words into the world, felt so good, so fluid and mesmerized, that I did not provide him an opportunity to respond, did not afford him the chance to refute any of my charges. I felt so righteous in my confidence. I felt so holy in my crusade against this man's soul and history and identity. I felt so godly in my desire, in my wish, to stamp this man out and leave him in a pile of bones on the sidewalk to be gawked at like some dead rhinoceros. And when he eventually tired of my rantings, he smiled again, in his pretty and dashing way, thanked me for the cigarette, and turned towards home.

I, too, stumbled home, along the highway, and when headlights crested a hill, I would retreat to the ditch so the drivers would not see me. The stars were out, and the wind was calm. I already felt the alcohol seep from my skin and felt the anger dissolve back into anxiety and fear and doubt, and I knew as the night progressed into morning and then the morning into day, I would further dissolve into a puddle of shame and humiliation and would pray I would never have to see the dancing, handsome man for the rest of my life. Before I turned down my concession road, I made out the billboard broadcast in the moonlight: "The Crown has stolen our land." And as I entered my house on our settled property, which sheltered me during my settled childhood, I did not think much on the shakiness of my position.

I think about these things—the fogginess of moral positions, the impossibility of innocence—when the guide's father parks the car outside of Bulawayo Club, and I shake his hand and thank him for the ride and his daughter for the tour. I stand in front of the gates, and they open for me. The club's grandeur extends its hand, and I imagine the old Rhodesian ghosts mingling and socializing over whiskies and cocktails and talking about the bush and how much better everything was when the white man was in charge. The receptionist asks me how my day was and whether I will be joining them for dinner. I politely decline and climb the stairs to my room, the silence only broken by my shoes on the wooden floors. And as I turn the key in its hole and the door to my one-hundred-dollar-a-night room opens, I remember the white woman I saw the day before outside the Pick N' Pay grocery store sitting on the ground. Her lower legs had swollen to the size of tree trunks, and she sat with a sign explaining her condition and the dire situation she was in. She was asking for money to help her.

Around her, Black people with shopping bags raced towards their respective buses and tried to cram themselves and their belongings into the tiny spaces. They did not acknowledge the white woman and neither did I. I did not know how to feel about her. I did not know where to put her in my order of things.

Lying in my bed and wrapping myself in the soft blankets, I wonder if she sees herself as the rhinoceros. Once so plentiful and powerful, she now survives only on the philanthropy of others. Once, the bush was hers and hers alone. Or does she crave the attention the rhinoceros engenders among the conservationists and the international network of animal rights activists? Does she desire that concern? Does she want those resources amassed on her behalf to save her and her kind from extinction? Does she secretly whisper to passersby "Think of me as you would a rhinoceros"? Or can a white person, despite their suffering and hardship, ever be compared to a rhinoceros? What person in Zimbabwe deserves the attention and worry given to the fate of the rhinoceros? What person in Zimbabwe deserves such compassion? Such empathy?

Pennywise cottages sit at a distance from the A8 highway—a snaky piece of asphalt leading the world towards the Zimbabwe-Zambia border, to the voracious Zambezi, and to the mighty Victoria Falls. And the remarkable thing about Victoria Falls is not the falls itself, but the town rising from its edge, the tourist centre of Zimbabwe, which despite the country's decades of suffering has survived and grown here at the country's periphery. The town possesses all the characteristics one expects from such a tourist showstopper: the hotels, the souvenir shops, the booking and tour agencies, the restaurants, the bars, the touts. It seems that no matter what is happening to the south in Harare or in Bulawayo, it has little effect on the tourists who drive over from Botswana or Zambia or fly in from South Africa. Regardless of the ruinous nature of the country's infrastructure, the poverty, and gross human rights violations, tourists will still amble along the A8 and book their helicopter flights, their bungee jumps, their white-water rafting, their crocodile cage dives, their lion and elephants walks, and their Zambezi sunset cruises. The A8 is a veritable buffet of adventure opportunities and once-in-a-life-time opportunities.

But Pennywise is not located on the main drag; it stands on Kingsway Lane, a short road connecting Soper's Cress to Reynard Road, which runs in the shape of a horseshoe and eventually connects right back to itself. Such is the fate of the roads on the edge of the world: There is nowhere to go except inwards. The streets here are residential and relatively calm. The houses are spaced at a reasonable distance from one another. Everything is roomy and spacious. The sun is out; the flowers are pink and red. Along the pavement, shadows shuffle in the light breeze. Trees rise proudly from the ground and hold lovely canopies of green. The neighbourhood is peaceful, a welcomed antidote to the hustle of the A8.

My taxi driver hums a church song about the benevolence of Jesus Christ as he points me to Pennywise's gates. He asks me if I have already planned my Victoria Falls activities, and I tell him I have.

Pennywise is managed by a young Black man named Joseph, who takes my bag and shows me my room. He is enthusiastic and spry and patient, the kind of disposition one would want from a hotel proprietor, the kind of person who never tires from hearing the same questions again and again, never dulled from the same conversations, which is why I appreciate his restraint when I ask him, as every other guest surely does, whether the ATMs are, indeed, not working.

"It is true," he says. "I always advise my guests to save their American dollars and put as much as they can on their credit card."

He looks around the room with a degree of satisfaction, as if surprised himself that he has kept his guesthouse alive and breathing through disaster and calamity.

"Yes, things are not easy."

"Are you hopeful about the election?" I ask.

He is thoughtful and reflective and lets his words rest on his lips before releasing them into the world.

"The old man had been in charge for so long it's now difficult to think about the country without him."

I had never heard Mugabe referred to as an old man. The phrasing possesses a wonderful paradox. Sons call their fathers "old man" usually from a feeling of muted affection, usually from a sense of deference to the father's wisdom and experience, usually from, maybe, a sense of love, a love that cannot be expressed in any other way except in those forms deemed permissible by masculinity—cold, distant, ironic. Yet the phrasing also hints at decline, atrophy. The man has passed his prime; he is no longer young or vital or, even, relevant. He has weakened, softened. What was once muscle has turned to fat. What was once visionary has turned to cliché. What was once vital has turned to parody. And I think there really is no better way to describe Mugabe than as an old man, an authoritative father figure, belt in hand, who beat his children out of some warped sense of love and duty and manhood. Mugabe is now only tragedy, another cautionary tale, a warning of the corrupting burden of power, how heavy and destructive lies the crown.

I sense a melancholy in the way Joseph talks about the old man. He is disappointed in him, embarrassed at what he has become, saddened by what he could have been.

"Listen to the man speak one-on-one with someone," Joseph says, "and you will see how lucid and piercing his intellect still is. Get him away from the cameras and the crowds—his mob base that he had to placate to survive, the liberation war veterans, his bush generals—and you will see how nuanced his arguments can be."

I think about Mugabe and his ragtag guerilla army emerging from the bush in the 1970s after a long and brutal liberation war. I think about the optimism that must have swirled through the urban centres, the rural towns, through the farms and mines. I think about what it must have meant to see white Rhodesia brought down from its pedestal, to see whiteness bleed red. I think about the 1979 Lancaster Agreement—the post-war negotiations that transformed Rhodesia and minority white rule into Zimbabwe and majority Black rule—and how land was so central to the independence struggle, how in 1980, around six thousand white farmers owned 15.5 million hectares, whereas some 4.5 million Black farmers had only 16.4 million. I think about how the Lancaster provisions hamstrung meaningful land reform from the outset, about how Britain and the United States applied pressure, how Joshua Nkomo and Mugabe resigned themselves to accept "willing buyer, willing seller" land-reform provisions, and how white Rhodesian fears were allayed, their privilege and power maintained and protected. And I think about how twenty years later, on the eve of the farm invasions, 40 per cent of the peasantry were landless, and about how forty years after independence, those land invasions seem almost inevitable.

"It's hard to picture Zimbabwe without the old man," Joseph says.

I nod and wonder what Mugabe himself thinks about his situation. I derive certain satisfaction thinking about the old man tucked away in his mansion surrounded by his personal memorabilia denoting his former greatness. I think about his million-dollar bank accounts and his expensive suits and sunglasses and cannot help but smile. I think that to be exiled in his own country and to be forced to watch younger and fitter men take his country's reign serves, in a sense, as a form of punishment. Mugabe must watch as he becomes increasingly irrelevant, as his minions die and sink away, and as historians write his story not to placate his megalomania, not to twist Zimbabwe's history to serve his nationalistic agenda, but to expose him as the tragic man he is—the Macbeth of

Africa—to reveal in all his complexity the gargantuan monster he had become sitting on his throne and overseeing Zimbabwe slide into madness.

Victoria Falls is angry. It is the tail-end of the wet season, and the Zambezi has more water than it knows what to do with. And tonnes of it fall over the edge to the gorge below. Everything is wonderfully bright and fecund, so green and healthy. The surrounding trees soak up the light, the leaves bathe in the falls' spit and mist. The falls are so powerful and strong that the spray becomes a downpour and soaks the tourists who stand at the brink and try to snap photos of the world wonder through the wetness. It feels so odd to be soaked in the sun.

At one scenic overlook, where the mist is not so terrible, I take one picture that almost captures the power of the place, the sheer volume of water pounding over the cliff's edge. But what intrigues me more is what stands behind me—another statue of another white man. This one is named David Livingstone. David dresses in clothing ideal for the bush: long pants, overcoat, a hat with earflaps. He leans on a walking stick. Little of his skin is left vulnerable to the elements, exposed to the creepy crawlers that seemed to love the taste of white skin and seemed to kill the white man with the ease of a bomb. He towers above his viewer with his serious, experienced visage, yet his unshaven and gaunt face hints at his humbleness—that Christlike devotion to service and the alleviation of suffering. He is a man of passion, compassion: the white man who dedicated his life to uplifting and healing African souls, the man who made it his mission to connect the son of Africa to the son of God, the man who never met a body beyond his saving.

Below Livingston sits a plaque informing the reader that this statue was erected in 1955 to celebrate the centenary of Livingstone's discovery of the falls: "On the occasion of the centenary of David Livingstone's discovery of the Victoria Falls men and women of all races and from all parts of the Federation of Rhodesia and Nyasaland assembled solemnly to dedicate themselves and their country to carry on the high Christian aims and ideals which inspired David Livingstone in his mission here." Would Livingstone be satisfied with 1955 Rhodesia had he seen it? Had he walked through the wide boulevards of Salisbury and Bulawayo and noted the industry and churches, the tranquility and order, would he have been impressed? Had he experienced the transformation from dark forests to roads and cars, from the pit of the slave trade and malaria to the ascendancy of civilization and Christianity, would he have smiled and thought what better proof of God's magnificence could there be?

Above the roar of the falls, I hear the helicopters buzz in the sky flying tourists over the Zambezi so they may enjoy Victoria Falls from every vantage point imaginable. Other tourists snap a photo of Livingstone before they follow the trail along the cliff's edge, before they disappear into the mist and into the green trees. And as I follow them along the trail, the water falling from the sky increases and increases until I get wetter and wetter, until the falls and all its glory no longer hold any interest for me, and I turn back.

I am walking the A8, and I pass the tourists drinking their four-dollar coffees, booking their lion tours, preparing for their round of golf overlooking the Zambezi, returning to their five-star hotels after a morning safari, all of us, Livingstone's children, playing in this playground for the rich on the precipice of incredible poverty.

A Black man approaches me and spouts a litany of things he has for sale: cheap tours, crafts, a one-trillion-dollar bill, other curios, and, of course, marijuana. I politely decline and keep walking, keep moving, keep moving, I tell myself, just get away, please, please. But he follows, persistent, persistent in his right to be recognized, persistent in his desire to make me acknowledge him. He calls me his brother. "Brother," he says, "Give me one dollar for bread. Just give me one dollar so I can buy Zimbabwean bread. It's cheaper. Only one dollar." He walks next to me for ten, twenty, thirty metres, and it must look to an outsider, or maybe not, that we are friends engaged in an animated, wonderfully interesting conversation. He is relentless, dogged in his desire for his dollar. And then it confronts me hard that I am willing to pay this man one dollar to leave me alone. I am willing to pay this man to go away. I am willing to pay this man to stop harassing me at Victoria Falls, a natural wonder of the world, a place of adventure, excitement, unimaginable beauty. I pull out my wallet, remove a dollar bill, and hand it to him. He takes it and smiles. To myself I say, now, please, brother, just go away. My brother, go away. Go away.

Endnotes

1. Lessing, Doris. *African Laughter: Four Visits to Zimbabwe.* Harper, 2009. Kindle Edition.
2. Bulawayo, NoViolet. *We Need New Names.* Back Bay Books, 2014. Kindle Edition.
3. This and the previous three quotations were taken from Mlambo, Alois. *A History of Zimbabwe.* Cambridge, 2014. Kindle Edition.

9.

Tanzania

It's summer 2019, and I am thirty-five years old. I have returned to Africa to visit two places I intensely studied during my graduate career: Zanzibar and Ghana. I haven't come to soak in the sun on a Zanzibari beach or track elephants in Mole National Park. I have come to feel the weight of the African slave trade. I have come to visit the marketplaces and castles that transported millions of Africans from their homelands to work without respect or renumeration in distant, hostile lands the world over. I want to pay respect to these sites of barbarity and reflect upon how this trade shaped and moulded modernity and how I fit into slavery's long echoes.

Indeed, I have come to Zanzibar armed with the history I learned so many years ago. I have come to put an image to a word. I have come to feel Zanzibar beyond what is evoked by books and their sentences. I have come to witness how the island's history of slavery has etched itself on the streets and buildings of this dreamy and heavenly paradise.

I have not come as a tourist, but, of course, I am one. I look like the other tourists milling about the beach on this August 2019 morning waiting for our dhows to arrive. There are dozens of us in shorts, flipflops, and sunglasses. We are almost indistinguishable. We will spend the day visiting nearby islands and relaxing on the sand and in the sun. We will spend the day in a postcard.

Slavery should be the furthest thing from my mind, yet my imagination often wanders and plays.

In 1749, Ahmad ibn Said became sultan of Oman and set to work building an empire that would cast the nascent House of Said into the annals of history forever. His was a vision of ambition and scope. Said saw potential where others only saw nature. He gazed out at the world from his capital at Muscat and realized, more so than most of his contemporaries, that those tiny little islands bobbing so peacefully off the coast of East Africa could serve as the perfect entrepôts for trading Africa's riches to Asia and beyond. They could become islands connecting one vast continent to another. They could tilt the tide towards the East, erode the West's hegemony, and make the Indian Ocean the centre of the universe. In 1822, he took Pemba from the Mazar'i family through stealth and cunning and ruthlessness; five years later, he did the same in Mombasa. The next year, he visited Zanzibar and purchased two clove plantations, and the island's rich soil, its unharvested potential, so wowed and enticed him that by 1834 rumours were circulating in Muscat that he desired to make Zanzibar the capital of his burgeoning empire. Al-Said wanted to blast the impenetrable forests of Africa wide open; he wanted to suck its rich meat from its bones; he wanted to grow fat from its lush lands, healthy animals, and muscular male bodies. He needed slaves. He needed more bodies to work the lands. He sponsored caravans to carve through Tanzania's innards all the way to Lake Tanganyika and into modern Uganda. The traders returned with ivory and slaves and deposited them in the markets of Zanzibar, from where, these products further afield to every corner of the Indian Ocean. By the 1840s, Zanzibar had become the Mecca of commerce in the western Indian Ocean, which gave credence to Al Said's often made claim that he was nothing but a merchant. Zanzibar had become a cosmopolitan island in which its residents bought slaves and sold cloves.

Zanzibar is idyllic, a slice of heaven that has fallen to earth, as the sayings go. On Zanzibar, the sun is hot, constant, and generous. The sand's as soft as a slipper. The water's as warm as a bath on a winter's morning. Etcetera. On the island of Zanzibar, the sea has a dozen shades of blue. The sky is clean, except for the drifting chunks of cloud, which seem as threatening as a kitten attacking a spool of yarn. The wind is lazy. No gales disturb the palms. No gusts bother the fisherpersons hunting the waters for their daily sustenance with only a hook and determination.

From our motorized dhows, they look quaint in their small boats, like an antique in a gift shop, and when a muscled white South African waves at them, they do not wave back. The Yamaha motor cuts a white wound through the blue sea, as the captain, who wears a colourful kofia and a plain blue shirt directs our vessel towards Sandbar Island, a sandy stretch of about a kilometre that breaks the sea's surface at low tide. He stays focused on the horizon while the tourists, about fifteen or so, chatter among themselves in English, Italian, Portuguese, and Afrikaans. I sit next to the captain and do not say a word.

When other crewmembers pass around plastic cups to be used later on the island for wine and other refreshments, his left hand stays clasped to the outboard motor's handle, adjusting the speed when needed. Behind us, dozens of dhows follow in our watery trail, as if we were leading a race or fleeing from a crime. Each dhow's covering has advertisements painted in big lettering. One says Blue Wave, another Facebook, another Baba Bora, another Fortlina, another Sting Ray. This fleet of dhows, carrying hundreds of tourists, follows us through paradise as if our shadow. I feel as if we're being hunted.

One hundred and fifty years ago, a fleet of dhows, too, would have crisscrossed this section of sea separating East Africa from Zanzibar. They, too, would have traversed these waters with the sun on their faces and the wind ruffling their hair. They, too, perhaps, would have cooed and sighed at the beauty of it all.

These dhows, though, did not carry tourists eager to breathe in the tranquility of sun and sea. Instead, they transported men, women, and children, who though dressed in a manner befitting a day at the beach—little clothing, exposed skin—were not fleeted across the sea so as to partake in a week's holiday on the fabled island of Zanzibar. No. They were sent to Stone Town to be sold as slaves to the cosmopolitan crew of merchants—Indians, Arabs, Europeans—awaiting their arrival at Mkunazini, one of the great slave markets of the nineteenth century. And these slaves, unlike the contemporary visitors, did not begin their journey to paradise from North America, Europe, or even East Asia; rather, they started their long sojourn from the African interior, from areas as far west as Lake Victoria and today's eastern Democratic Republic of the Congo, and were brought to the coast by caravans—long lines of shackled human beings controlled by whips and further threats of violence—that grew fatter the closer they lumbered to the Indian Ocean. One little boy described his journey to the coast as such: "We travelled on ... for more than a month ... and a great many of the people died on the way.... They would go on walking for sixteen days at a stretch, hardly able to get any water.... Only the little children had no slave-sticks or chains, but the grown-up people were all fastened to prevent their running away."[1] But those who did survive the arduous trek to the coast were rewarded with that legendary dhow trip—the quintessential Zanzibari experience—and one does wonder, with the risk of sounding crass, if the experience of being enslaved, of having a life shredded, could really have ruined the joy of sailing atop the Indian Ocean and witnessing the sun, sand, and sea in all their spectacular glory. And maybe, just maybe, if they caught the sight of the sun sinking into the sea, they would ignore their chains and, like the many tourists to come, would simply forget about their worries, live a bit more in the present, a little more mindful, maybe, and enjoy the view.

In the shallows, a crewmember tosses an anchor and then lowers a ladder. We stand, toss our shoes and sandals to the floor, and wait to descend. And then once our feet touch water and then sink into sand, I watch, as if on cue or mandated by law, the tourists strip to their essentials—men to shorts and speedos and women to the tiniest yet most elaborate of bikinis. Exposed skin moves everywhere here on the sandbar. The beach has freed these thighs, torsos, and buttocks from clothing's constraining fabrics. Some skin jiggles; some glistens from sweat or cream; some stays as still as rock. Most is as brown as varnished wood. Here, inhibition is a foreign, curious thing. Ass is on full display.

Yet the bare body parts feel almost aggressive, a passive assault on the more modest attire of Stone Town's inhabitants, the city that though sitting a few kilometres to the west feels almost a world away. Neither the mosques' minarets nor the churches' steeples hold any sway along the beach: Tourists only worship the sun and strip in profound reverence. There is only one God, the sun, and the tourist is his messenger.

A British captain named Smee arrived to Zanzibar in 1811, and very much like future travellers to the spice island, he wanted to visit the market. The show commenced at four o'clock in the afternoon, Smee writes, which is, undoubtedly, a fine piece of information to provide readers and other interested parties, for without the basics—the who, what, where, why and how—visitors would be at a loss over how to participate in such an event. Yet hours before the show started, Smee hints, the traders had already started preparing and polishing their wares for potential customers. They applied coconut oil to their property's skin in liberal and generous amounts to ensure these bodies glistened in the afternoon sun. It was, to be sure, a little wasteful, a little too extravagant, perhaps, yet the traders must have seen the oil and its application a wise investment, a sound business calculation, because eyes are naturally attracted to what glitters and sparkles, and the only thing better than a well-built torso is one that shines. Despite the modern mantra to the contrary, it has always been perfectly acceptable to judge a book by its cover, which is why, tellingly, the traders did not stop their beautification efforts with oil. On the contrary, and as noted by Smee, the traders decorated their goods with bracelets as well as gold and silver jewels and ornamented these bodies to such an extent that their hands, noses, ears, and feet transformed from perfunctory, dull things into appendages and parts that bedazzled the eye. Only when the traders were satisfied with how everything looked, once they had that feeling, only mastered after years of successful and profitable commerce, that their things would attract the interest of prospective clients and that all their effort and time and labour would not prove futile but lucrative did they arrange these pieces of merchandise from youngest to oldest and march them into the marketplace and present them to the rapacious stares of the eager and agitated buyers.

Everyone poses. Everyone smiles. A woman in a black bikini squats, drops her head to the sand, rests her knees on her elbows, and then shoots her legs into the sky. While she balances in an incredible show of agility and strength, her friend kneels in front of her, aims her camera at her glistening torso, and snaps a photo for posterity. A Zanzibari handstand. Others wander into the shallows, up to their knees, and raise their hands to the sky or present the ocean in the palm of their hand, as if a painting they had created with the most vivid of colours.

And vivid the colours are. The water is so translucent and light that it resembles a pool, as if God himself had descended from his throne and disinfected the island for us, sprinkling the shoreline with chlorine to kill all the bacteria and viruses, the dark matter, by shattering their chemical bonds. An Italian couple lie in the sand, eyes to the sky, while the gentleman fiddles with a remote control controlling a drone fluttering a dozen or so metres above him. I hear it hovering above me, and I imagine its camera primed towards my creamy skin, thirsty for images, ready to drink me in as if I were milk poured into a glass for their enjoyment.

The merchants were a cosmopolitan bunch. Along the market's edges stood buyers from India as well as the islands of Mauritius and Reunion, Arabs from the Gulf, some Catholics, and even ordinary island residents. Among the melee, as the traders sashayed into the marketplace with their pretty products tied in a line, the buyers craned their necks and contorted their bodies to see what was on offer and to get a feel for what today's shopping had in store. If a particular body caught the eye of a spectator, he yelled for the line to stop, which it did, immediately, allowing for ample time for the buyer to examine the men, women, and children who stood silently in front of him. The buyer placed his hands on whichever bodies had piqued his curiosity, without permission, of course, for the simple yet profound reason that merchandise and machines do not give consent and the purveyor of such products need not, repeat, need not, request permission from things without the mental fortitude or the spiritual strength to grant it.

Although these objects resembled humans in their construction and appearance, in their gait and stride, they did not possess the sentience, an inner spark, separating man from beast, which, naturally enough, was their primary attraction, their edge in the marketplace: Men cannot be worked to death, whereas bodies can be. Yet bodies are only as useful as their health and vitality, so the buyer took his time with his hands, rubbing them, as he did over their black, shiny skin, hunting and searching for a diseased or sickly or unsightly part, which would render his investment unwise and would make him question whether these bodies could perform the labour asked of them. He had to be thorough, so the merchant did not interject when the buyer's finger entered a mouth, grabbed a buttock, or caressed a breast—a thoroughness and attention to detail that, according to Smee, were "unequalled in any cattle market in Europe." After all, a broken body sold as whole jeopardizes the trust of the buyer and endangers the entire operation.

So the seller granted the buyer his inspection, as he was painfully cognizant that he with his money and buying power ultimately decided the fate of the system, since without any demand, the supply, no matter the quality or price, would be made superfluous. Capital, and its associated privileges, was what in reality separated buyer and bought and seller from sold, regardless of all the racist discourses circulating like butterflies on a summer's afternoon; racism was the tool to justify the horror, yet it was capital, and its history of accruement through exploitation, which granted the power to decide who could sell and who could be sold. So when the buyer finally settled on a male—after exploring with the detail of a poet his legs, arms, chest, and shoulders—to work on his clove plantation and the buyer paid the merchant the price due, the two shook hands in the marketplace not only to conclude the transaction but to remind themselves that they were only as good, only as human, as the money lining their pockets.

Zanzibar is known as the spice island, yet for all the spices the bountiful island produces, the clove has affected and shaped the island's development the greatest. Made from the flower buds of the Syzygium aromaticum, cloves are a versatile spice used in cooking, medicine, and cosmetics. Clove production is arduous work. Trees can grow up to fifteen metres high, which forces workers, mainly men, to scale the trunk, with nothing but a rope and determination, to pull branches from the tougher-to-reach parts and let them tumble to the ground. There, women and children gather the cloves into gunny sacks, and, together, families carry them from the farms to the villages, where experienced fingers separate the buds from the branches. Both are left to dry for three days in the sun, and as the cloves harden, they transform into a brownish, almost rusted colour, which for visitors from colder climates, easily resembles the fallen leaves of a late October morning. As they dry, the buds release a sweet, intoxicating aroma, which drifts and wafts throughout Zanzibar, en-chanting both resident and tourist alike.

Yet it would be fair to speculate whether such a pleasing smell ever lessened the burden of those made to harvest the clove under a ruthless sun. It would be even more apropos to wonder about the relationship between the clove and its workers before the abolition of slavery in 1897 when the conditions were even more brutal and merciless. Between the 1840s and 1870s, at the height of Zanzibar's clove production, when the mortality rate on clove plantations skyrocketed to 20 per cent a year and the arrival of slaves greatly increased (nine to twelve thousand per year) to compensate for the unrelenting death, did those smells—one of nature's playful little gifts—soften the pain of the slaves' travail? As Zanzibar became the world's foremost supplier of cloves, did the slaves stop to consider the joy and pleasure their work brought to those people in those distant countries who dressed and doused themselves in the clove's extracts so that their appearance and smell could be a little less natural and a lot more gratifying to the senses? Did some of those soft scents rub off on the slaves themselves so that at the end of a day's turmoil their hands and fingers and limbs would smell a little less of sweat and grim and more of the flagrances of a person befitting a more dignified and becoming stature? Amid all that plantation death, did those rotting bodies worked to death actually smell lovely?

The starfish and crabs at my feet stop me from pursuing this line of inquiry further, as do the young people strolling in the horizon, where the light blue meets the darker variety, the point where the shallows plummet to unseen depths. One strolls in front of me at a distance of about half a kilometre. His clothing is functional—blue shorts, a grey t-shirt, and a white cap. In his left hand, dangles a sack, and his right grips a stick. He walks among the shallow weeds, whose green ends peak above the water's surface, and then carefully steps among the exposed coral bed. He glares among the rocks and pools of water, hunting for crustaceans and a livelihood, and clutches his stick so strongly that his entire arm explodes in definition, in muscle. Neither the sun nor the heat seems to bother him, as his body has ingratiated itself in the conditions of the ocean. His physique is the result of work, not pride. Underneath his feet, the sandbar resembles a chessboard drawn by a drunk: Pools of the clearest of water merge with pieces of rough coral, and weedy sections blur into patches of soft sand. It mirrors a continent whose borders have finally succumbed to the natural rhythms of life and circumstance. The European voices explode in laughter and happiness. The men of the reef do not seem disturbed by them; they work these coral beds every day just as the tourists come every day to snorkel above them.

The only reminders of Zanzibar's proximity are the crewmembers who have quickly begun to work: laying out the snorkelling gear, pitching large tents, cutting fruit, preparing a seafood lunch. And it is not just for our group. Along the sandbar, similar tents go up—makeshift tents of carpets attached to a few poles—similar fruits are cut, and similar seafood is prepared. They erect an entire village on a piece of sand. And the villagers do come, descending from dhows in the dozens, climbing up the sandy embankments, and then stripping in the sun. Soon, the barren little strip plays hosts to hundreds of tourists eagerly salivating for more sun, drink, play.

The British are an odd bunch. With the monarchy's blessing, the inhabitants of that dreary island set out to first know the world as well as its residents and to understand its workings, limitations, and mysteries—and then to enslave them. It's a curious fact that as modernity rose from the ashes of ignorance and superstition, as cultures worldwide developed and mastered more sophisticated forms of transportation—making journeys that once seemed only achievable by God pedestrian and commonplace—that rendered the world knowable and exploitable, only a map to memorize, and as human beings became more aware of one another, brutality and horror increased at a rapid pace. It's as if the more people, particularly Europeans, learned about the world's vast richness in terms of culture and language and art, the more they wished to see it destroyed and its adherents, the peoples of the world, made into a thing to be used to make more things. Yet, even more curiously, the British who had mastered the art of enslavement better than any of their predecessors, who had witnessed their empire and wealth grow on the backs of the enslaved from Jamaica to Cape Town, and who had, in fact, ushered in the Industrial Revolution through sugar and the whip, suddenly, towards the turn of the nineteenth century, developed serious reservations about slavery. They outlawed the trade in 1807, abolished the practice throughout the empire in 1833, and then set about policing the seas and stopping any ship suspected of carrying human cargo. Overnight, it seemed, the British had gone from champions of slavery to its most steadfast foe, which, understandably, must have irked some of the more recently arrived slave-holding societies, who did not have over two hundred years of mass slaving under their belts, nor had they, obviously, yet benefited from the practice the same way the British had. The British had created the game, won remarkable prizes, yet when more participants arrived to try their luck, the British declared the game illegal, which was hardly keeping with the British sense of fair play.

Unsurprisingly, then, the little island of Zanzibar and its slave ships caught the attention of the British navy, and between 1822 and the end of the century, just as slavery was blossoming, the British government used domestic pressure through a series of treaties, degrees, and regulations to pressure the Omani Sultanate into weakening the slave trade and eventually outlawing it in 1873. The British wanted legitimate commerce; the British wanted the trade in humans to be replaced by the trade in cloves and ivory. The British wanted the slaves, who would be emancipated twenty-four years later in 1897, to become men who hired out their labour for a wage. The British wanted free men dependent on their own labour power to survive. They wanted men who could freely choose, without the fear of the whip, to work for a living or to starve to death.

In many ways, though, slavery was the gift that kept on giving—not only for the British but a host of European powers. Despite the valiant efforts to curtail slavery in the African interior, the practice still flourished, with slavers like Tippu Tip becoming the most powerful men on the continent. Obviously, the British, in the name of humanitarianism and concern for the suffering of their human brethren, could not let Africa slip back into savagery but had to, with great courage and ingenuity, shine a bright light into the blackest of recesses. Africa, more so than ever, needed the West's three great presents to the world: Christianity, commerce, and civilization. In the name of emancipation and uplift, then, the British penetrated the African wilds, threatened or slaughtered the more reactionary and recalcitrant elements, and stayed for eighty years.

Zanzibar is a case in point. In the mad scramble for Africa, the island lost its mainland possessions and, eventually, became a mere protectorate of the British Empire in 1890. Even after destroying both the slave trade and slavery and planting the Union Jack on Zanzibari soil, the British still demanded further concessions from their wards, especially the final say over who ruled the island's residents, which drew the ire of one sultan, Kalid ibn Barghash, who took the Zanzibari throne upon the death of his uncle in 1896, even though the British had desired to install their own candidate as sultan. The British were outraged and reacted how a father, albeit a more traditional and antiquarian one, would react to a petulant child, who could no longer claim innocence or ignorance as to why they had disobeyed Daddy and who could no longer cry oppression when the blows rained down on their skin, for they knew better not to challenge what could not be challenged: the wisdom of he who holds the whip. Despite such a shocking and disrespectful gesture, the British, being a fair-minded lot, presented Kalid with an ultimatum: surrender the throne or face war with the world's mightiest naval power.

The royal marines and sailors went ashore to join the pro-British Zanzibari troops pacing the pathways of Stone Town. Rear Admiral Harry Rawson arrived in port aboard the cruiser St. George and gave the sultan five minutes to submit. And when Khalid did not, when he stayed stubbornly hidden in his palace, when he refused to realize the impossibility of his position, facing the divine providence of British superiority, Rawson ordered the bombardment of Khalid's wooden palace. As a last gasp of resistance, a playful ribbing at the British's expense, Khalid deployed Glasgow, an armed yacht which Queen Victoria had gifted the previous sultan. And although the St. George easily destroyed the ship and its parts fell to the ocean's bottom and although Khlaid surrendered a mere forty minutes later—the shortest war in human history, according to some accounts—Khlaid must have derived a certain satisfaction from hearing that the British had indeed sunk one of its own. They had decimated a gift given by Victoria herself.

The British had won and not just in Zanzibar but throughout the continent. They won so much and so quickly that the more ambitious of imperialists among them were dreaming of railways that would connect Cape Town to Cairo. They devoured so much land so rapidly and disrupted ways of life so efficiently that it was said that the sun never set on the British Empire, meaning, one would guess, that at every second, somewhere among the darker nations, the benevolence and beauty of Her Majesty's people—shining through her armies of soldiers and missionaries and colonial bureaucrats—brightened the dreary lives of her charges and inched them ever closer to status of man: a fully formed human body who prayed to Jesus Christ, spoke English, and worked for his money.

Under the makeshift tents and along the covered tables, the staff have assembled an assortment of dishes—seafood, meats, and the most delicious local fruits—and when the lead guide announces lunch is ready, a great wave of white, not to mention nearly naked, bodies descend upon the food and its makers. The chefs and servers speak in a mixture of Italian, English, and Swahili and encourage their guests to sample from each dish. And we do. We pick and pick and pick from the buffet until our plates are full. We stuff ourselves on fruit and seafood until the juices run from our lips and we wipe our mouths with the back of our hands. We drink and drink and drink until everything appears hazy and sublime, until all movement and thought are effortless and carefree like a beach. We indulge ourselves until we are like a beach. We laugh and stumble over the sand and out into the sun. We have reverted back to our primordial selves before we fell victim to the sin of knowledge, before everything was made complicated by the sheer fact of existence, before life seemed like one big tragedy or, worse, a joke, full of unspeakable horror and terror, which you could only laugh at because to stop and actually think about it and reflect on its true significance would be tantamount to putting a gun your mouth and pulling the trigger. And no one commits suicide on a beach. It's unheard of. No one can die on a beautiful, sandy beach. It is forbidden. It is not allowed. So on the beach, we lie on our backs half-naked and drunk and let all the juices fall from us, since we are only laughter and giggles and no thoughts, never thoughts. On the beach, thinking is forbidden.

On the journey back to Stone Town, the holiday makers clothe their bodies and hide their tanned skin with shorts, t-shirts, and tank tops. Minarets and steeples come closer and closer as the dhow zips back into town. Nakedness has returned to the closet. Respect for the local culture, after all, necessitates a level of prudence and modesty, especially in more conservative places preaching a level of restraint in revealing God's creation in all its shameful glory. Feet still lie naked under the afternoon sun, though, and hands still lather exposed skin with more lotion.

The cups are returned, and the wine has stopped. The only evidence of alcohol remains those traces swimming in the blood, still making everything dreamlike and hallucinatory and unreal, as well as those glassy, happy eyes ensconced behind pairs of black sunglasses.

The crew members lead us in a song, and we all clap and smile and mangle the Swahili words.

"Hakuna Matata," the guide says.

"Hakuna Matata," we shout.

We thank the crew and disembark.

The town disorients even more after the tranquility and privacy of the sandbar. The curio shops and bazars all beckon with their spices and artwork and trinkets. Scooters buzz past usually carrying three times the recommended load. Hawkers sell Messi jerseys and bracelets. The noise of commerce deafens the sounds of the wind and water.

Some holidaymakers make plans for dinner and further drinks. Others confirm with the guide about a dhow sunset cruise. Still others disappear into restaurants and hotels. A few others, though, drift silently into the narrow alleyways of exchange that circle and spiral in no discernible clarity or route, often leaving visitors frustrated yet eventually content to simply disappear into Zanzibar.

These holidaymakers up ahead do not mind the maze, as they saunter about stopping at which ever stall or store catches their fancy, until, for whatever reason, the group splinters at an intersection, with a few going left and the others right. The latter drift and float through the labyrinth and fall further away from the tourist mobs, until they find themselves in a more residential quarter, being blasted by construction workers, apparently, readying this section of town for more tourist development. One house, in particular, draws a long stare from the guests—a three-story dwelling covered in the filmiest of scaffolding. A renovation, or indeed a resurrection, appears to be on the way, as men in mud-stained jeans and shirts carry logs about while others debate and discuss the building in some animation. Could it be another hotel, maybe? One tourist spots a plaque nearby and sashays towards it in her sarong. There, in fading lettering, she reads the following:

> Residence of the famous Arab trader Hamed Muhammed Al-Marjebi (Tipu Tip) who built up a large trading empire in the Eastern Congo in the 19th century with Belgian Colonization of the Congo. He returned to Zanzibar where he acquired many clove plantations and built his house. He died in Zanzibar and is buried nearby.

"Interesting," she whispers to herself and motions for her companions to join her. Interesting, they too, agree, after reading. After asking a few locals, and with a great degree of luck, they find his burial site.

Hamed earned his nicknamed from the sounds of his guns—Tippu Tip, Tippu Tip, Tippu Tip—which during the second half of the nineteenth century fired frequently and with great precision. Tip controlled great swaths of land between the Indian Ocean and Lake Victoria; he ruled over a veritable empire in the African interior. And wherever he went, slaves and ivory would follow. Wherever he went, people would disappear. He served as a guide for European travellers, who became impressed by his business savvy as well as negotiation skills. They liked him, very much so.

Tip's burial site lies hidden on some nondescript side street between ongoing renovation projects. No opportunities for quiet contemplation or sombre reflection exist here; the sounds of drilling and hammering disturb each thought. The tourists note how no markers or plaques adorn his tomb; time and erosion have eaten away at its base, leaving ugly and unsightly holes and blemishes, as if termites had taken it upon themselves to keep the great Tip company. The tomb rests atop rubble and sits at the base of two walls—one iron corrugated, the other cement—that separate Tip's grave from an attractive three-storey building, which from the rooftop, the Indian Ocean must surely be visible. Here on the ground, however, the tourists can only see rocks and a few listless trees. The afternoon sun, though, has broken its way through the leafy canopy and for a moment, its rays illuminate the white, forgotten grave and bathe its cold surface in light. Yet the sunlight only momentarily dissuades the onlookers from noting the obvious: Tip has been set aside. And then after the tourists have had their fill of the burial site, something truly extraordinary happens: They simply walk on and rejoin the rest of Zanzibar's tourists shopping for souvenirs and wave at the second group of tourists, with whom they had just visited the sandbar.

This second group has already made purchases, evident by the large number of bags they carry, and they stroll with a delightful air about them, so content to be here, so content to be experiencing it all. They wander into the old slave market area, and where bodies were once auctioned off to the highest bidder now stands the massive Anglican Church, yet the sombreness of the sight does not diminish the spirit of the tourists—on the contrary. For when they open their guidebooks and turn to the pages dedicated to the church and its history, the visitors learn that its construction began on Christmas day 1873, the same year the market was closed. No creeping sadness hinders their springy gait because the history of this church is the history of the triumph of good over evil. Light conquered darkness. Good men vanquished evil ones. Christianity relegated slavery to the dustbin of history. So when they saunter around the church's perimeter, noting its size and grandeur, they feel comforted in the knowledge that everything that had to happen has, indeed, happened. The world is right. The world is as it should be. Such feelings of security are why the tourists do not look askance at the five stone torsos tied together by chains and sitting in the sunken ground. "Kumbukumbu Ya Historia Ya Watumwa," the plaque reads. "Memory for the slaves." They do not stare into their vacant and cold eyes and beg for forgiveness because such savagery belongs to the past, and the present has no business stirring up history's ghosts. That violence is not of their making, and tourists are not responsible for the sins of their father. They choose instead to align themselves with the church and its symbolism. Inside, their guidebook informs them that the high alter was built on the site of the market's whipping post, where slaves' blood was often spilled. They read, too, that above the pulpit hangs a crucifix made from a tree at Chitambo, in Zambia, the site where David Livingstone's heart lies buried. The tourists like this connection. David Livingstone, a man with the heart and tenacity and ambition of Christ himself, walked into the darkest recesses of Africa and swore to bring light. And he did. He was light embodied. His spirit cut down ignorance and laid waste to barbarity. He nursed the sick back to health. He cured and he healed. But of most of all, he railed against the ungodliness of slavery and its trade. He fought the gospel that preached certain men were nothing but beasts to be beaten. He shamed those who profited from chains and blood and death. He cursed those who used the Bible and its teachings to justify the enslavement of God's finest creature, even though that fine book had always inspired men to do the most un-Christian of things. And men headed his call, and they followed him into deepest and darkest Africa to deliver what is promised to all of God's children: a chance to worship him.

In Livingstone's wake, they have all come to Africa in the name of humanity and progress—in the name of universalism. The West has always tried to replicate itself wherever it has gone and has always endeavoured to implant its traditions and values and gods in places and in people that had not had the good fortune of having them revealed to them across the sky. So just as the Indigenous peoples in sixteenth-century Mexico and Peru could not be punished for not knowing God, Africans in nineteenth-century Tanzania and Uganda and Kenya could not be rebuked for not knowing how to live, which is why all those men arrived to Zanzibar and why they continue to do so. Missionaries, teachers, bureaucrats, investors and entrepreneurs, politicians, technocrats and economists, aid workers, volunteers, tourists have all, in their own ways, helped Africans reach the West. From planting cloves to implementing neoliberal reforms, the West and its adherents have been ever so gracious with their time and expertise in transforming Africa from a Conradian nightmare to a playground for half-naked Westerners. And in return, all they ask for is everything.

These tourists at the Anglican Church do not stay long, nor do they dedicate much thought to its history, for they know the long story is over, the long walk from slavery to freedom has finished. There is nothing left to contemplate. Livingstone won, and Tippu Tip lost. Light trampled darkness, as it always does.

In the evening, they return to their respective hotels, and I return to mine. We take a drink on the patio and watch the sun fade into the sea as it has done forever. And in the distance, the dhows glide across the waters as they, too, have done forever. Only today, they carry people looking a lot like us, a lot like me.

Endnotes

1. All direct quotations about the slave trade in East Africa were taken from the Slave Market Memorial in Stone Town, Zanzibar.

10.

Ghana

Phillip Quaque, né Kweku, was born in the Cape Coast community on the Gold Coast in 1741. This settlement sat on the outskirts of the Cape Coast Castle, one of the largest British slave castles on the West African coast. The date of his birth must have been a Wednesday as Kweku was a common Fante name given to a boy born on that day of the week. The Fante lived along the coast and belonged to the larger Akan cultural group. They diligently served as middlemen between the Europeans on the coast and African merchants further inland. Exchanging guns and other exotic European goods for human cargo, the Fante found themselves operating along a steep cultural divide. Indeed, these forts served as a site for the transaction of humans and goods (although that distinction was seldom made), but also as a place of cultural exchange—a meeting place between two alien cultures, one African and the other European. As the Fante and other Akan groups eagerly vied with each other for the newest European import, some segments of the European population, in this case the British, saw the Gold Coast as an ideal choice site for the advancement of European culture, notably Christianity, into the African continent. In 1754, at the tender and impressionable age of thirteen, young Kweku was sent to England for education as part of a treaty made between the Fante and British. Sponsored by the Society for the Propagation of the Gospel (SPG), Kweku spent eleven years in England and returned Philip Quaque, the new and first African chaplain of Cape Coast Castle. His goal was to proselytize his former countrymen and introduce European culture to an area, apparently, in desperate need of it. He was an alien in his former homeland.

Kweku was greatly influenced by the eleven years he spent in London and by the education he received there. He was baptized in Islington Parish Church in 1759 where his tutor was Mr. Hickman, the local schoolmaster. Afterwards, he came under the tutelage of Reverend John Moore of St Sepulchre's Church, who was impressed by the advancement of young Kweku's learning. On March 25,

1764, Quaque was ordained deacon by the Bishop of Exeter, and on May 1 of the same year, he was ordained priest by the Bishop of London. Now a full-fledged Christian and sufficiently indoctrinated in European culture, Phillip Quaque confidently returned to Cape Coast Cast in February 1766 prepared to eradicate the culture that gave birth to him. His confidence was to be short-lived.

He returned a changed man; he lived in European fashion, with books and mahogany furniture and his first wife was an Englishwoman. Like many others at the fort, he engaged in trade including that lucrative one in humans. And it soon became apparent that a large rife was growing between him and his traditional origins. He ceased to be fluent in Fante or any African language, relied on an interpreter, and mercilessly attacked traditional Akan religious practices. He soon realized that it would take a lot more than the words and work of one man to dislodge these traditional Akan practices, which included the worship of a Supreme Being, widespread ancestor veneration, and investing natural objects with spiritual qualities. The state of the mission was in such disarray that it led Quaque to write the following: "No argument can move their obdulent hearts to a better mode of thinking; it therefore seems to me that the justice of God's proceedings with impenitent sinners still pursues this race of men, if I may be allowed this expression, for their unjust dealings and practices."[1] Quaque was, indeed, facing an uphill battle.

One of the traditional practices that particularly irked Phillip was their funerary rites. On October 20, 1778, the funeral of Caboceer (chief or big man) Cudjo (an Akan day name for a boy born on a Monday) was exhibited. This event was characterized by firing of muskets, shouting of songs, an abundance of drinking, exuberant dancing, the visitation of many other coastal Caboceerw, and the sacrifice of many individuals. This occasion had such a joyous feeling to it that it prompted Quaque to write that the scene appeared to him "more like harvest feats than that of mourning or sorrow." The sight of individuals being sacrificed greatly alarmed Quaque, but he was, of course, unaware of the significance of these events for Akan religion beliefs. Because the Akan held that both the living and the dead were linked together and the dead influenced the course of events for the living, the departed had to be constantly placated to ensure a favourable outcome. Thomas Thompson, the predecessor to Quaque and often called the first missionary to the Gold Coast, understood this better than Quaque. In the early 1750s he wrote, "They rather think that the soul, after Death, keeps Haunt of the Body, and is latent in, or near its Repository; and it must be grounded upon the Imagination, that they have a Custom of setting Pots and Basons, with other such Furniture and Utensils, at the Graves of their Kindred; there to stand and remain for the Uses of the Dead."[2] In any event, Quaque simply found these practices a hindrance to his work.

Towards the end of Quaque's life, a profound, spiritual and moral crisis enveloped him. After being a victim of European cultural imperialism and then an agent of that very same system, Philip Quaque reverted back to his ancestral culture and religion. By the 1790s, he left the castle walls and built a family house in the Cape Coast town. Moreover, his second and third wives were both African women and the Western concept of individualism seemed to have chided with his newfound duties to his extended family. Although Quaque's return to his African roots is well attested, his contemporaries steadfastly denied it and attributed his transformation to senile dementia. Quaque was the SPG's pride and joy, and it would not behoove them to promote or acknowledge his choice of a return to Akan practices and beliefs. Having been forcibly straddled across the cultural divide from that day in 1753, when his relatives had pledged him to the British, Quaque decided to opt for the customs of his childhood. In 1811, on his death bed, Phillip wrote, "The state of this unsuccessful mission, I formerly had some hopes of its growth, but at present on the face of things bears but an indifferent aspect." Death was quickly approaching and Quaque was once again born anew—he was Kweku again.

I wrote those lines over ten years ago as an introduction to my master's thesis on the contributions of the Akan cultural group to the religious practices of enslaved Africans in Jamaica. Kweku represented a life pulled in different directions; he felt torn between the culture of his childhood and the culture of his new European overlords. It was as if some cruel person had tied each of his limbs to a horse and shouted "March!" He chided his earlier African beliefs, yet returned to them as death approached, as if they were his own personal hospice, providing the necessary comfort and security before the long sleep. For me, his life served as a perfect metaphor for the resiliency of culture, as even under the brutalist of conditions and under the threat of the severest punishments, people, their hearts and minds, remember what it was they once believed and loved. Even under slavery, people remember what had long been forbidden.

I had never been to Ghana (or anywhere in Africa for that manner) nor Jamaica. Yet I pieced together my thesis from hundreds of secondary sources and a handful of primary accounts of Europeans who had visited West Africa or had resided in Jamaica. Yet a book is not a place. A page can never capture the magnitude of a moment. A sentence can never truly resuscitate what was taken or breathe life back into what was stolen. A word is never truly what it represents. Literature, at its best, can only represent a sliver of life. Writing can only hold history, its weight, for a moment before cracking and then spilling its contents. Language does not yet have the power to articulate certain horrors, which are best experienced as a wave of sensations creeping over the body and through the skin before settling within.

Along the coast of Ghana, the sun is shining, and the sky is cloudless. But I am standing in darkness, deep underground, in the slave dungeons of Cape Coast Castle. Sunlight still bursts through small openings to illuminate the damp and dreary confines. The dimness makes the streams more revealing, robust, and explosive. Their presence here is cruel, a mockery. The light magnifies what no longer is allowed. The light burns and then destroys what it touches as it does with ants held under a piece of glass.

Today, the dungeons are empty, except for us. No slaves lie shackled to the walls or languish in puddles of their own excrement. Piles of dried human bodies, hundreds on top of hundreds, do not wait for the ships to arrive offshore, do not twitch or shudder at the thought of being sent to the New World. The naked bodies succumbed to disease or death are not taken by fully-clothed officers and thrown to the waters and their sharks. Today, it is only us: the guide and his tourists.

The guide has a languid air and a breezy step. He seems unperturbed by the heat and suffocating humidity that quietly and strategically licks away at my sustenance. Fifteen of us follow the guide through the barren rooms. Five of us are white, myself included, and we sweat the most. The other four seem to be a family, and the mother and father, dressed in light, breathable cotton, wear nametags advertising their affiliation with a church. They stand at attention and follow the guide's words as if he were the teacher and they the students, they the conscientious and diligent pupils, like me, committing to memory every date and person mentioned so to ace the inevitable pop quiz and to separate themselves, the special ones, from the merely mundane.

We are in class, they and I, and when the teacher, a white man, shouts a question, we bark the answer in unison:

"Who were the first Europeans to arrive to Cape Coast?"

"The Portuguese!"

"What were they primarily interested in""

"Gold and ivory!"

"Who came after the Portuguese?"

"The Dutch, Brits, Swedes, Danes, French!"

"And what were they interested in?"

"Slaves. Slaves. Slaves."

Such hardworking students would know, and they, the white family, know too. I bet they know. I bet they know that this castle once had a church located just above where we now stand, in a sunnier and breezier spot, and just a few floors above from where the slaves slept. I bet they know that between 1664 and 1807—the 143 years that this castle belonged to the British and served as the grand emporium of the British slave trade—Biblical phrases, God's word, were whispered in the halls and rooms and chambers and floated over the dungeons and cannons and the staircase leading to the canoes and then to the ships and then to the Americas. I bet they know that for forty-two of those years, the Castle's chaplain was a man named Philip Quaque, an African from the Gold Coast who was taken and taught about God in England, and then was returned during the height of the slave trade to speak lovingly about God right here in this castle. I stop myself and return my gaze to our guide. Such anger is not mine to have. I have been wrong, too. I have been wrong in deep and profound ways.

Many years earlier in my African diaspora course, I watched a documentary of Henry Louis Gates, the great African American scholar and Harvard professor, travelling along the Niger River in Mali towards the fabled city of Timbuktu. He spoke about how the city had been one of the great centres of learning, how scholars the world over had come to this place to study. It was the West African epicentre of Islamic erudition. He spoke about these things to counter depressingly common views of Africa as a place bereft of culture and history. He spoke about these things to challenge hurtful stereotypes and lazy representations. Yet in parts of the documentary, he wears a Harvard shirt while speaking to people or to the camera about African culture and African history. And when our Jamaican Canadian professor asked the class what we thought about his choice of attire, we all agreed it was distasteful and passive aggressive—arrogant. Yet a few years later, in one of my depressingly common drunken rants, I took this critique a step too far when I suggested that Louis Gates had somehow forgotten what it meant to be African. He had somehow betrayed his ancestors by selling his, as well as their soul, to the cult of American individuality and scorning a collectivist ethos central to many African cultural groups and communities. In those few sentences, I had thrown my allegiance behind a train of thought whose terminus is racism: There is only way to be African, and there is only one way to be a member of its diaspora. In those few sentences, I had tried to take the complexities of history, the tangled and harsh legacies of slavery, and reduce them to a guidebook. As a white man living in the long shadow of slavery, I had attempted to offer advice on what it meant to be a member of the African diaspora because I had a read a few books. I had entered a conversation not mine to have.

This episode still shames me yet also provides a lens for me to analyse my own thinking about Africa and its diaspora as a white man. The episode reminds that I will never understand the complexity of that relationship, nor will I discover it in a book, for that relationship is first lived and then written about.

In a secluded corner of the castle, our guide lingers near a heavy door, slightly ajar, revealing the darkness behind. "This is where misbehaving slaves were kept, and this is where they died."

Our guide opens the door a little more. And then a little more.

"Please step carefully, and watch your head."

We shuffle inside, a little reluctant, a little nervous, and in the cell, the pit, a true heart of darkness, we stand in a half-circle in silence. When the guide closes the door and the humidity and the blackness descend, I feel as if I have punched in the gut. I feel my body become alert to the danger, the place's explicit threat. I feel my body sweat more and more, trying to cool itself down, yet no amount of perspiration can provide relief from this room. It is powerfully suffocating. I feel my body lying under a mountain of dirt, buried alive, and I feel my hands working through the soil desperately searching for the surface but nothing, only more dirt in my fingers, in my nostrils, mouth, and lungs. It is such a visceral, unexpected reaction that I wonder if this is what dying feels like: light pushed aside to welcome a never-ending darkness.

"Slaves were left here to die," the guide says. "No food. No water." He scans our sweating, suffering bodies. "It wouldn't take long, right?" We nod. "Europeans would come to check every so often to see if they were still alive. And when they were dead, their bodies were tossed into the ocean. For the sharks."

Silence amid the stones and memories.

"To honour the memory of those who died here, let us have a minute of silence. One minute please of silence."

When I was a boy, and due to an error of judgment, I found myself locked in my apartment's basement storage room. I pounded on the door and screamed until I was hoarse. I begged invisible forces to come to my aid and deliver me from the darkness into the light. Beyond my sobbing and shouting, what I remember most was the palpable sense of doom that gripped my little body. I thought I would die in that little room. My skin and flesh would become food for the rats that surely slept somewhere among the garbage bags. I would never see my friends and family again. Everything I loved was gone. My life was over. I knew it and could do nothing. Only wait. Only watch.

Is that what it was like? Was it the palpable sense that life was about to end? Inside these walls, would an enslaved person only think of what might have been? Would they soothe themselves with memories of their past, a kind word, a loving gesture? Or would they hold onto their righteous indignation and their rebellious spirit until life finally departed them? And for those who marched through the Door of No Return, boarded the ships, and then descended into the hull, that hellish belly, to exist in excrement and hunger for months on end, would they experience a measure of solace when they escaped their chains and tossed themselves into the Atlantic's waves? In graduate school, based on a thorough review of the literature, I argued that suicide among the enslaved was an act of resistance—a rebellion against the slavery forced upon them. I reasoned, in my comfortable chair, that to die by one's own hands was an assault on the very essence of servitude. You cannot have my body, they said. My body is not yours to have.

But as I stand and sweat in this tomb, I cannot say anything about the thoughts and actions of those who perished here or in the Atlantic. Empathy is a virtue. To think upon how you may feel standing in the shoes of another is a noble intellectual pursuit. Yet it remains purely intellectual, completely of the mind. Sometimes the experiences are so far removed, the suffering so distant and unknowable, that to ascribe feelings to those with whom you empathize renders thought mute. Nothing in my world can relate to the experiences of those who died here. Any attempt at empathy is an insult to their history. I cannot know their suffering, and to try to feel what they did is to only pity them, and pity extinguishes all thought. Empathy transforms into fantasy and the unreal—where monsters roam and heroes die tragic but noble deaths. Instead, I want to extend the world of Cape Coast Castle into my own. I want to understand how those who died in this room or drowned in the Atlantic or were worked to death in Brazil, Jamaica, or Canada connect to my corporeal existence in the here and now. What is remarkable about slavery is not its suffering but how the institution has been confined to the past, how its abolition has been celebrated as evidence of humanity's march towards greater enlightenment and benevolence. What is remarkable is how some think that simply turning the page on slavery means underscoring its contemporary irrelevance—a mere castle to visit to reflect on how awful things once were. Yet slavery's consequences are real and reach past these white walls into the fabric of the modern world. Slavery built the modern world. I can understand this intellectually, but I can never understand it as corporeally, as in the flesh, as those who feel the legacies of racialized slavery in their skin and deep in their bones. And no amount empathy will ever make me.

Phillip Quaque is buried in the courtyard in a nondescript, perfunctory grave. Marked off by rope, the site consists of four flattened stones shaped as a cross, on the left one is carved "P" and on the right "Q."

"Phillip Quaque" the guide says, "Hero or traitor"?

"Traitor," a Black man answers, and a few others agree. He wears a light blue t-shirt with a map of Africa emblazoned across it. The continent appears as a stitching of different colourful threads bisecting one another, a knitting of a kaleidoscope, a vibrant sweater, a million different hues flowing together as one.

"He was a traitor," the Black man repeats, and I thought so, too, when I read about him in the library over a decade ago. Now, I equivocate. He was certainly not a hero, but nor was he a traitor. A hero for whom? A traitor to what? These designations reduce the complexities of time and place to mere rhetoric. Standing over his grave, I sense simple condemnation is far too simple a reaction to a life as complex as his, to a body and mind that was forced to take a mishmash of competing ideas, somehow balance them, and live a moral, Christian life in milieus—both in Europe and Africa—that had taken these teachings and made them compatible with condemning any practices unfamiliar to the church and condoning those practices related to the buying and selling of human beings. His self was split, and he had not the tools to stich himself together. And I wonder if his eternal punishment for his participation in the slave trade—being branded a traitor by returning diasporans—is just or excessive.

At the castle's rear, we pass through the Door of No Return and see the stone staircase leading into the water, the last few steps of Africa. The Black man in the Africa t-shirt steps towards the gently moving Atlantic—that great highway of blood, bodies, and culture—and turns to face the castle and his friend holding a camera. He does not smile. He does not wave. He only stands on the staircase that led millions of his ancestors to the New World. I do not know how he processes this moment—his return to the place from which his ancestors were stolen centuries ago.

At the foot of the stone staircase, where land and sea meet, the ocean softly lathers the rocky ground. The waters are calm—a flat field of cerulean blue. The sky is cloudless and hazy with heat. Everything feels languid and slow, the simplest task an impossible chore. A few gulls swoop in the gentle breeze that mercifully swats the humidity away if only for a second or two. One glides away from shore, hovering between the ocean and the sky, and as its wings flutter further from shore, flying into the horizon, the blues become indistinguishable and form a great palisade just beyond my sight, and there the world seems to stop; there it would seem no ship could pass, no man or woman could enter.

Behind the man in the Africa shirt, a shirtless local descends the steps and wades into the water to his waist. His head glances to the surface as if he were looking for something, as if he had just dropped a bracelet or a coin into the water, nothing too serious or alarming but a trinket still worthy of a search, no matter how perfunctory the effort. He splashes some water over his face and chest, and I imagine what the water would feel like over my skin. Another local dressed in a red top and bottoms joins him in the water, and the mingling of red with the sparkling, light blue reveals a contrast I cannot help but note. He carries a green bag filled with clothing to be washed. The two men stand behind each other as I am sure they have countless times before. Another day. Only another day.

To the left of the staircase, dozens of fishing boats painted in blues, greens, and reds rest. For my eyes, they look like oversized canoes. Few men mingle between them lifting and sorting white nets that when bundled together resemble gigantic cotton balls. Differently styled flags adorn the boats, symbolic of each's personality, perhaps, the secret qualities that keep them safe when they drift miles from shore or are caught in the most dangerous of currents. One flies the American flag, the significance of which I can only guess. A smaller boat is called "Hazard," a gentle rebuke, I hope, to the notion that size equals strength. Ten or so wooden benches bisect each, and from the stern to the bow, they grow and then shrink in size following the curvature of the boat's body. I reckon each could fit a dozen men comfortably, fifteen if pressed, and I wonder if these beautifully crafted vessels resemble at all the ones that only a few hundred years ago transported the human cargo from these stony steps to the ships awaiting offshore. And if they indeed bore some resemblance, did the slave traders worry about overloading the vessels with human bodies, not necessarily out of concern for the safety of the passengers, but because their future return on their investment necessitated the safe, within reason of course, transport of their property from here to there. Did it still make financial sense to try and fit forty men in one boat, if in all likelihood four or five would fall and disappear into the waves en route? I have heard some stories that when some men and women saw those larger ships bobbing in the distance, they jumped from the boats transporting them to the sea and simply sank to the bottom, preferring instead to have their lungs fill with salty water than to breathe in whatever hell awaited them among the white men who spoke in strange tongues and traded in guns and flesh.

"We now call this the Door of Return," the guide says. We adjust our eyes on his lithe body and his slender arms waving at the imposing door behind him.

"Some have begun their return journey home to Africa."

He tells us that in 1998, the remains of two enslaved Africans—Samuel Carson and Crystal—were returned to Ghana and laid to rest at Assin Manso, once an important trading site on the slave route, located about a thirty minute drive north of Cape Coast. Carson's remains were disinterred from the Brooklyn Naval Cemetery in New York, where Samuel, it is believed, escaped to after the planned 1822 Denmark Vesey rebellion was foiled in Charleston South Carolina. Vesey, a former slave turned carpenter, was a gifted orator, who held meetings at the African Methodist Episcopal Church and at his home. There, he would read from the Bible how the children of Israel were delivered out of Egypt from bondage, and then he would proceed to organize the largest slave rebellion in American history, in which his nine thousand followers planned to set fire to the city and kill every white man in sight. And although Vesey was betrayed and executed and the church was burned and Black life was further curtailed, it is possible that Carson was at Vesey's meetings and took those ideas with him to New York, where he lived as a free man and then back to Africa as a deceased one.

Crystal did not have a name when her remains were unearthed in Jamaica at the enslaved quarters of Seville Plantation. Researchers named her Crystal because they found a pecked crystal stopper among her remains that they believed was associated with her burial. They determined she died as a teenager from chronic anemia, likely resulting from deficiencies in iron and vitamins. Beyond these cursory details about her cause of death, nothing else is known about her brief life, except that in 1998, she was returned to Africa—an event laced with spiritual and symbolic significance. New world slaveholders understood the significance Africa held for the enslaved; they knew what the continent represented for those who toiled day in and day out under the hot sun and whip. Jamaican slave masters, in particular, developed cruel tactics to remove the memory of Africa, or its idea, from those who worked under their control.

I had read about how the enslaved upon death believed their spirit would return to Africa. They believed their days of torment were over, slavery only a nightmare for the living, and soon they would find themselves among family, friends, and ancestors. They believed in this return so much that they did not hesitate to cut their own throats or throw their bodies into the ocean whenever the opportunity presented itself because the extinguishing of the corporeal body—the avenue towards enrichment for their overseers—was a small price to pay for total liberation. And even when the masters hung the bodies of the suicides from trees to illustrate to the living that the dead did not in fact get to return to their homelands, the enslaved did not drop their razors because they knew that in death, the fleshy body meant next to nothing; it was their spirit that returned to Africa.

"The remains of the two Africans were returned through the Door of No Return," the guide says, and we follow him from the sea, boats, and steps through the door and back into the castle to symbolize the diaspora's return home and to consecrate a link that slavery and the slave trade had sought to sever. And even as an outsider, for whom Africa existed only as an intellectual project to disentangle, I sense the significance of this act of return for the New World diasporans, whose histories they were repeatedly told began in chains and bondage and not in the stories and traditions of Africa.

Near the castle's exit, the guide stops at a plaque fastened to the stone wall. "Here is a written apology from the local chiefs for the role their ancestors played in the slave trade and in aiding the Europeans to take so many Africans to the New World." Among us, there is silence. "More than that, this is a reminder that slavery still exists all over the world and it is hell on earth." There is still silence. "We need to ensure that what happened here at Cape Coast Castle never happens again."

"Who wrote that?" a large Black man in sunglasses asks, pointing at the plaque.

"The descendants of the chiefs who participated in the slave trade," the guide repeats.

"They apologized?"

"Yes."

Among us, there is silence.

"In every transaction and in every trade," the guide continues, "you need buyers and sellers. There are always two parties. There is always a shared responsibility."

I feel myself become agitated. I look to the ground, then to the distance, and then to the ground again. The diplomacy of the guide unsettles me; his reluctance to cast blame and judgment bothers me. I worry he does this for my benefit. I worry he dares not offend white sensibilities, infamous the world over for their acute defence mechanisms. I worry he dares not upset me.

"I blame the buyers," the man says. "I blame the buyers," he repeats. "There was something in their heads," he says. "Something in their heads."

The guide smiles.

"We could argue this all day," he says by way of conclusion and proceeds to thank everyone for coming.

I stare at the row of cannons aiming towards the sea, and I ask myself who benefitted. I ask myself who prospered in this trade of human beings, in this transaction that took millions upon millions of bodies from these lands and transplanted them in Brazil, Jamaica, the United States. I ask myself who benefits from this discourse of mutual responsibility in which buyers used human flesh to finance the Industrial Revolution and modernity and the sellers suffered through depopulation, underdevelopment, resource scarcity, and war. I ask myself who benefits from this erasure of cause and effect, this historic myopia surrounding consequence, and this wishful thinking that relegates slavery and its effects to morality lessons, informative museums, and sombre slave castles. Who benefits from the separation of the past and present?

In the Cape Coast Castle washroom, I remove my sweat-soaked t-shirt and replace it with the extra one I bought just for this occasion. I do not do well in the heat. My sweat exposes me and casts me as vulnerable, a body unable to adapt to the local conditions. I run the tap and splash some water over my face. I stare at myself in the mirror for a second and watch the beads of sweat return. I remember a decade earlier when I would take breaks from reading and writing at Scott Library and would go to the washroom and then for a cigarette. These little breaks broke my twelve-hour library days up into manageable pieces, and I savoured each one. They gave me an opportunity to reflect not only on how much I had accomplished and how good it would feel to finally finish my thesis and be done with it all but also on how my argument was taking shape, how strong was my evidence, how lucid the structure. I thought about how well I linked Ghana to Jamaica—two countries I had never been to but had read dozens of books about—and about how well I matched the accounts of slave traders along the west coast of Africa with the accounts of slaveholders residing in Jamaica. Should that quote really go in that chapter, I would ask myself. Maybe I should add it earlier. But amid my persistent questioning and never-ending self-doubt, I would always congratulate myself for pulling together a coherent argument concerning the relationship between Africa and the Americas. I took disparate and seemingly unrelated pieces of history and stuck them together to create something unique, tangible, and worthwhile, with a logical conclusion. I felt myself an artist who makes sense of the world through creation. I felt myself an archaeologist who resurrects a disappeared people through combing through their remains. I felt I understood.

In Cape Coast Castle, those feelings have dissolved into frustration. I wish to understand beyond the books and the dates and the numbers. I wish to feel the pull of return. I wish to be part of it. But for that, I must be another person with another set of experiences, another understanding of the past and present. It is foolish and disrespectful to even try. There is no one way to interpret Cape Coast Castle, just as there is no way to ignore its significance.

Before I reenter the outside world, I turn to face the castle's interior. Should I go back in? Have I spent long enough inside? Should I revisit the museum, the dungeons, the governor's room, the Door of No Return? I hear the outside world barking for my attention. I hear Ghana going about its business, fighting forwards. And I step towards the noise and life and away from the castle because I can.

Standing amid the voices and motorbikes, the taxicabs and merchants, I remember the flush of pride I felt when I finished writing the final paragraph of my thesis and felt satisfied with the way I concluded my argument and the way I tied together all its different parts—how my sentences and syntax made history seem so tidy and finite, with a clear beginning and end:

> *In slave-holding Jamaica, therefore, various traditional African religions came together and worked towards a coherent religiosity that suited their needs under the conditions of slavery. The interplay among enslaved Africans with different yet closely related religious beliefs fostered the development of Pan-African religious experience in Jamaica.*

I felt I had engaged the literature and pinpointed a significant gap. I felt I had combined an adequate number of primary and secondary sources from both sides of the Atlantic:

> *In the slaveholding context of Jamaica, where ethnic identities eventually succumbed to the assimilative influences of Pan-Africanization, these Pan-African practices were new in the sense that they required the input of a variety of African religious viewpoints but old in*

the sense that they incorporated African religious principles.

I had met the requirements of history. My methodology was sound; its shortcomings were duly noted. Each fact was meticulously noted, emulating the best practices of the most thorough and fastidious of scholars:

> *The transformation, therefore, that these African religious principles and practices underwent in Jamaica did not make them any less African. The religious practices of the Akan certainly played a part in these emergent Pan-African practices, but the Akan element was only one ingredient in a broader Pan-African mixture that was recreated on Jamaican soil.*

And when I finally handed in my thesis, I smiled and whispered to myself "On to the next." I had finished with Cape Coast, Ghana, Africa. From that history, I had found what I needed and taken what I required. I had achieved my master's degree; I was an expert in slavery, a master of the arts. I could choose to further my studies of slavery at the PhD level, or I could choose a different topic entirely. I felt free.

When I finally turn my back to Cape Coast Castle and get into a taxi and drive away, a similar choice presents itself to me. I could further reflect on the castle's significance in shaping the world I see before me. I could further do my part to create awareness of slavery's legacies, its continued grip on the modern world. I could further work to unpack the privileges that have afforded me the freedom to visit Ghana as a well-to-do white man. Or I could simply put it from my mind. I could choose to think about more pleasant, sunnier things.

And although this book represents my attempt to situate myself in a world largely defined by slavery's weight and to trace my own story in relation to Africa through unlearning many of the harmful lessons my Canadian upbringing taught me about the continent, this project, nonetheless, remains a choice I was free to make. For many, Cape Coast's significance simply cannot be ignored; its effects are non-negotiable. They cannot easily move on to the next topic. Racism is not a mere topic of investigation; its significance is not found in books or in the archives. Racism is lived, and its effects are felt.

I know that despite my earnest efforts to learn about slavery and its legacies, my whiteness protects me from certain realities. I am shielded from certain harms; I am sheltered from certain storms. These words of mine can only express so much.

Endnotes

1. The quotations attributed to Quaque are from Priestly, Margaret, "Philip Quaque of Cape Coast." *Africa Remembered: Narratives by West Africans from the Era of the Slave Trade*, edited by Philip Curtin, University of Wisconsin Press, 1968, pp. 99-139.
2. Thompson, Thomas. *An Account of Two Missionary Voyages by the Appointment of the Society for the Propagation of the Gospel in Foreign Parts. The one to New Jersey in North America, the Other from America to the Coast of Guiney.* London, 1758.

Afterword

Rwanda

Twenty-one-year-old Patrick Wood Crusius drove from Allen, Texas, a suburb of Dallas, to El Paso on the American-Mexican border, around a thousand kilometres away. The most direct route between the cities follows the I-20, a relatively straight stretch of asphalt that traverses barren desert, the loneliness only reprieved by mid-sized communities such as Odessa and Midland, whose lights in the desert night must appear as the warmest of friends after a long, solemn drive. Crusius, though, was not technically alone on his journey: He had his phone of course, a portal to people all over the world, as well as his AK-47.

Upon arriving in the multicultural city of seven hundred thousand in the mid-morning hours of August 3, 2019, Crusius uploaded a four-page manifesto to an 8Chan message board at approximately 10:15 a.m. He warns of an impending attack in response to the "Hispanic invasion of Texas," an attack which he himself will perpetrate to defend his country from "cultural and ethnic replacement."[1] For Crusius, El Paso represented the epicentre of such an invasion, the locus where migrants amassed like locusts along the Rio Grande and planned to lay the plentiful fields of America fallow.

Around 10:30 a.m., Crusius parked his car at the local Walmart, grabbed his weapon, and walked towards the entrance.

By 11:00 a.m., over twenty people would be dead, dozens more injured.

Four months earlier in May, at a rally in Florida, the president of the United States, Donald Trump, stood at a podium in front of an adoring audience of supporters. Behind him, rallygoers wore white hats with USA emblazoned on them; a child of no more than ten held a "Make America Great Again" sign. The president spoke about them, about them who had walked from El Salvador, Honduras, and Guatemala, about them who hadnow arrived to the southern borders of Texas, New Mexico, and Arizona.[2]

"The wall would stop it," the president corrected an audience member, who had suggested Trump's proposed border wall would slow them down.

"When you have fifteen thousand people marching up, and you have hundreds and hundreds of people, and you have two or three border security guards ... people who can't use weapons ... how do you stop these people?"

As the president uttered the words "fifteen thousand," he shot his right arm forwards into the crowd, his hand opened, fingers wide apart. At "hundreds and hundreds," he straightened it again, shooting his hand towards his fans, as if to indicate a dangerous force encroaching upon their land, families, lives, a marauding army ready to colonize and then destroy everything they hold dear—values, language, culture—and a looming threat prepared to destroy the America they know and love.

An invasion.

How do you stop an invasion?

Donald Trump had worried about this invasion for some time.

In July 2015, Trump tweeted "WHAT U REALLY SHOULD B ANGRY ABT IS THE INVASION OF MILLIONS OF ILLEGALS TKING OVER AMERICA! NOT Donald Trump." In the same year at a Houston-area event, Trump said "Everything's coming across the border. The illegals, the cars, the whole thing—it's like a big mess, blah. It's like vomit."[3]

One supporter at the Florida rally must have sensed the president's frustration at the many legal and political hurdles that have kept his wall unfinished and the invasion unstopped. This ally must have thought that the president had exhausted all existing channels and that extraordinary measures were needed for extraordinary times. And this devotee must have realized Trump was the only authority figure who would entertain such an idea, the only person brave enough to endorse what needed to be done.

"How do you stop these people?" the president asked.

"Shoot them!" the supporter suggested.

The advice stopped the president in mid-sentence. He chuckled but was then momentarily rendered silent. He turned away from the crowd, closed his eyes, and let a smirk form across his lips. In those few seconds of quiet and introspection, what thoughts must have drifted through his mind? He had the crowd at his mercy. He had legitimized their long-standing grievances. And now, here in Florida, a supporter had suggested what was previously only thought or maybe whispered among similarly thinking friends and allies. What was Trump responsible for?

"Shoot them."

He gazed at his crowd. Behind him, the men and women tentatively grinned, unsure of the reactions allowed, unsure of whether murder was something the president would joke about. The few children wore blank expressions, young faces ready to be instructed about the appropriate emotions to form, a smile, a scowl.

"Shoot them."

The president smiled and gripped the podium.

"Only in the Panhandle can you get away with that stuff."

The men and women smiled and cheered and laughed. They clapped and clapped and clapped.

"Only in the Panhandle," the president repeated.

He smiled.

On August 9, less than a week after the El Paso shooting, I walk through the rooms of the Kigali Genocide Memorial. Twenty-five years earlier, between April and July 1994, Hutu extremists marched through Kigali and the surrounding countryside armed with machetes and lists of opponents and proceeded to slaughter close to a million Tutsis, Twa, and moderate Hutus. The militias received lists of prominent Tutsis and hunted them down. They set up roadblocks, checked IDs, and murdered anyone whose cards read Tutsi. Thousands seeking sanctuary in churches were massacred. Neighbours murdered neighbours. Families turned on families. For four months in 1994, Rwanda ate itself while the world watched.

The remains of close to 250,000 people are buried at the centre. Researchers still try to determine the identities of those buried. Much space still exists on the memorial walls, ready to be filled with names, identities, histories, and remembrance. The blank, black spaces profoundly reveal the work still needed to be done—the lives needed to be exhumed and etched into the annals of history. To the left of the name Kayiranga Janvier, for example, and all that name evokes for those who knew Janvier, is only cold, black rock. Below the name Kundumukiza Alice is only more ample room.

The memorial displays the history of the genocide in a chronological fashion and traces it antecedents to the German and Belgian colonial periods. The colonialists, armed with the latest racial classification theories and a keen desire to extract Rwanda's riches with the least amount of resistance, cemented and reified what had only been tangentially adhered to: ethnic difference. Seemingly overnight, the Europeans took the history of Rwanda and reduced it to Hutu and Tutsi. The former, and the colony's largest cultural group, were said to be natural farmers and worked best without education or access to positions of power; the latter, meanwhile, were said to be natural rulers who excelled at administration, leadership, and ruling. Naturally, such favouritism did not sit well with the Hutu majority, and resentment brewed and strengthened as the colonial period drew to a close. The Hutu Revolution, tacitly supported by both Roman Catholic clergy as well as some Belgian personnel, started on November 1, 1959, when rumours of the death of a Hutu leader by Tutsi hands spread throughout the hills and mountains. Vengeance sprang from bodies as naturally as saliva, sweat, and blood, and Hutus took their grievances out on thousands of Tutsi bodies. On January 28, 1961, a Hutu coup finally abolished the Tutsi monarchy; an independent republic was declared, and an all-Hutu government was born.

The Tutsis who survived fled to neighbouring Uganda, and between 1959 and 1973, they were joined by 700,000 other Tutsis, whom the ruling Hutus had ethnically cleansed. The exiled Tutsis formed an army named the Rwanda Patriotic Force (RPC), and on October 1, 1990, they invaded Rwanda, launching the country into civil war and internally displacing thousands.

The propaganda room is particularly enthralling. Within the swirling rumours of an imminent Tutsi attack, Hutu propagandists went to work. In the lead up to the genocide, the radio and newspapers were just as destructive as the machete and bullet. The memorial focuses on one publication in particular—*Kangura*, the marrow of anti-Tutsi hate speech. The French- and Kinyarwanda-language magazine was founded in 1990 by Hassan Ngeze, who won notoriety for becoming one of the most vicious propagandists during the genocide's build up. For only 100 Rwanda francs, a Hutu could have all their fears, biases, and hatreds confirmed and then magnified. For only 100 Rwanda francs, a Hutu could peer at cartoons depicting Paul Kagame, leader of the RPF, and his army marching over coffins filled with Hutu bodies. For only 100 Rwanda francs, a Hutu could absorb advice from Negze himself, including his infamous Hutu ten commandments, in which he instructs his followers, among other admonishments, to never marry a Tutsi woman, an act tantamount to treason, and to never pity a Tutsi.

Charles never pitied the Tutsi when he killed one with his bare hands. He never pitied his Tutsi neighbours when he pointed them out to the

Hutu mobs ransacking their property, homes, and families. He never pitied the Tutsi because you do not pity the villain, the usurper, the cockroach. This is what he learned from the radio and the newspapers and the leaders. This is what he learned for 100 Rwanda francs.

I am sitting on a bench under a leafy, shady tree in the village of Mybo, part of the Mayange village cluster in Rwanda's Bugesera district, located forty kilometres south of Kigali. The landscape here is flatter, browner—a sharp contrast to the rolling, verdant hills of the capital. Such topography has made the area more prone to poverty, unemployment, and illness. The Rwandan government has targeted the Mayange cluster for development programs and economic initiatives not only because of the area's unfortunate geography but also because this district has become an experiment in reconciliation: In these villages, perpetrators and victims of the genocide live and work side by side.

Around me, children kick a football around, and adults ride past on bicycles. Women sweep the dust away from the doors to their square-shaped homes. Everywhere, the unmistakable leaves of banana trees droop and dangle above the ground and next to containers used to haul water. Chickens strut through the brush, and the familiar call of cows breaks the silence. The village has the air of a farming community—one determined to survive against the odds. Yet Mybo is different from other farming settlements I have visited, as every now and then, and despite my efforts, I find myself gazing at the adults, particularly the men milling about, and wondering whether they killed anyone in April 1994.

Mybo is a reconciliation village, one of seven established by Prison Fellowship International, a Christian organization, in the aftermath of the genocide. The initiative was spearheaded by Pastor Déo Gashagaza after he visited men responsible for killing his forty-five family members in prison. In 1995, God told Gashagaza to go into the prisons, and he did—on the condition God grant him love for the killers. Behind the bars, the génocidaires mocked and threatened Gashagaza and wished he had been among those they had killed. But as he recited lines from Isaiah 61:1, about bringing light to the dark places, the men behind bars quieted and listened to his words.

Charles has labourer hands, large and strong. He has worked these fields most of his life—harvesting mangoes, avocadoes, and bananas—save for the seven years he spent in prison for participating in the genocide. There, he says he still harboured nothing but resentment and hatred while waiting for his victims to take their vengeance on him. I watch his hands while he speaks because it feels safer than watching him, lest he turn and accidentally see the judgment draped across my face, which I so desperately try to hide.

Seven years after the genocide, in 2001, Rwanda's prisons sheltered 125,000 génocidaires awaiting trial. With the country's criminal justice system overburdened—some estimated it would take hundreds of years for each perpetrator to be tried—local leaders, including Gashagaza, turned to the gacaca courts, an ancient form of community-centred justice in which elders conduct open-air hearings with the offenders and community members to determine the punishment. The gacaca tradition encourages offenders to confess to their crimes so that their truth may eventually lead to a sense of closure, a feeling of peace, for their victims' families as well as their own redemption.

Charles grew up with Tutsis. They were his neighbours and friends. In school, he remembers Tutsis and Hutus being identified by their ethnicity, but he had no animosity for the Tutsis, no hatred for a boy simply because he was Tutsi. This changed over time, Charles says, as the RPF gained strength in Uganda and finally invaded in 1990. His neighbours were no longer his neighbours with names, personalities, opinions, histories. They were a threat. They were an enemy. They were Tutsi. He believed what he read, and he believed what he heard. And by the time Habyarmina's plane was shot down on April 6, 1994, and the Hutu president was dead, Charles had been primed to betray his neighbour and massacre him.

The gacaca courts strived to provide not only a measure of justice for the victims but to carve out a path towards a post-genocide future by promoting truth, peace, healing, and forgiveness. To facilitate the gacaca process, Gashagaza and his team launched the Umuvumu Tree Project, an in-prison program that brought perpetrators and victims face to face to discuss ways to secure restitution while fostering healing.

What frightens me most about Charles is not the details of his story but how banal he appears. He is ordinary. His shirt, pants, and shoes are workmanlike, perfunctory. Something I myself might wear. He speaks softly without agitation or any lingering trace of anger or malice. Charles resembles any number of men I have met. I did not expect a génocidaire to appear so average. So human. I was expecting horns, hoofs, and a pitch-fork. Where was the devil I had read so much about? Where was the monster who roamed these hills cutting men and women to pieces? And when I shake hands with Charles, I do not feel the coarse, calloused, and scabby hands of evil incarnate. I do not shake hands with the devil. Charles is not a monster, and this terrifies me.

At first, prisoners were suspicious of the program's aims, and only a handful confessed to their crimes even when knowing an admission of guilt could lead to a lighter sentence. But gradually word of the project passed throughout the prisons, and prisoners thought more about its concepts of responsibility, forgiveness, and reconciliation. And with time, the number of confessions rose, and along with those words of veracity, more unmarked graves were unearthed, more piles of bones were given names and remembrance, and more survivors were given the opportunity to grieve honestly and heal more completely. And as time went on, survivors were given the chance to forgive those who had taken everything from them.

I want to ask Charles a question, but I dare not interrupt him or my guide's translation of his words. I want Charles to be more specific about his transformation from farmer to killer. What was it specifically about the propaganda he heard that so resonated with him that he took a machete to his neighbour? When did he know he would do it? What made him think he was justified? What words made his neighbours change from a human being into a cockroach? I feel Charles can offer something, a warning. Yes, Charles is a warning of how easily a human being can turn monstrous.

Monsters neither think nor feel. Monsters simply scare because that is what they do. In that sense, then, monsters are beyond thought. They require no subsequent explanation. They simply terrify and destroy, and people best stay clear from them. To call someone a monster, thus, is to silence all discussion and to render mute any mention of context, any talk of history. Monsters require no elaboration because how could their acts ever be rationalized. Monsters should be killed or locked away, not listened to. Monsters only speak death and mayhem. And to try to explain their actions is only a small step from justification, and no monster deserves such sympathy and certainly not forgiveness. You cannot forgive a monster just as you cannot forgive an earthquake.

Katherine speaks after Charles and recounts in gruelling detail how she managed to survive those few weeks in April. She describes the forests she crawled through, the few strangers who briefly took pity on her by offering some food and/or sanctuary, and the génocidaires who did not kill her because they thought she was close enough to death already due to her physical appearance and was not worth the effort of killing. She eventually fled to Burundi but did not feel safe there. Upon returning to her village at the genocide's close, she learned she had lost 98 per cent of her immediate family.

She forgives Charles, she says. She forgives him for the role he played in the murder of her family. She forgives him because to cherish hatred and vengeance is to die a slow death. She forgives him because God led her back to light and helped lift the weight of recriminations from her shoulders until she felt free and merciful in her heart, body, and soul. She forgives Charles because forgiveness is the only path forwards.

Across from me, a white woman from Charleston, South Carolina, thanks Katherine for her story and her words. She says Katherine is so incredibly brave for allowing God to bring forgiveness into her heart. She says she, too, is a Christian, and she, too, knows, albeit in slightly different ways, the power of forgiveness to block the encroaching forces of darkness from encamping in the mind and soul. The woman from Charleston recounts the night of June 15, 2015, when a twenty-one-year-old white man named Dylan Roof entered the Emanuel African Methodist Episcopal Church during an evening prayer. He sat down among the worshippers, who welcomed him and gave him a sheet with religious verses. For fifteen minutes, Roof sat with the congregation and listened while they sang God's praises. For fifteen minutes, he enjoyed their hospitality and warmth. For fifteen minutes, he summoned the strength to ignore what he saw around him, the communality and generosity of spirit, and decided to follow those feelings of supremacy he had nurtured over the previous months and had learned from the internet's darkest chat rooms, those whispers that said his neighbours were not his neighbours but rather cockroaches threatening infestation, cockroaches in need of extermination. Roof took out his Glock .45 calibre and fired seventy rounds into the crowd, reloading five different times. While shooting the unarmed worshippers, the gunman shouted, "I have to do it. You rape our women, and you're taking over our country, and you have to go."[4] And go some did that night. Nine of them.

The woman from South Carolina says what was truly remarkable was how some members of the Black congregation and family members of the slain immediately forgave Roof. We are built on love, they said. We have no room for hate, they said, so we have to forgive. Of course, not all forgave Roof. On January 11, 2017, Roof was formally sentenced to death and was made to stand and listen as the relatives of the men and women he stole addressed him personally. Yet he did not face them; he did not look at any of those he so terribly wronged. The daughter of the murdered Reverend Depayne Middleton-Doctor told Roof directly "You will rot in hell where you belong. I hope your guilt eats you alive. While you're pleading for life and begging for your life, I hope God forgives you, the one sin I'm not sure even he can forgive." She said, "This spawn of Satan will not steal our joy."[5]

Roof himself showed no remorse for what he did. At his sentencing, the twenty-one-year-old said he still felt he had to do what he did. This boyish-looking man with his dirty-blonde hair and blank expression, this thin waif full of malice and vehemence, who walked into a house of worship and betrayed its hospitality, this vicious little puppy dog who stole the lives of nine human beings because he believed the racist propagandists he read on the internet and let their words pillage his soul and spirit, said after the state promised to take his life in retribution and vengeance that he still felt he had to kill to protect his whiteness and his white kin and, undoubtedly, would slaughter again if given the opportunity.

"I forgive Charles," Katherine says. "I forgive him." A part of me questions her sincerity. A part of me wonders how much of this is staged. A part of me thinks these plays of reconciliations and villages of forgiveness and second chances are nothing but propaganda material for the Kagame regime, the man who has ruled Rwanda since 1994 with an steadfast resolve, the autocrat who had stifled freedom of expression in the name of stability and overcoming the past, the former commander of the RPF who himself has remained unaccountable for the massacres he and his army committed during and after the genocide—the hunting and massacring of civilian Hutus in northern Rwanda and the neighbouring DRC.

"I asked for forgiveness," Charles says. A part of me finds his remorse disingenuous, almost disgusting. A part of me finds his punishment too light—seven years for murder and then allowed to return to the community of his birth, given the opportunity to live in relative peace and security and then put on pedestal as an example of a repenting butcher, a contrite and apologetic murderer, a reformed génocidaire who now amazes tourists the world over with his tale of metamorphosis from man to machete and then back to man. I know the numbers. Of the twenty-seven thousand perpetrators convicted of crimes related to genocide, fewer than one in four have showed any remorse or a desire to apologize for what they did. Some even claim that no genocide took place.

When I was a child, I associated Africa with *The Lion King* and Rwanda with nightmares. Each time, I sang Hakuna Matata along with Timon and Pumba, my favourite characters, I heard voices and read sentences describing in the most horrific detail about how hell had crept over the land of a thousand rolling hills, how blood had splashed across its verdant mountains, how bone had been buried in its rich soil, how its people had begun to slaughter each other seemingly for sport. I was too young and too naïve to put the violence in its appropriate context or to realize that genocide—depressingly—was not something unique to Africa and had, in fact, transpired in less headline-grabbing ways in my country of Canada. For me, at the time, Rwanda was darkness and fire. It was the epitome of terror and horror. It was the place my school friends read about in their Bibles and heard about at their Sunday-school classes. Rwanda was hell.

The closest I have come to experiencing what hell could possibly feel like was walking among the pews of Nyamata Catholic Church under the watchful eye of a statue of the Virgin Mary. As a result of Belgian colonialism and the insertion of Catholicism as the new harbinger of spiritual salvation, Rwanda had transformed itself into one of the world's most pious countries. So when genocide descended in April 1994, thousands upon thousands of men, women, and children flocked to churches throughout the cities and countryside and prayed that these holy abodes would provide them with refuge from the violence—sanctuary from the slaughter. On April 10, an announcement sprang from the Nyamata radio encouraging residents to take shelter in the church, where they would find food, water, and protection. Thousands of people arrived terrified but hopeful they had finally found safety; ten thousand settled in the church itself while another thirty thousand lingered around outside. The Hutu militias arrived in the evening carrying machetes, clubs, guns, and hand grenades. When they left, forty thousand were dead.

Walking towards the entrance, I find it difficult to believe that fifty thousand refugees stood here twenty-five years ago. I find it difficult to believe that ten thousand of them had fit inside this small, red-bricked building. I find it difficult to believe they were all butchered within those walls. I have visited Dachau and Auswitchz; I have walked across the killing fields of Cambodia, paid my respects to the victims of Srebrenica, and thought about the legacy of slavery at Cape Coast Castle, Ouidah, and Gorée. I have watched the flame flicker at the Armenian genocide memorial at Yerevan and reflected on cultural genocide at the sites of former of Canadian residential schools. But nothing has prepared me for the inside of Nyamata Church.

Thin streams of light leak through the roof-top holes left by bullets. Along the pews, piles and piles of unwashed and unsorted and unfolded clothing rest in requiem to those who once wore them. At particular angles, I have trouble not imagining that each red shirt or brown jacket covers a person bowing in prayer in pure submission to the celestial beings whom they hold sacred in their heart for mercy from the encroaching trucks carrying calamity. I have trouble not imagining these terrified people offering the most desperate of pleas to the Virgin Mary—whose statue stands above me and who stares at the dirty floor in a violently quiet way—for protection from the men whose voices they now hear outside the church's walls.

Mary does not look at her congregation but stays frustratingly silent in prayer and reflection. But I wonder if she looked up that day in April to see those mobs enter her church and spill blood on her floor. Did she watch those men who had professed to love her hack and hack and hack against the skin of innocents? Did she recognize those priests who led these lambs to their slaughter?

Now, twenty-five years later, does she pray for the souls of the murderers who killed so many here? Does she pray for the souls of the priests who betrayed their followers? Does she pray for the souls of the missionaries who first brought her here and used the teachings of her book to instill and then foster feelings of shame and resentment? And does she reflect on how words appearing so good and decent on paper can embolden such passionate hatred? Do gods ever apologize to their believers? Do they ever beg their followers' forgiveness for not being better? Does Mary now ask for forgiveness from those piles and piles of unworn clothes?

Outside the church and beneath the earth sits the mass burial site. The steps below are narrow and steep and terminate in a white chamber filled with coffins stacked on top of one another. Some coffins have a family name scrawled in black marker—I wonder who the famile Karangwa Simeon was—while others do not. The lids of some are ajar, and I can see bones and bones and bones. I have heard that the remains of close to forty-five thousand people are buried here. Around me is what remains of an entire community. And I question whether what remains can ever truly be reconciled.

Katherine says she forgive Charles. And when I shake Charles's hand to thank him for sharing his story, I would like to think I would forgive the person who took everything from me. I would like to think that in my grief and despair, I would realize hatred only begets more hatred and any semblance of a future requires the soul to be cleansed of acrimony. But I do not know if I could forgive Charles. I do not know what type of future a genocide can produce.

But I choose to believe Katherine. I am in no position to question the sincerity of her words. I choose to believe her and what she says. I choose to believe she is not merely the RPF's puppet or a servile devotee to a god who has acted so indifferently towards her. I choose to believe Katherine because I catch of glimpse of her and Charles sitting next to each other. They are no longer representatives of a reconciled village; they are no longer spokespersons for genocide and survival. Charles says something and Katherine smiles, and she touches his shoulder. I choose to believe Katherine because what she thinks and feels belong to no one but herself. I choose to believe Katherine because her future is not written in some book. Only she is its author.

Before I leave the village, I purchase a woven bracelet from a local women's cooperative. It costs one American dollar. I wish to remember certain things from my time here. I wish to remember that the qualities that define us as sentient beings—language, thought, compassion, and love—can so easily become polluted and tarred. I wish to remember that every act of violence has a history that must be traced and mapped. And I wish to remember that to contextualize a monstrous act—and even to forgive one—is not to condone it and simply erase its happening. Rather, to provide a past to monstrosity is to promote a future of love. But love here does not resemble faith in the providence of god; love is only the work that promises nothing but hope and a chance of tomorrow.

Rwanda has tried to unshackle itself from its past and make peace with its ghosts. The country has tried to rebrand itself, twenty-five years later, as a bastion of stability amid perpetually warring countries. In Kigali, development is contagious; foreign investment has poured in from abroad. New, flashy buildings rise from the rolling green hills. Everywhere smells of money. Everything exists under Kagame's looming shadow.

Rwanda itself has become a boutique tourist destination—a place where the more discerning traveller can hunt the Big Five from the comfort of his safari vehicle one day and trek in search for mountain gorillas the next—such remarkable diversity for such a small country. And it must be a jarring experience for those travellers to photograph a lion or buffalo in the morning and then to visit the Genocide Memorial in the afternoon. It must be challenging for them to hold those two conflicting images of Africa together in their mind—one of wildness and beauty and the other of barbarity and violence. It must be daunting to reconcile the majesty of a mountain gorilla with caskets of skulls and bones—beautiful animals and dead Africans. They know of no other reality, no other narrative. For in the West, the quintessential stories about Africa are the ones that contain no Africans—only its animals, only its resources, only its beauty. And in the stories in which Africans play a paramount role, they are either bloodthirsty killers or their victims.

Rwanda is so much more complex than its animals and its history of genocide.

Africans themselves—writers from each corner of this diverse continent—continue to offer a corrective to these stories; they continue to lead lives honouring their traditions while navigating the uncertain terrain of modernity as well as neocolonialist powers emanating now from both the West and the East. They continue to strive for self-determination and lives full of dignity and purpose. They continue to balk at the white man's simplistic and self-serving stories.

I am confident about Africa's future. I met a man in Morocco who told me that the future belongs to Africa—not the West. In the wake of the refugee crisis and the West's slamming its doors shut, the West has lost its moral superiority. "We want bridges," the man said. Bridges. Trump and his ilk—the Orbans, Bolsonaros, Netanyhus, Johnsons, Salvinis—will continue to lay bare the West's fraudulent image of itself, its continuous eroding of decency and solidarity, its penchant for never-ending war and lust for the latest weaponry. But in their stead, as the West slowly seeps into further irrelevancy, other creative spaces of hope could emerge around the world, which may offer alternatives to walls and which may seek to render more fluid the arbitrary borders of the present.

"I have no interest in the West," the man said. "No interest."

I hope the continent can grow outside the West's long shadow and become better than it. I hope the continent can plan and support mobile communities transcending the old colonial borders, communities that embrace and foster the creative and productive potential of mobility. The West has begun its long descent into history; its cracks have begun to show. It has turned its back on the world and has started the long process of eating itself to death.

As for me, I no longer seek protection from books or see them as mere fodder in an argument. Books open pathways and new understandings, absolutely, but they can never replace the work of self-reflection or the efforts required to situate the reader in relation to the words on the page.

After spending some time in Africa, I can safely say that books can never substitute for the real, maddening nature of reality. Reading all I did about the slave trade or about migration from Zimbabwe or about the Rwanda genocide could never have adequately prepared me for Cape Coast Castle or Harare or Nyamata Catholic Church. The world beyond the page is so much more fraught with complexity and tension. You can never close the door on a place, the way you can close a book. Books are bracketed by their covers; life merely goes forth.

I am sitting at a campsite deep within the Okavango Delta, Botswana's primary tourist attraction. Night has come, and I eat my rice and meat at a small table by lamplight. My three guides sit around the fire and talk in their native Tswana language. I finish my meal, scrape the remnants into the garbage, and clean and rinse my dish and cutlery in two containers full of water. After I finish and leave my dishes to dry, the guides stand and move to the table with the makeshift buffet and serve themselves their dinner. From my table, I watch them return to the fire with their plates full of food and continue their conversation from, seemingly, where they left off. I have not the faintest idea about what they speak, but there's a wonderful democratic rhythm to the conversation. One man speaks for a minute or so, without interruption, and then another begins, and then another. They all speak with their eyes on the fire. Voices are never raised; no judgement or scorn creeps into the conversation. The calm is only broken by occasional laughter.

"Jesse, come sit with us," Tan, the lead guide, says, and I take a seat next to them and rest my eyes on the flames. The four of us sit in silence around the fire; the light briefly illuminates our faces.

"We call this the bush television," he says, and I smile, and watch the fire slowly eat the kindling, slowly devour and disintegrate the wood into ember and then ash. The stars above are in the thousands, and Tan asks me if there are such stars in Canada. I smile but do not answer. Every now and then, something moves just outside the camp, in the dark, and I turn to its direction, but the others around the fire still sit and watch the fire, and pay the noise, the unknown, no attention. I decide only to worry if they worry. Around us, the hippos begin their grunting.

Across from me, the young guide with dreadlocks speaks in a low, soothing baritone. He speaks in slow Tswana; every word, it seems, is deliberately picked and softly pronounced. The others listen, as do I, in silence, around the fire. I hear his unknown words drift and float above the fire, piercing the darkness and wilds. I listen intently, not for meaning, but for the sounds, his sounds, the sounds of his home, here in the Delta. I listen because I am here.

Tan suddenly laughs as do the other two men. He tells me they are speaking about the old times, before the arrival of the white man, the time of their great-grandfathers and the stories that were passed on, the time when things started to change. I smile and feel the fire's warmth along my skin, upon my face. I listen more and more. I do not say a word. In the fire's glow, in the wilds of Africa, I hear Tswana and the grunts of hippos, getting closer and closer, but never so close that I cannot hear the voices of the Delta.

Endnotes

1. These quotes can be found here: https://www.nytimes.com/2019/08/03/us/patrick-crusius-el-paso-shooter-manifesto.html.
2. This sequence of events can be seen here: https://www.bbc.com/news/av/world-us-canada-48218887.
3. This quote can be found here: https://www.nytimes.com/2019/08/04/us/politics/trump-mass-shootings.html.
4. This quote can be found here: https://www.washingtonpost.com/posteverything/wp/2015/06/21/how-benevolent-sexism-drove-dylann-roofs-racist-massacre/.
5. This quote can be found here: https://abcnews.go.com/US/charleston-victims-mother-tells-dylann-roof-forgive/story?id=44704096.

Deepest appreciation to
Demeter's monthly Donors

DEMETER

Daughters

Rebecca Bromwich
Summer Cunningham
Tatjana Takseva
Debbie Byrd
Fiona Green
Tanya Cassidy
Vicki Noble
Bridget Boland
Naomi McPherson
Myrel Chernick

Sisters

Amber Kinser
Nicole Willey
Christine Peets